THE POVERTY OF NATIONS
A Relational Perspective

Paul Spicker

First published in Great Britain in 2020 by

Policy Press
University of Bristol
1-9 Old Park Hill
Bristol
BS2 8BB
UK
t: +44 (0)117 954 5940
pp-info@bristol.ac.uk
www.policypress.co.uk

North America office:
Policy Press
c/o The University of Chicago Press
1427 East 60th Street
Chicago, IL 60637, USA
t: +1 773 702 7700
f: +1 773-702-9756
sales@press.uchicago.edu
www.press.uchicago.edu

British Library Cataloguing in Publication Data
A catalogue record for this book is available from the British Library

Library of Congress Cataloging-in-Publication Data
A catalog record for this book has been requested

ISBN 978-1-4473-4332-5 hardback
ISBN 978-1-4473-4333-2 paperback
ISBN 978-1-4473-4335-6 ePub
ISBN 978-1-4473-4334-9 ePDF

Cover design by Clifford Hayes
Front cover image: Getty/Artur Widak/NurPhoto
Printed and bound in Great Britain by CMP, Poole
Policy Press uses environmentally responsible print partners

Contents

List of figures and tables

Figures

Tables

About the author

Paul Spicker is Emeritus Professor of Public Policy at the Robert Gordon University, Aberdeen. His research includes studies of poverty, need, disadvantage and service delivery; he has worked as a consultant for a range of agencies in social welfare provision. His books include:

- *Stigma and social welfare* (Croom Helm, 1984)
- *Principles of social welfare* (Routledge, 1988)
- *Social housing and the social services* (Longmans, 1989)
- *Poverty and social security: concepts and principles* (Routledge, 1993)
- *Planning for the needs of people with dementia* (with D S Gordon, Avebury, 1997)
- *Social protection: a bilingual glossary* (co-editor with J-P Révauger, Mission-Recherche, 1998)
- *Social policy in a changing society* (with Maurice Mullard, Routledge, 1998)
- *The welfare state: a general theory* (Sage, 2000)
- *Policy analysis for practice* (Policy Press, 2006)
- *Liberty, equality and fraternity* (Policy Press, 2006)
- *Poverty: an international glossary* (co-editor with Sonia Alvarez Leguizamon and David Gordon, Zed, 2007)
- *The idea of poverty* (Policy Press, 2007)
- *The origins of modern welfare* (Peter Lang, 2010)
- *How social security works* (Policy Press, 2011)
- *Reclaiming individualism* (Policy Press, 2013)
- *Social policy: theory and practice* (Policy Press, 2014)
- *Arguments for welfare* (Rowman and Littlefield, 2017)
- *What's wrong with social security benefits?* (Policy Press, 2017)
- *Thinking collectively: social policy, collective action and the common good* (Policy Press, 2019)

A range of his published work is available on open access at http://spicker.uk

Introduction:
Representations of poverty

This book is about poverty. It is distinctive in two ways: in the case it makes for a relational view of poverty, and in its attempt to draw out common themes relating to developed and developing countries.

Poverty is represented in many different ways. Here are some examples from around the world.

'Many of the world's poorest people are women who must, as the primary family caretakers and producers of food, shoulder the burden of tilling land, grinding grain, carrying water and cooking. This is no easy burden. In Kenya, women can burn up to 85 percent of their daily calorie intake just fetching water.'[1]

'Poverty is a persistent problem for over 20% of the children in the United States. Child development is shaped by children's interactions within and across social contexts. The social contexts in which children from impoverished backgrounds live can be devastatingly harmful: growing up in poverty exposes children to more stress or abuse in the home, neighborhood crime, and school violence. Exposure to environmental conditions associated with poverty profoundly shapes their development, and the effects become more pronounced the longer the exposure to poverty. Empirical studies from multiple social science disciplines … have consistently documented crippling disadvantages across a number of developmental domains, showing that the disadvantages associated with poverty are entrenched, wide-reaching, and constitute an immediate and pressing policy challenge.'[2]

'In our world, one in eight people live in slums. In total, around a billion people live in slum conditions today. …

---

[1] Team Kenya, 2015, Focusing on girls and women to reduce poverty, https://www.teamkenya.org.uk/2015/08/10/focusongirls/, accessed 11.4.2018.

[2] A McCarty, 2016, Child poverty in the United States, *Sociology Compass*, 10(7): 623–39.

The impact of living in these areas is life threatening. Slums are marginalised, large agglomerations of dilapidated housing often located in the most hazardous urban land – e.g. riverbanks; sandy and degraded soils, near industries and dump sites, in swamps, flood-prone zones and steep slopes – disengaged from broader urban systems and from the formal supply of basic infrastructure and services, including public space and green areas. Slum dwellers experience constant discrimination and disadvantage, lack of recognition by governance frameworks, limited access to land and property, tenure insecurity and the threat of eviction, precarious livelihoods, high exposure to disease and violence and, due to slums' location, high vulnerability to the adverse impacts of climate change and natural disasters.'[3]

'Poverty is both a cause and a consequence of poor health. Poverty increases the chances of poor health. Poor health in turn traps communities in poverty. Infectious and neglected tropical diseases kill and weaken millions of the poorest and most vulnerable people each year. … Very poor and vulnerable people may have to make harsh choices – knowingly putting their health at risk because they cannot see their children go hungry, for example. … The cost of doctors' fees, a course of drugs and transport to reach a health centre can be devastating, both for an individual and their relatives who need to care for them or help them reach and pay for treatment. In the worst cases, the burden of illness may mean that families sell their property, take children out of school to earn a living or even start begging. … Overcrowded and poor living conditions can contribute to the spread of airborne diseases such as tuberculosis and respiratory infections such as pneumonia. … A lack of food, clean water and sanitation can also be fatal.'[4]

'The United Kingdom, the world's fifth largest economy, is a leading centre of global finance, boasts a "fundamentally

---

[3] UN Habitat, 2016, *Slum almanac 2015–2016*, Nairobi: UN-Habitat, pp 2, 4.

[4] Health Poverty Action, n.d., *Key facts: poverty and poor health*, www.healthpovertyaction. org/policy-and-resources/the-cycle-of-poverty-and-poor-health/the-cycle-of-poverty-and-poor-health1/, accessed 11.4.2018.

strong" economy and currently enjoys record low levels of unemployment. But despite such prosperity, one fifth of its population (14 million people) live in poverty. Four million of those are more than 50 per cent below the poverty line and 1.5 million experienced destitution in 2017, unable to afford basic essentials. ... Official denials notwithstanding, it is obvious to anyone who opens their eyes. There has been a shocking increase in the number of food banks and major increases in homelessness and rough sleeping; a growing number of homeless families ... have been dispatched to live in accommodation far from their schools, jobs and community networks; life expectancy is falling for certain groups; and the legal aid system has been decimated, thus shutting out large numbers of low-income persons from the once-proud justice system.'[5]

'Poverty remains firmly entrenched in rural areas, which are home to 84 per cent of Ugandans. About 27 per cent of all rural people – some 8 million men, women and children – still live below the national rural poverty line. Uganda's poorest people include hundreds of thousands of smallholder farmers living in remote areas scattered throughout the country. Remoteness makes people poor ... In remote rural areas, smallholder farmers do not have access to the vehicles and roads they need to transport their produce, and market linkages are weak or non-existent. These farmers lack inputs and technology to help them increase their production and reduce pests and disease. They also lack access to financial services, which would enable them to boost their incomes – both by improving and expanding their production, and by establishing small enterprises. The poorest areas of the country are in the north, where poverty incidence is consistently above 40 per cent and exceeds 60 per cent in many districts – and where outbreaks of civil strife have disrupted farmers' lives and agricultural production. ... Changing climate patterns ... have a serious impact upon

---

[5] United Nations Human Rights Council, 2019, *Visit to the United Kingdom of Great Britain and Northern Ireland: report of the special rapporteur on extreme poverty and human rights*, A/HRC/41/39/Add.1 pp 3–4.

water and other natural resources, agricultural production and rural livelihoods.'[6]

'Poverty causes families to send children to work, often in hazardous and low-wage jobs, such as brick-chipping, construction and waste-picking. Children are paid less than adults, with many working up to twelve hours a day. Full-time work frequently prevents children from attending school, contributing to drop-out rates. According to the Labour Law of Bangladesh 2006, the minimum legal age for employment is 14. However, as 93 per cent of child labourers work in the informal sector – in small factories and workshops, on the street, in home-based businesses and domestic employment – the enforcement of labour laws is virtually impossible.'[7]

The first thing that springs out from such examples is their diversity. There are some common themes here – deprivation, lack of resources, the way that problems in one part of life generate problems in others – but we need to avoid the assumption that it all boils down to one thing, or that everything shares a common cause. Poverty is not a single condition. It has been understood in different ways at different times. It is multi-headed; for every problem that is reduced or resolved, another one seems to take its place. It occurs in many different ways, often at the same time. It often happens that when people talk about poverty, they are not talking about the same thing. Some people talk about lack of rights, others about dependency; some are concerned with low income, others with long-term problems; for some, participation in society is central, and for others it is whether people own things.

Understanding poverty in relational terms

A considerable amount of work has been done in recent years to establish a view of poverty as a multidimensional concept and set of experiences. The argument in this book begins from there, but it

---

[6] International Fund for Agricultural Development, n.d., *Rural poverty in Uganda*, https://operations.ifad.org/web/ifad/operations/country/project/tags/uganda, accessed 19.12.2019.

[7] UNICEF Bangladesh, n.d., *Child labor*, www.unicef.org/bangladesh/children_4863.htm, accessed 11.4.2018.

goes further. The representations of poverty I have been citing are concerned to some extent with poverty as a lack of resources, but there is a lot more to them. They refer, with no less force, to a wide range of social issues - the position of women, child development, health care systems, child labour, access to law and justice, financial services, remoteness, discrimination and disadvantage.

Much of the academic literature has attempted to explain the relational issues in poverty as consequences of lack of resources and material deprivation. I thought so, too, when I wrote my first book on poverty.[8] Over time, partly as a result of exposure to ideas from other countries, partly through policy work, and partly through research that called for listening to poor people, I have come to think that this is a mistake. It is not only that poverty needs to be thought about in its economic, social and political context; nor is it just a matter of finding it difficult to separate the material aspects of poverty from the consequences of deprivation. The idea of poverty refers in itself to a complex set of social relationships. The relational elements of poverty tell us what poverty is – what poverty consists of, what poor people are experiencing, and what kind of problems there are to be addressed.

Describing poverty as a relational concept is already a departure from conventional treatments of the subject, but this book is also doing something rather different from previous writing on 'relational poverty'. Some of the writing on relational poverty has been concerned with the psychology of social interactions: for Robert Walker, poverty is 'relational in the sense that the experience of poverty is determined by others as well as by self'.[9] Other relational arguments have been conflated with structural explanations for poverty.[10] Frances Fox Piven, for example, says this:

> The concept of 'relational poverty' implies a theory or theories about causality. In contrast to prevalent understandings which root economic hardships in the deficits of individuals or families or subcultures, the theory asserts that poverty is best explained by patterns of human relationships, and by the social institutions that organise those relationships. And in contrast to understandings that ascribe hardship to the consequences of social exclusion

---

[8] P Spicker, 1993, *Poverty and social security: concepts and principles*, London: Routledge.

[9] R Walker, 2014, *The shame of poverty*, Oxford: Oxford University Press, p 120.

[10] G Feldman, 2018, Towards a relational approach to poverty in social work, *British Journal of Social Work*, doi: 10.1093/bjsw/bcy111 1–18.

or isolation, it asserts that poverty is importantly the result of the different terms and conditions on which people are included in social life.[11]

Her position, as I understand it, is that a relational perspective posits a social explanation for the causes of poverty; that it stands in opposition to individualistic or pathological understandings of poverty; and that poverty is the consequence of social structures and social institutions. None of those propositions is inherent in a relational approach. The point is not that poverty *results* from social relationships; lots of things do. Nor is it that some social relationships *lead* to poverty. Relational concepts might be explanatory, but they do not need to be, any more than other relational categories such as 'status' or 'gender' are intrinsically explanatory. The case I want to make is that poverty is *constituted* by social relationships – relationships such as class, low status, social exclusion, insecurity and lack of rights.

The plan of the book

A full relational account of poverty needs to consider relationships that are social, economic, legal and political; the material considered in Part 1 is partly contextual, but principally it is concerned with the relationships that delineate the nature of poverty in contemporary societies. Chapter 1 makes the core theoretical argument for understanding poverty from a relational perspective. The subsequent chapters in Part I examine aspects of those relationships. Chapter 2 considers the links between poverty and the world economy. Some of the core definitions of poverty centre on people's economic position; the structures and institutions of the economy have a general and pervasive influence on the experience of poverty. The chapter reviews the implications for poverty of the structure of the world economy – the formal market economy, access to finance, and the framework governing transactions and exchange – and considers the arguments for considering poverty as a product of economic relationships.

Chapter 3 continues the discussion of economic relationships, considering economic development, growth, and human development. Development is about much more than production or income generation; the term covers a complex set of processes, which have a profound effect on social, economic and political relationships. It

---

[11] F Piven, 2018, Introduction, in V Lawson, S Elwood, 2018, *Relational poverty politics*, Athens, Georgia: University of Georgia Press, p ix.

follows that development, too, is relational, and that it is intimately linked to relationships of poverty.

Inequality is another relational term, and while it is somewhat broader than poverty, there are substantial links and overlaps between them. Chapter 4 discusses the links. Poverty is strongly identified with inequality, and some concepts, including class and economic distance, effectively treat poverty as a form of inequality. At times it can be difficult to tell the concepts apart; there are forms of disadvantage which are not part of poverty, but almost every instance of poverty is also an instance of disadvantage.

Chapter 5 considers social exclusion. The discourse of exclusion has emerged as an alternative to discourses about poverty, largely because it opens debate to the examination of relational issues in ways that many social scientists have been determined to reject. Many of the themes raised by poor people are about social relationships – isolation, powerlessness, gender and the problem of government. As the policy communities dealing with poverty – governments, international organisations, voluntary NGOs and practitioners – have come to be aware of the relational elements of poverty, many of them have changed the way they talk about poverty. The idea of exclusion is rooted in a distinct view of society, based on networks of social solidarity; the experience of exclusion is defined in terms of those networks; the primary remedy is 'insertion', integration or inclusion, rather than resources, equality or redistribution. These are all relational issues; the idea of exclusion is rooted in a relational understanding of people's circumstances. And that means that discussions of exclusion often come closer to the idea of poverty than much of the literature on poverty in itself, offering a way to escape from the limitations of the academic analysis of poverty. The concept of exclusion has become a major part of anti-poverty policy in international organisations, including the European Union and the United Nations.

Another developing relational discourse has been the increasing emphasis, especially in the international organisations, on rights. This is discussed in Chapter 6. Poverty is about relationships, and rights are rules that govern such relationships; Amartya Sen links the idea of poverty directly to entitlements.[12] Discussions of citizenship, legal rights, collective and human rights have become part of the armoury of anti-poverty campaigns. This all takes the idea of poverty some way from the traditional focus on deprivation and resources.

---

[12] A Sen, 1981, *Poverty and famines: an essay on entitlement and deprivation*, Oxford: Clarendon Press, Oxford.

Chapter 7 considers the implications of the relational perspective for social policy. If poverty is a matter of resources, then the way to deal with poverty is to increase people's resources, either directly – providing money, goods and services – or indirectly, for example by promoting employment so that people can earn more resources. From a relational perspective, by contrast, anti-poverty policies have to advance people's integration into social networks, for example relationships of work, family, education and ethnicity – and to reduce vulnerability, through human development and systems of social protection. In so far as poverty is viewed as being about resources, some responses and remedies might be considered without reference to the political and social context where they are applied; but in so far as poverty is relational, they cannot be.

The second main element of the book is an attempt to combine evidence and argument from developed economies together with insights from the global South. Much of the literature on poverty begins from a resource-based understanding. If that is taken as the starting point, the differences between countries and societies are glaring; poverty in every society, Townsend argues, has to be considered in terms that are distinctive to that society.[13] Viewed from a relational perspective, the situation is not so clear-cut. The relationships that characterise poverty – relationships of exclusion, low status, lack of rights, economic marginality and insecurity – are experienced in countries with markedly different resources and wide variations in their social norms. Part 2 discusses how the relationships that constitute poverty are constructed in rich and poor countries, how those are affected in turn by the relationships between countries, and so how both rich and poor countries can respond to the problems of poverty.

The focus of the second part falls on nations and countries – literally, the poverty of nations – and that calls for some justification. Chapter 8 examines the case for doing this. There has been a tendency in much of the literature to treat poverty as an individual matter, a condition or status that attaches to particular people; poverty has been treated as an issue that mainly affects individuals, families and households.[14] That has prompted some distrust of 'methodological nationalism'. There is a sense that national boundaries can get in the way of understanding the

---

[13] P Townsend, 1979, *Poverty in the United Kingdom*, Harmondsworth: Penguin, p 36.
[14] For example, S Ringen, 1988, Direct and indirect measures of poverty, *Journal of Social Policy*, 17(3): 351–65.

position of poor people, and that the distinctions between countries need to be broken down rather than reinforced.[15] There are limits to how far that can be taken. The relationships which constitute poverty are structured and understood within a national context. Countries are about much more than lines on the map; their boundaries mark out a political community, typically governed by a framework of laws that are made at a national level. The data we hold reflect those structures; much of what we know about poverty, and much of the supportive evidence referred to in this book, has been developed to serve governments. Policy responses are often made on the national level, and writing on social policy is usually concerned with identifying and understanding the role of government in the provision of social welfare – what governments ought to be doing, and how they can make a difference. Methodological nationalism is central to effective responses to the problems of poverty.

Countries define the scope for legitimate social action, the limits of social responsibility and the effective means of achieving social ends. Chapter 9 discusses the role of government in the political community. All democratic countries attempt to reduce or at least to relieve poverty. This role is interpreted in different ways, but almost all governments accept the principle that they are responsible to some degree for the quality of people's lives – a view which would not have applied to most governments in history, and one which is still resisted by some. Governments are limited by their constitutional roles, their practical capacity and their economic powers. Policy is a disputed area; most governments proceed, not by coercion, but through negotiation, partnership and planning with a range of actors.

Chapter 10 considers the nature of poverty in richer countries. The persistence of poverty in rich countries is something of a puzzle for those who see poverty in terms of resources; from a relational perspective, it should be unsurprising. Although public discussion is sometimes dominated by moral judgements about the poor, governments in developed countries have come to see responses to poverty and the protection of people's circumstances as basic elements in the role of a democratic government, and if governments do not ensure that basic living standards are protected, they have failed. Debates tend to centre in practice on money, markets and commodification.

Chapter 11 considers poverty in poorer countries. Countries are poor, not just because they have many poor people, but because they are less developed than others; development reshapes the economic,

---

[15] N Yeates and C Holden, 2009, *The global social policy reader*, Bristol: Policy Press.

social and political relationships in a country. Some accounts treat underdevelopment as something which is pathological or endemic in a country, but there are also strong structural reasons for a lack of development, including domination by other countries and structural dependency.

Chapter 12 considers the relationship between rich and poor countries. The position of poor countries reflects international relationships governing economic exchange, debt, and markets. No less important are the dominance of ideas from abroad, such as the Washington Consensus, and the role of international organisations in enforcing its principles. Policies have shifted from the self-direction of the Poverty Reduction Strategies towards the top-down priorities represented by the Sustainable Development Goals.

Chapter 13 ends the second part of the book with a consideration of what this might mean for social policy. The experience of developed countries tells us that markets are not enough; that targeting does not work; and that systems are always mixed. The experience of the developing world is that local ownership of policies, participation and empowerment, and social protection can make a huge difference to lifestyles, in a way that economic growth alone cannot. The relationships of poverty will be expressed differently in different countries, but it cannot be assumed that different standards are being applied. In rich and poor countries alike, people might be socially excluded, lacking in rights, insecure or disadvantaged.

The concluding chapter reviews the implications of the book's arguments for social science. The analysis of poverty raises strong passions, and some commentators have taken the view that treating poverty as anything other than a lack of command over resources is inconsistent with a scientific approach. They may judge that this book is not scientific; they might even say it is not about poverty, because it is not about poverty as they define it. When the dust settles, however, I think that many readers will understand that the ideas that have informed this analysis are all rather more familiar than conventional understandings of poverty, or a literal reading of the seminal texts, might suggest. There has been a growing emphasis on poverty as a multidimensional set of issues, and a shift towards considering social exclusion together with poverty. The data which are currently being used in poverty studies have already shifted to provide insights into 'poverty and social exclusion'; responses to poverty are increasingly informed by ideas of voice and empowerment, and a focus on exclusionary processes. These trends point to an implicit recognition of a change in the paradigms which underlie the analysis of poverty. The conceptualisation of poverty that underpins mainstream social science on the subject, with its relentless focus on material deprivation, has not yet caught up with what social scientists are actually doing.

The Poverty of Nations is primarily a work of theory: it offers a reinterpretation of existing evidence, a synthesis of material, and a framework for further discussion. I mainly work in the field of social policy, and the method of the book is fairly typical of studies in that subject – a pragmatic combination of the interpretation of evidence, insights from a range of social sciences, and moral evaluations of policy responses. I have also borrowed liberally from development studies, another eclectic field. The two subject areas used rarely to refer to each other, but the division of labour has been slowly breaking down in recent years. They share common interests in a wide range of topics – among them, multidimensional views of poverty, social exclusion, safety nets, universality, the scope of markets, targeting, planning, partnership and service evaluation. My discipline still has a great deal to learn from the world beyond Europe and America. Identifying the common ground and the gaps offers a hope of glimpsing new perspectives on an old set of problems.

PART I

Poverty: economic and social relationships

1

Poverty

Poverty is complex and multi-faceted, a constellation of issues rather than a single problem. There are more concepts of poverty than it is possible to discuss in this book, but in previous work I have argued that it is possible to see several clusters of meaning – 'families' of interrelated concepts.[1] Some concepts of poverty relate to *material conditions*:

- A generally low standard of living, where poverty becomes a struggle to manage in everyday life. The World Bank has described poverty as 'the inability to attain a minimal standard of living'.[2]
- The lack of specific goods and items, such as housing, fuel, or food. For Vic George, this depended on 'a core of basic necessities as well as a list of other necessities that change over time and place'.[3]
- A pattern or 'web' of deprivation, where people have multiple deprivations, or they may be frequently deprived, though there may be considerable fluctuations in circumstances.[4]

Some concepts of poverty are based in *economic circumstances*:

- A lack of resources. For Townsend, people were poor because they lacked the resources to have access to the conditions of life that other people have. 'If they lack or are denied the incomes, or more exactly the resources, including income and assets or goods or services in kind to obtain access to these conditions of life … they are in poverty.'[5]

---

[1] P Spicker, 2007, Definitions of poverty: twelve clusters of meaning, in P Spicker, S Alvarez Leguizamon and D Gordon (eds) *Poverty: an international glossary*, London: Zed Books.

[2] World Bank, 1990, *World development report 1990: poverty*, Washington DC: World Bank, p 26.

[3] V George, 1988, *Wealth, poverty and starvation*, Hemel Hempstead: Wheatsheaf Books, p 208.

[4] D Narayan, R Chambers, M Shah and P Petesch, 2000, *Voices of the poor: crying out for change*, Oxford: World Bank/Oxford University Press, Chapter 11.

[5] P Townsend, 1979, *Poverty in the United Kingdom*, Harmondsworth: Penguin, p 915.

- An 'economic distance' from the rest of the population, or a degree of inequality, which means that people are unable to buy the things that others can buy.[6]
- Economic class – an economic status, or relationship to production and the labour market, which means that people are consistently likely to be disadvantaged or deprived. Ralph Miliband wrote: 'The basic fact is that the poor are an integral part of the working class – its poorest and most disadvantaged stratum. ... Poverty is a class thing, closely linked to a general situation of class inequality.'[7]

Then there are *social relationships*:

- Poverty understood as dependency on financial support and state benefits.[8]
- Poverty as a social class – a set of inferior social roles and statuses, exemplified in the idea of the 'underclass'.[9]
- The problem of exclusion, which implies not simply that poor people are rejected, but that they are not part of the networks of social solidarity and support than most people in a society rely on.[10]
- A 'lack of basic security', 'the absence of one of more factors that enable individuals and families to assume basic responsibilities and to enjoy fundamental rights'.[11]
- A lack of entitlement, in the sense that poor people do not have the rights to access and use resources that others can. The concept is linked, by Sen or Nussbaum, to a lack of capabilities.[12]

---

[6] M O'Higgins, S Jenkins, 1990, Poverty in the EC: 1975, 1980, 1985, in R Teekens and B van Praag (eds) *Analysing poverty in the European Community*, (Eurostat News Special Edition 1–1990), Luxembourg: European Communities.

[7] R Miliband, 1974, Politics and poverty, in D Wedderburn (ed) *Poverty, inequality and class structure*, Cambridge: CUP, pp 184–85.

[8] G Simmel, 1908, The poor, *Social Problems*, 1965, 13(2): 118–39.

[9] See L Morris, 1994, *Dangerous classes: the underclass and social citizenship*, London: Routledge.

[10] S Paugam, 1993, La disqualification sociale: essai sur la nouvelle pauvreté, Paris: Presses Universitaires de France.

[11] J Wresinski, 1987, Grande pauvreté et précarité économique et sociale, *Journal officiel de la république française*, 6 fev. 1987.

[12] A Sen, 1981, *Poverty and famines: an essay on entitlement and deprivation*, Oxford: Clarendon Press; M Nussbaum, 2006, Poverty and human functioning: capabilities as fundamental entitlements, in D Grusky and R Kanbur (eds), *Poverty and inequality*, Stanford: Stanford University Press.

It is difficult to separate many, if not most, of the ideas, from the final category: the position of poverty as a moral evaluation. Poverty refers to severe hardship or a situation that is morally unacceptable. The moral content of poverty implies not simply that poverty is approved or disapproved of, but that the simple fact of accepting the term also carries a moral imperative – a sense that something must be done. That might be countered by denying that people are poor, or finding some other moral reason for rejecting the claim for support, but neither of those positions shakes the fact that a moral claim is being made.

It is not really possible to offer an authoritative 'definition' of poverty, and it makes little sense to impose a single, uniform interpretation, because that would exclude many of the issues which matter. There is an overlap between the concepts, but that reflects the complex, varied nature of the phenomena that are being considered. Figure 1.1 shows, schematically, the main clusters.

Some clusters of meaning are close to each other, and they can be difficult to untangle in practice; each of the clusters is close to its

Figure 1.1: Poverty – twelve clusters of meaning

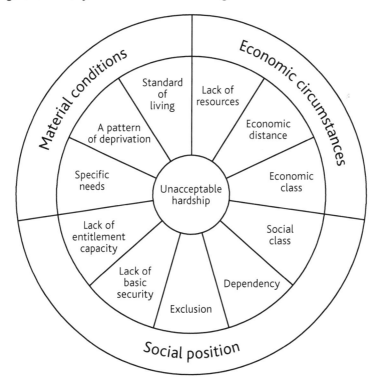

Source: Spicker, 2007, p 240

neighbours, and there is an evident relationship between needs and a pattern of deprivation, or economic and social class. As we move round the circle, however, the distance between the clusters becomes clearer and stronger. Dependency or exclusion are not at all the same as a lack of resources; economic and social class are not evidence of lack of entitlement. Although poverty is not a single, unified idea, several of these issues can apply at the same time. Poverty refers to material deprivation, economic circumstances or social circumstances; it refers to hardship; and its use entails a judgement, that the situations it refers to are normatively serious.

Many of the advocates of a 'scientific' discourse about poverty think that it is possible to say things much more exactly, to command general agreement about meanings and definitions, and to agree policies internationally on that basis. This is from a declaration signed, a little over twenty years ago, by Peter Townsend and more than seventy of the leading researchers in the field:

> EUROPEAN SOCIAL SCIENTISTS are critical of the unwillingness at international level to introduce a cross-country and therefore more scientific operational definition of poverty. In recent years, a variety of different definitions have been reviewed and evaluated. They apply only to countries or groups of countries. Many are conceptually unclear: some confuse cause and effect. ... Poverty is primarily an income- or resource-driven concept. It is more than having a relatively low income. ... If criteria independent of income can be further developed and agreed, measures of the severity and extent of the phenomenon of poverty can be properly grounded. That will lead to better investigation of cause and more reliable choice of priorities in policy. SCIENTIFIC PROGRESS can be made if material deprivation is also distinguished from both social deprivation and social exclusion. ... All countries should introduce international measures of these basic concepts and take immediate steps to improve the accepted meanings, measurement and explanation of poverty, paving the way for more effective policies.[13]

---

[13] P Townsend and others, 1997, An international approach to the measurement and explanation of poverty: statement by European social scientists, in D Gordon, P Townsend, 2000, *Breadline Europe*, Bristol: Policy Press.

If we can all agree that poverty has a clear, set meaning, the Declaration supposes, it should be possible to identify its relationship to other social problems, and to respond appropriately.

There are three powerful objections to this approach. The first is philosophical. The meaning of a word depends on how that word is actually used, not on the definition that some people wish to impose upon it. Insisting that poverty is about material deprivation, and about nothing else, does violence to the way the word is actually used. It should be clear even from the opening quotations that poverty is not adequately defined by specific forms of deprivation, and that it extends far beyond income and resources. Patterns of deprivation, such as low income, asset deprivation or standard of living, may be useful indicators of poverty, but they are not the whole story.

The second objection is scientific. The reason why so many social scientists are determined to impose a firm definition on the term is rooted in the belief that firm definitions are basic to measurement and analysis. Concepts have to be 'operationalised', or translated into terms which lend themselves to empirical analysis. This aim is made explicit in the Declaration, when it claims that an agreement about definitions will make it possible for 'measures' to be 'properly grounded'. There are two kinds of error being made here. One is to assume that the things which are conventionally measured and analysed are the things we need to focus on. The central focus on income in poverty studies is a notorious example of the 'streetlight effect': looking for answers in the place where the light is shining, instead of the place where the object in question might be found. Robert Chambers complains:

> poverty is then not what people living in poverty experience. Nor does it reflect the expression of their priorities. Poverty is economic, to do with reported income or consumption. ... Those who plough this furrow dig themselves into a reductionist rut. Wider and more complex realities disappear out of sight and out of mind. ... Poverty becomes what has been measured.[14]

The other mistake is to assume that using empirical data depends on 'measuring' complex phenomena; it does not. Empirical analysis in social science mainly works, not by precise specification of an issue, but by 'triangulation' – accumulating evidence that corroborates and

---

[14] R Chambers, 2007, *Poverty research: methods, mindsets and methodologies*, Brighton: University of Sussex Institute of Development Studies, p 18.

tallies with other evidence. Quantitative data are useful, not decisive; no single 'metric' can stand on its own. The figures provide social scientists, not with measures, and not with unassailable 'facts', but with indicators – pointers, signposts and guides to interpretation.

The third objection is ethical. Poverty researchers need to respect the views, experience and voice of people who are poor. An interpretation of poverty that imposes a single, authoritative definition does not square with what people say, and the assumption that this is possible or desirable is not consistent with an empowering ethical approach.

What, then, do poor people say about poverty? A good starting point is *Voices of the Poor*,[15] a set of studies by the World Bank. The studies were based on participative poverty assessments – on a process of engaging and listening to poor people. It reports the feelings and concerns of poor people in their own words. They conducted meetings and interviews with groups of people; more than 20,000 subjects participated in 23 countries. The second volume, *Crying out for Change*, identifies a series of major themes. Some of the themes are concerned with material deprivation; they include a concern with precarious livelihoods, problems of physical health and living in excluded locations. Other themes put great emphasis on social relationships – relationships of gender, social exclusion and lack of security. And then there are political issues – limited communal organisations and abuse of power. They describe a 'web' of poverty – a tissue of interconnected issues that affect people in poverty in different ways.[16]

Some people do strongly emphasise the role of resources, but that is not universally the case. Poor people do not see the experience of poverty as being solely, or even mainly, a matter of managing resources. Take, for example, access to water, one of several issues raised at the start of this discussion. There are powerful statements in *Voices* about water: 'Water is life, and because we have no water, life is miserable.'[17] Despite that, access to water does not feature enough in the responses to be presented as a major theme in its own right. It gets three pages of Volume Two, and half of that is about irrigation – that is, the general problem of getting enough water to support agriculture. So what is

---

[15] D Narayan, R Chambers, M Shah and P Petesch, 2000, *Voices of the poor*, vols 1–3, Oxford: World Bank/Oxford University Press.

[16] D Narayan, R Chambers, M Shah and P Petesch, 2000, *Voices of the poor: crying out for change*, Oxford: World Bank/Oxford University Press.

[17] D Narayan, R Chambers, M Shah and P Petesch, 2000, *Voices of the poor: from many lands*, Oxford: World Bank/Oxford University Press, p 37.

going on? One possible answer might be that problems which outsiders might suppose are pre-eminent are not necessarily the problems that people most clearly identify. Collecting water, for many, is a part of daily life; there is no more point in complaining about it than there is about having to cook. Halleröd suggests:

> the longer a difficult economic situation lasts, the more people adjust their aspirations. Hence, it would seem that people adapt their preferences in relation to their economic circumstances.[18]

However, when poor people are asked more specifically about deprivations they experience, they don't adapt their preferences to their situation – they interpret it in terms of the expectations of their society. Research in Benin found that the items poor people identified as essential were the same items identified by other non-poor people in that society; the researchers see that as a direct contradiction of Halleröd's contention.[19]

All this is concerned with the priorities people don't have. The other side of the question concerns the priorities that they actually do have. The point is not that water is not important, but that other things appear to be even more important. One of the key methods developed to establish which resources are most essential to people has been the 'consensual' approach, which asks the general public what is essential, and then establishes which things poor people cannot afford. The places where consensual accounts of poverty have been made, such as Britain,[20] Australia,[21] Finland and Sweden,[22] yield some similarities among the wealthiest countries; and it is difficult to make a comparison with, say, the study in Vietnam, which rated having a buffalo or cow as being much more essential than a bathroom.[23] This could be interpreted simply as an example of a difference in norms or standards, but I think it is showing us something else –

---

[18] B Halleröd, 2006, Sour grapes: relative deprivation, adaptive preferences and the measurement of poverty, *Journal of Social Policy*, 35(3): 371–90, pp 377–8.

[19] S Nandy and M Pamati, 2015, Applying the consensual method of estimating poverty in a low income African setting, *Social Indicators Research*, 124(3): 693–726.

[20] J Mack and S Lansley, 2015, *Breadline Britain*, London: Oneworld.

[21] P Saunders, 2011, *Down and out: poverty and exclusion in Australia*, Bristol: Policy Press.

[22] B Halleröd, D Larsson, D Gordon and V Ritakaillio, 2006, Relative deprivation: a comparative analysis of Britain, Finland and Sweden, *Journal of European Social Policy*, 16(4): 328–45, p 333.

[23] R Davies and W Smith, 1998, *The basic necessities survey*, Hanoi: Action Aid.

something that goes beyond either resources or social values. The differences reflect the social, political and economic organisation of different countries. The reason why the consensual surveys of poverty in countries like the UK and Australia yield such similar results is not that the UK and Australia have just the same resources, but that they have very similar forms of social organisation. Vietnam is different, not primarily because its norms or values are different, but because its social organisation is different. The buffalo is the clue.

There are many other examples of how different patterns of social organisation shape poverty. The reason why the expenses of health care make people poor in the United States is not that United States has low levels of health care resource; it is because they have a social organisation of health care that leaves people without the basic levels of support that they will find in most other developed countries. (Being able to get a doctor to visit the sick was ranked as the most essential factor in Vietnam, too.) In Mali, Malawi and Tanzania, the deprivations that children experience are different again:

> Mali, for example, defined Child Labour as a separate dimension (29% deprived), reflecting a national priority, while Tanzania and Malawi opted to include it in a broader dimension of child protection (10% and 66% deprived, respectively), which includes also early marriage (in both countries) and child registration (in Tanzania). For the same reason Malawi included a separate dimension of food security for children from 5 to 13 years old.[24]

Child labour, early marriage and child registration are, of course, a matter of social organisation; only food security is clearly about resources. When poor people are asked to explain what poverty means to them, they talk about social relationships far more than they talk about material deprivation. People in poverty consistently point to problems in their society – problems such as isolation, lack of power, gender relationships, or mistreatment by people in authority.

Poverty, the *International Declaration* grandly states, 'is primarily an income- or resource-driven concept.'[25] It is easy enough to suppose that people who take a different view from social scientists ought to

---

[24] L Ferrone, 2017, Do the Seven Kingdoms of Westeros need seven measures of child deprivation? https://blogs.unicef.org/evidence-for-action/do-the-seven-kingdoms-of-westeros-need-seven-measures-of-child-deprivation/, accessed 19.12.2019.

[25] Townsend and others, 1997.

adjust their thinking. That can only work by leaving out consideration of issues that matter to people profoundly. Poverty is a subject that raises passions; people care very much about the subject. Telling them that they have misunderstood their own situation will make some people angry, but for others it will only confirm how powerless they are. Hardly anything that gets discussed under the banner of poverty does not really matter, even if at times attention tends to get diverted towards myths and stereotypes rather than the major problems. The things that people do complain about – the aspects of their hardship that are unacceptable – are more typically the things they expect to be different, such as being unwell, being exposed to violence, or being persecuted by people in authority. And those are things that poor people in richer countries complain of too.

Relative poverty

One of the standard distinctions made in textbooks twenty or thirty years ago was a distinction between 'absolute' and 'relative' poverty – there are still some throwbacks in contemporary work. Absolute poverty was supposed to relate to basic needs. The OECD defined it as 'a level of minimum need, below which people are regarded as poor, for the purpose of social and government concern, and which does not change over time.'[26] This is closely tied to an idea of poverty as basic subsistence. People had physiological needs, for example for a basic calorific intake each day, and if they were not able to afford that, they could be counted as poor. Because those needs were part of the make-up of human beings, they could be considered to be constant over time. That was never a satisfactory way of describing subsistence. The levels of minimum need are not fixed; any focus on 'basic needs' has to be stretched to take into account the social and economic conditions where poverty is experienced.[27] And even the most basic needs that people have – such as food, clothing and shelter – cannot be considered wholly in isolation from the society they lived in. So, in the 1970s, the idea of absolute poverty was moderated through a concept of basic needs. Basic needs extended beyond minimum subsistence:

[26] OECD (Organisation for Economic Cooperation and Development), 1976, *Public expenditure on income maintenance programmes*, Paris: OECD, p 69.
[27] D Ghai, A Khan, E Lee, and T Alfthan, 1976, *The basic needs approach to development*, Geneva: ILO.

> Firstly, they include certain minimum requirements of a family for private consumption: adequate food, shelter and clothing, as well as certain household furniture and equipment. Second, they include essential services provided by and for the community at large, such as safe drinking water, sanitation, public transport and health, education and cultural facilities.[28]

In the Copenhagen Declaration, absolute poverty was described as 'a condition characterised by severe deprivation of basic human needs, including food, safe drinking water, sanitation facilities, health, shelter, education and information'.[29]

The idea of relative poverty was developed mainly as a critique of these approaches. It might have meant at least three quite distinct positions, rather too often assumed to be equivalent to each other. In the first place, relative poverty might be taken to mean that the tests for poverty are based in social norms and expectations, and are liable to change. Absolute poverty was supposed to describe a fixed, constant state of being; the idea of relative poverty, by contrast, supposes that the tests might need to adjust to those conditions, and that as some needs were met, others would become apparent. Poverty is a moving target. This is the way that Martin Ravallion uses the idea of relative poverty: so, in his view, there is absolute poverty in the poorest places, and relative poverty, defined to a less restrictive standard, in developed economies.[30]

A second view of relative poverty was that the nature of poverty should be considered to reflect the standards of the society where it applied. Poverty is defined socially, because the rules that govern people's behaviour depend on understandings and arrangements that differ between societies. Richer societies are able to demand and impose higher minimum standards for food, consumer goods, sanitation, public safety and so on. Critically important issues like access to land, shelter, education and employment are socially defined. This is not just about expectations; limiting the range of acceptable conduct determines what is possible in a particular place. People are

---

[28] International Labour Office, 1976, *Employment growth and basic needs: a one world problem*, Geneva: ILO, p 243.

[29] United Nations, 1995, Report of the World Summit for Social Development (Copenhagen Declaration), https://www.un.org/en/development/desa/population/migration/generalassembly/docs/globalcompact/A_CONF.166_9_Declaration.pdf, p 41, accessed 19.12.2019.

[30] M Ravallion, 2016, *The economics of poverty*, Oxford: Oxford University Press.

homeless, not just because there are no homes, but because the rules governing access and entitlement are defined socially. For example, in many societies, people with nowhere to live can squat. In much of the developed world, that is not an option, and people have to live on the street instead.

Amartya Sen's understanding of capabilities and commodities recognises these issues. The idea of a capability represents, in abstract terms, the things that people need to do – to have food, the capacity to move around, communications, and so forth. Commodities represent the specific means by which these capabilities can be recognised, but the commodities through which capabilities like 'shelter' or 'communication' are realised are different in different societies.[31] Peter Townsend also emphasised relative differences in norms, in a different way. He explained relative deprivation in these terms:

> People are relatively deprived if they cannot obtain, at all or sufficiently, the conditions of life – that is, the diets, amenities, standards and services which allow them to play the roles, participate in the relationships and follow the customary behaviour which is expected of them by virtue of their membership of society.[32]

The question of what makes poverty depends on the way that entitlements, amenities and services are shaped by the standards of each society. Townsend argued for a 'thorough-going relativity'.[33] He emphasised the relationship of poverty to social norms – the expectations, patterns of behaviour and customs that are accepted 'in the societies to which they belong'.[34] That implies, in turn, that the experience and character of poverty will be different in different societies.

A third view of relative poverty is that it describes a form of inequality. Poverty, Townsend insisted, is not inequality,[35] and the idea of inequality is much wider than the idea of poverty; but in the statement I have just cited, Townsend identifies poverty explicitly in terms of disadvantage, and that is just another way of saying that it

---

[31] A Sen, 1999, *Commodities and capabilities*, Oxford: Oxford University Press.

[32] P Townsend, 1993, *The international analysis of poverty*, London: Harvester Wheatsheaf, p 36.

[33] P Townsend, 1985, A sociological approach to the measurement of poverty, *Oxford Economic Papers*, 37(4): 669–76.

[34] P Townsend, 1979, *Poverty in the United Kingdom*, Harmondsworth: Penguin, p 31.

[35] Townsend, 1979, p 57.

is unequal. The idea of 'economic distance', referred to earlier, is an example of the same kind of reasoning. It is generally expressed as a percentage of median household income, usually 50% or 60%; that is a test of dispersion, not of adequacy. The rationale is not that poverty is being precisely measured, but that at certain levels of income people are so far removed from the mainstream pattern of life that they can be considered to be poor. The test of economic distance directly reflects income inequality within a particular society.

There are three different kinds of relativist argument here, and there is a good case for all of them; standards are not fixed, they are socially constructed, and unavoidably they do reflect issues of inequality. The absolutist position has not been able to stand against any of the three, and that is why it is far less often referred to than it was twenty-five years ago. If poverty is relative, it has to be understood within the context of the society where it takes place. There are some intellectual problems with that, and I will return to those issues in due course. For the present, however, I am more concerned with the way that concepts of poverty shape our understanding of the experience of poor people, and the idea that poverty is 'relative' in any of these senses does not go far enough.

Absolute and relative poverty begin from a common position. They both describe poverty as a situation, a set of circumstances or a state of being – a position that can be considered exclusively from the perspective of the individual who experiences it. If, for example, a person has less money than a poverty threshold, does not have access to specific facilities or amenities, or lacks key resources, that person might be considered to be poor, both on relative and absolute definitions. There are reasons to think this kind of representation of poverty is misleading, and that is the subject of the next section.

Poverty as a relational concept

Conventional economic theory treats individuals as if they lived on desert islands, in isolation from other people: 'a collection of Robinson Crusoes, as it were.'[36] The Copenhagen definition of absolute poverty begins with an innocuous word: poverty is a 'condition', a property of the poor person. When the primary issue in world poverty was subsistence agriculture, this might have made some sense, because the condition of subsistence farmers is remarkably self-contained: the

---

[36] M Friedman, 1962, *Capitalism and freedom*, Chicago: University of Chicago Press, p 13.

resources, assets and income derived can usually be described in terms of unique households. It is not coincidental that the strongest adherents of the absolute model of poverty have been those who worked in the poorest countries, such as Lipton and Ravallion.[37] However, most countries have moved away from that kind of world. Poverty in contemporary societies is defined and experienced in terms of the way that people live in relation to other people.

There are some concepts of poverty – the web of deprivation, a low standard of living, and a lack of resources – which refer to a situation that poor people find themselves in; the terms might in principle be applied to people living in isolation from society. However, most of the definitions of poverty considered so far in this chapter are relational, not situational; they are concerned not with material conditions, or the things that people have or do not have, but with relationships between poor people and others. The word 'relational' sounds a bit like 'relative', which is liable to confuse, but they have different implications. Relative poverty, while it might mean several things, is essentially poverty that is relative to the society where it occurs. That might well be something like the level of income, the things that someone owns, the capabilities of the poor person. People might be considered 'relatively' poor if, for example, they do not have a warm overcoat or a bed for every child.[38] On this account, the idea of poverty is much like the idea of ill health: it is a condition or a state of being, which can be considered individually, person by person.

'Relational' concepts call for a different way of thinking about the issues. They are constructed in terms of relationships with other people. Poverty is not so much like ill health – a condition or situation that the person has – as it is like ideas of social class, status or power; a complex set of circumstances, defined by that person's relationships to other people. Other examples of relational concepts might include, for example, being part of a family, being employed, or having membership of a club; they do not mean anything at all unless other people are included in the idea. If poverty is unusual in this, it is not because it is relational – lots of other concepts are – but because it is so complex. It manifests itself in many different ways. It is not consistent over time – people can be poor at some times and not at others. People may not recognise themselves as being in relationships of poverty; sometimes they just do not want to think of themselves as

---

[37] M Lipton and M Ravallion, 1995, Poverty and policy, in J Behrman and T Srinivasan (eds), *Handbook of development economics*, vol 3B, Amsterdam: Elsevier.

[38] See for example, J Mack and S Lansley, 2015, *Breadline Britain*, London: Oneworld.

being poor. Despite that, poverty is just as real, and just as important, as being a member of a class, a family or an ethnic group.

It is easiest to show what the relational aspects of poverty might be by example. *Voices of the Poor* identifies a long series of relational issues – power, gender and social organisation among them.[39] Table 1.1 re-presents material used by the researchers to describe the 'web' of poverty; it was initially drawn up in a rather attractive diagram, but apparently the team decided not to use it, and it only found its way later into a working paper by Robert Chambers.[40]

Some of the factors in the table are self-evidently relational, and I have listed them in the middle column. They include issues like debt, corruption, gender relations, legal issues, political organisation, and much more. Some others are not evidently relational. (There are nevertheless some very strong arguments to say that issues like disability, old age, pollution, sickness and hunger should be thought of as relational nevertheless. Sen reviews relational accounts of hunger as part of his discussion of social exclusion.[41]) The key point to take away is a simple one: the issues in the table that are clearly and directly relational outnumber the rest by more than two to one.

Several writers in recent years have been feeling their way towards a relational understanding of poverty, often linked to the idea of exclusion. Others refer to the relational dimensions of the subject obliquely; that is only to be expected, because any empirical research is likely to encounter some of the relational issues. The writers who have come closest to a relational understanding of the subject are Amartya Sen and Ruth Lister, though both in their own ways stop a little way short of declaring that poverty is relational. Sen attributes the relational elements of poverty to the concept of social exclusion. He holds that the concept of 'capability deprivation' or poverty has always incorporated relational elements; he has welcomed the idea of exclusion as a way of emphasising the importance of those issues. 'Some types of social exclusion must be seen as constitutive components of the idea of poverty – indeed must be counted among its core components.'[42] He distinguishes two types of process: exclusions which are 'instrumental', which can be seen as causes of

---

[39] Narayan and others, 2000.

[40] R Chambers, 2007, *Poverty research: methods, mindsets and methodologies*, Brighton: University of Sussex, p 37.

[41] A Sen, 2000, *Social exclusion: concept, application and scrutiny*, Manila: Asian Development Bank, pp 9–12.

[42] A Sen, 2000, *Social exclusion: concept, application and scrutiny*, Manila: Asian Development Bank, p 5.

Table 1.1: The web of poverty

Class of issues	Relational issues	Issues that are not self-evidently relational
Problems with institutions and access	Problems with documents Rude behaviour Extortion Corruption Poor service	
Poverty of time	Low earnings Family care/domestic dependents	Distances Travelling and waiting Time-laborious activities
Seasonal dimensions	Work Debt	Sickness Hunger
Place of the poor	Isolation Lack of infrastructure/services	Bad shelter Unhealthy Exposed Polluted
Insecurities	Work/livelihood Crime Civil disorder War Legal Macro-economic	Natural disasters
Physical ill-being	Appearance	Hunger/lack of food Sickness Exhaustion Disabled/old Lack of strength
Social relations	Widowhood Gender roles Individualism Lack of cohesion	
Material poverties	Lack of work Low returns Taxation Casual work Debt Dowry social code Lack of access	Lack of assets Lack of resources
Ascribed and legal inferiority	Gender Ethnicity Caste Refugees and displaced persons Children	
Lack of political clout	Behaviour of elites Lack of political organisation	
Lack of information	Weak networks	Physical isolation No TV, radio, newspaper
Lack of education	Poor quality Need children at home Cost	Distance

Source: Chambers, 2007, p 37, reworked by the author

poverty, and exclusions which are 'intrinsic' or 'constitutive' elements of deprivation. For example,

> 'The relational exclusions associated directly with unemployment can have constitutive importance through the connection of unemployment with social alienation, but they can also have instrumental significance because of the effects that unemployment may cause in leading to deprivations of other kinds.'[43]

Lister, for her part, accepts the principle that poverty can be defined in terms of material deprivation, but she argues for a relational perspective as a further component:

> The material – lack of the material resources needed to meet minimum needs, including social participation ... – is widely regarded by social scientists as the stuff of how we define poverty. But when we also conceptualise poverty in relational and symbolic terms, it changes the angle of vision to provide a more acute sociological and social psychological understanding.[44]

While material deprivation remains, in her view, at the heart of the concept of poverty, she classifies some aspects of poverty as 'relational-symbolic'. This includes such issues as disrespect, humiliation, stigma, the denial of rights and lack of voice. These are issues which, she has argued, should be considered as having 'parity and interdependence' with the material aspects of the term.[45] In her earlier work on the concept of poverty, she suggested that poverty was 'mediated and interpreted' through such relationships.[46] In the later paper, she has edged towards a stronger relational focus, re-emphasising the role of relational issues, both social and psychological, as important elements of poverty in their own right.[47] In many circumstances 'poverty' refers immediately and directly to social relationships. Stigma, exclusion,

---

[43] Sen, 2000, p 22.

[44] R Lister, 2015, To count for nothing: poverty beyond the statistics, *Journal of the British Academy*, 3: 139–165, p 140.

[45] R Lister, 2004, *Poverty*, Cambridge: Polity Press, p 8.

[46] Lister, 2004, p 8.

[47] Lister, 2015, p 141.

entitlement and lack of security are not just *mediated* through relationships; they *are* relationships.

Resources and relationships

If the experience of poverty is substantially a question of social relationships, it seems appropriate to question how that can be reconciled with the kinds of definition I have been discussing. Some of the clusters of meaning considered earlier are explicitly and directly concerned with social relationships: class (whether economic or social), dependency and exclusion. Some are statuses, that is, sets of social roles and norms – lack of entitlement and lack of basic security. As a moral evaluation, the idea of poverty implies social obligations, rights and responsibilities. In sum, seven of the twelve clusters of meaning identified earlier in this chapter are clearly and directly relational.

Even if many concepts of poverty have relational dimensions, it could still be argued that this is not typical of the way that poverty is most widely understood – that poverty is primarily framed, regardless, in terms of a lack of goods or resources. 'There is general agreement', David Gordon claims, 'that poverty can be defined as having "an insufficient command over resources through time."'[48] This is probably a fair representation of the mainstream view in social policy, but it bears re-examination. In five of the twelve clusters of meaning I have outlined, poverty is primarily understood in terms of access to resources. They are:

- the lack of specific goods and items;
- the web of deprivation;
- a low standard of living;
- a lack of resources; and
- economic distance. (This is a comparative lack of resources, but by the same token it is relative rather than relational.)

The relational elements of these concepts may not be immediately obvious, but they are there nevertheless. An insufficient command over resources might refer, not just to access to physical items, but to a range of relationships – services, facilities or participation in society. People's command of basic items such as housing, education, health

---

[48] D Gordon, 2006, The concept and measurement of poverty, in C Pantazis, D Gordon and R Levitas (eds), *Poverty and social exclusion in Britain*, Bristol: Policy Press, p 32.

care, transport and personal security is developed through a tissue of interwoven social and economic relationships. Often, despite an initial emphasis on resources, these concepts point at the same time to a set of economic and social relationships. Ideas such as the web of deprivation, patterns and standards of living, or economic distance are all ways of trying to capture a wider, broader sense of poverty.

The connections between resources and relationships go all the way through. Money may seem to be an unlikely example, but money too has relational dimensions. One of the most basic ideas in economics is the idea that the price of goods and services depends on demand as well as supply. Demand is defined in terms of the willingness of different participants to devote their financial resources to obtaining different commodities. Describing poverty in terms of a fixed level of income, such as $1.90 a day, seems to suggest that money is a fixed good with an inherent value. Money is not a fixed good; its value is relative. Even the cost of money itself varies:

> In Indian villages, power relations over many generations have solidified conditions of contrived scarcity, generating a rent-based distribution system in which the weaker sections cannot escape. Being a comparatively efficient medium of exchange, money is the most important scarce commodity. It thus has a high price, and those who possess it can exploit those who do not.[49]

What anyone's money is able to buy depends on the money that other people have. Wherever commodities are scarce, people with more money are able to obtain them before people with less. When 'targeted' programmes give money to some people and not others, it affects the balance of resources; this has an effect on what people who get the benefits are able to buy; that in turn affects the price of certain goods. A study in the Philippines for the World Bank found that, when some families with children got benefits, the price of protein-rich foods increased, and the nutrition of other children – the ones who did not get the benefits – got worse.[50]

Command over resources and the ability to obtain commodities are based in transactions, and transactions are relational. The fundamental

---

[49] S Davala, R Jhabvala, S Kappor Mehta and G Standing, 2015, *Basic Income: a transformative policy for India*, London: Bloomsbury, p 48.

[50] D Filmer, J Friedman, E Kandpal and J Onishi, 2018, *General equilibrium effects of targeted cash transfers*, Washington DC: World Bank.

question, Sen argues, is whether or not people are entitled to obtain the commodities that are there.[51] Entitlement cannot be understood in isolation. The web of deprivation, economic distance and a low standard of living call for consideration of relative purchasing power, while command over resources, the lack of resources and lack of specific goods are as much about entitlements as they are about the goods. It is hardly possible to do that without considering rights, relative purchasing power, access or basic security.

It follows that *all* the different ways of understanding poverty identified in this chapter, without exception, depend on statements about social and economic relationships. They may not be exclusively relational, but they all have relational elements, and the relational issues are not secondary to understanding the experience of poverty – they are integral to it. Social relationships are not just a reason for poverty – they are the stuff of poverty, what poverty is made of. Poverty is not just a relative concept; it is a relational one.

A relational perspective does not exclude consideration of material issues, but it does change the way that such issues need to be thought about. Social scientists have been likely to assume that the core of poverty is reducible to the question of resources, while other issues such as exclusion or insecurity are by-products; but that distinction, even if it is convenient for analysis, is arbitrary. It would make better sense – and it is arguably more faithful to the tenor of the mainstream argument – to say that poverty is both resource-based and dependent on social relationships. There are some issues associated with poverty which are not relational, such as clean water or sanitation; and some are relative without being relational, such as impaired health or early death. Resource-based concepts of poverty are not exclusively relational, then, and resource-based arguments that focus on those issues are still important in their own right. However, any focus on purely material issues is incomplete: well-being depends on an interaction between the person, the material circumstances and the social. Sarah White argues:

> Subjective, material and relational dimensions of wellbeing are revealed as co-constitutive. Wellbeing is emergent, the outcome of accommodation and interaction that happens in and over time through the dynamic interplay of personal, societal and environmental structures and processes.[52]

---

[51] Sen, 1981.

[52] S White, 2017, Relational wellbeing: re-centring the politics of happiness, policy and the self, *Policy & Politics*, 45(2): 121–36, p 133.

If we follow through the implications of this argument, the suggestion that resources are the fundamental issue, and that everything else is a consequence, is unsustainable. Poverty is not 'primarily an income- or resource-driven concept' that can be 'distinguished from social deprivation and social exclusion'.[53] It is a set of social relationships that manifest themselves in terms of deprivation, disadvantage, impaired economic relationships, lack of entitlements and social exclusion. There are many points in this book that refer to problems of resources or material deprivation, because those are some of the key ways in which relationships of poverty are expressed. Resources, however, cannot be considered in isolation from the social relationships. Leaving out the relational elements, as too many descriptions of poverty try to do, strips resources and goods of their meaning – of their place in people's lives.

---

[53] Townsend and others, 1997.

2

Poverty and the economy

The reason for beginning with the economy is partly that it provides a context for much of the argument that follows, but more importantly because it represents a framework of relationships in its own right. There is a direct connection between the structure of the economy and the resources that are available to people: the economy shapes how the resources are made, how they are distributed and what can be done with them. Beyond that, however, economic systems set the terms for how people live. This is not just a matter of material goods, but personal, social, economic and political relationships. The pattern of economic production shapes the key distinctions between agrarian and industrial societies, the pattern of urbanisation, communications and domestic life. There are strong links, too, between the pattern of economic organisation and social structures — structures of class, employment and labour, land and housing tenures, personal and social security, taxation and governance, and public services.

'Capitalism'

The way that the world works is often boiled down to a single word: capitalism. This is supposed to be a generic description of everything about the modern economy. As such, it is not terribly useful, because it fails to distinguish anything about the economy from everything else. If it is going to add anything to the discussion, it is because it is supposed to relate to a much more detailed, 'thicker' model of how the economy works.

Two competing models have dominated the discussion. On one hand, pro-market 'neoliberals' identify capitalism with the progressive development of the 'market economy'. On the other, there is the marxist model, which sees capitalism as a defence of a propertied class who own and control the means of production. The two models have some points of similarity, and some major differences; but neither of them, taken singly or together, represents the world as it actually is.

The key elements of 'capitalism' in neoliberal thought are:

- The establishment of 'markets': a system of production, exchange and distribution that develops through the free actions of a multitude of separate actors. Capitalism is identified by Milton Friedman as consisting of 'the organization of the bulk of economic activity through private enterprise operating in a free market'.[1]

- The profit motive. The various actors in a market aim to profit through self-interested decisions and choices. Adam Smith argued: 'It is not from the benevolence of the butcher, the brewer, or the baker, that we expect our dinner, but from their regard to their own interest.'[2]

- The use of money and the price mechanism to determine the process of communication and exchange in the market. According to Hayek,

  The whole acts as one market, not because any of its members survey the whole field, but because their limited individual fields of vision sufficiently overlap so that through many intermediaries the relevant information is communicated to all. … We must look at the price system as such a mechanism for communicating information.[3]

- The consequent development of a system of production that provides for everyone. Schumpeter explained:

  The capitalist engine is first and last an engine of mass production which unavoidably also means production for the masses. … It is the cheap cloth, the cheap cotton and rayon fabric, boots, motorcars and so on that are the typical achievements of capitalist production, and not as a rule improvements that would mean much to the rich man. Queen Elizabeth owned silk stockings. The capitalist achievement does not typically consist in providing more silk stockings for queens but in bringing them within reach of factory girls.[4]

- The dynamism and responsiveness to changing circumstances of the capitalist process, through a process of 'creative destruction'.[5]

This might be a fair representation of some part of most economies, but it has serious limitations. The first problem is that it relies on a questionable view of structures and institutions. Friedman's

---

[1] M Friedman, 1961, *Capitalism and freedom*, Chicago: University of Chicago Press, p 4.

[2] A Smith, 1776, *The wealth of nations*, Book 1, Chapter 2.

[3] F Hayek, 1948, *Individualism and economic order*, Chicago: University of Chicago Press, p 86.

[4] J Schumpeter, 1943, *Capitalism, socialism and democracy*, London: George Allen and Unwin, p 67.

[5] Schumpeter, 1943, Chapter 7.

characterisation of capitalism assumes that 'private enterprise' works by common principles, as if the owner of a corner shop, the Disney Corporation, a farmer, a landlord, a plumber were all engaged more or less in the same kind of activity. 'Capitalism' is supposed to cover a huge range of different sorts of economic organisation – commercial enterprise, manufacturing, finance, land management and so forth. The interplay of economic activity is characterised not just by diverse interests, but by different kinds of actor. Ownership has become dissociated from control, but both ownership and control are increasingly corporate rather than individually based. As systems of property holding and management have become more complex, it seems clear that much of the control rests, not with the owners, nor with shareholders, but with managers. Managers are nominally agents who have been invested with the authority to do things for their principals, but in reality they are self-interested actors in their own right. The structures of large-scale contemporary businesses are based on the principle that corporations are legal persons, and in the first instance they own themselves. Shareholders have rights to a share of the profits; that is not the same thing as owning the company. (This is something that some shareholders with executive responsibility find difficult to grasp, too; witness their astonishment when they are sent to gaol for using the assets of a public company as if it was their private wealth.) One of the key weaknesses of free market thinking is the assumption that business everywhere is motivated by the same kind of calculation – the pursuit of profit. Some businesses are, but there are many competing objectives: stability, personal income, security for managers and employees, company growth, long run rather than immediate profit maximisation and development of a field. We cannot take it for granted that any single motivation will dominate.

A great deal of what passes for economics is based on a theory about the way the world ought to be, rather than any understanding of how it is. Practical men, Keynes once wrote, are often the slaves of some defunct economist;[6] the 'common sense' of one generation is the radical theory of a century or more beforehand. In common with marxists, the commentaries of neoliberals are often fixated on a single view of what a 'capitalist' is like: either the idea of the owner-entrepreneur, or the self-interested producer. There are such people, of course, as there are still feudal landlords, merchant adventurers and patricians who would not have been out of place in the ancient

---

[6] J M Keynes, 1936, *The general theory of employment, interest and money*, London: Macmillan p 383.

Roman empire; but there are not so many of that that is could be credible to suggest that the economy is organised everywhere on the same dominant principle. 'Capitalist' financiers nestle cheek by jowl with artisans, small shopkeepers, agency services and multinational corporate structures. The production of an individual operator (like, say, the work of an independent medical practitioner) is governed by different criteria from that of a medium-sized firm, and differently again from a corporate enterprise. Even within the confines of the conventional model, the economy is complex, and does not actually work on a common set of principles at all. Different producers have different motivations and modes of activity. There are voluntary, non-profit and mutual organisations. 'Capitalism' is not a unified system.

The identification of capitalism with self-interest has to be considered in this light. Like much written in this area, this is partly right, and partly wrong. Self-interest takes the form of profit-seeking only in particular contexts; it can happen within organisations, but only when their structures and practice shape self-interest in that direction. Incorporation and the patterns of institutional structures are far more complex than that, and it follows that within a modern economy, there are many other motivations for action besides self-interest. For one thing, the ownership of many economic enterprises is separated from their management, with the effect that the profit motive may be subordinated to other criteria, like long-term growth, security or career development. For another, in most economies there are industries which work explicitly on a non-profit basis. This is most strikingly the case in the financial sector, where mutual organisations have played an important part in pensions, insurance and mortgages; non-profits are equally important in sectors like health care and education.

The next part of this model sees 'capitalism' as the primary source of prosperity of contemporary economies. Many advocates of the market system believe this to be true, but the story is not straightforward. If we look again at pensions, health care, or education, markets are not the core. In relation to the housing system, people in the UK were able to live in decent housing in most cases through one of two mechanisms: the building societies, which were mutual, non-profit organisations devoted to making home ownership possible, and social housing, mainly developed through local authorities. (Taken together, those two systems at their peak provided for more than 80% of the population. Many of the UK's current problems in housing relate to the ideologically led destruction of those systems.)

Another obvious omission is that the role of government has everywhere become a major element in most developed economies.[7] There is a widespread myth among free-marketeers that governments don't produce anything; private enterprise is 'productive' and government is 'non-productive'. 'Every dollar that the government spends means one less dollar in the productive sector of the economy.'[8] This is twaddle. Most governments in the developed world deliver services; many are engaged in production, to varying degrees, through subsidy, procurement, purchase of goods or support for private production; many more produce the conditions, including the infrastructure or the maintenance of the workforce, which makes production possible. Neoliberals tend to represent the state as an outside force, regulating, making up for 'market failures', 'intervening' as a last resort. The truth is that states are, much more fundamentally, an essential part of every developed economy, and that most countries which have developed large industries have done so through a process of government – Mariana Mazzucato's work on *The Entrepreneurial State* makes the case strongly.[9]

The marxist critique of capitalism begins from some of the same premises as the neoliberal argument – the emphasis on ownership and control, and on private enterprise and profit – and it follows that it is subject to many of the same criticisms. The key elements of capitalism in marxist analysis have been:

- the central role of capital as the determining economic factor;
- the dominance of the bourgeoisie, the 'capitalist' class;
- the commodification of goods, services and labour;
- the dominance of the profit motive, fuelled by self-interest; and
- the accumulation and concentration of capital by the dominant class.

For marxists, capitalism was both intrinsically disempowering and inherently unstable. Marx identified what he saw as the emergence of a new world order, based on the dominance of a class of business owner, the 'bourgeoisie'. The bourgeoisie had 'broken the fetters' of the feudal system, which gave authority to a ruling class on the basis

---

[7] C A R Crosland, 1956, *The future of socialism*, London: Jonathan Cape.

[8] D Mitchell, 2005, *The impact of government spending on economic growth*, Washington DC: Heritage Foundation, p 1.

[9] M Mazzucato, 2015, *The entrepreneurial state*, New York: Anthem Press; and see H-J Chang, 2007, *Bad Samaritans*, London: Random House Business Books.

of their birth. Capitalism was motivated by the pursuit of money, in the form of a 'cash nexus', and the basis aim for any business was to make profits for the owners. Marx's view was that the system held 'the seeds of its own destruction'. His position was intrinsically pessimistic. The progressive immiseration of the population would bring about the collapse of the system. Capitalism, Marx argued, would inevitably be followed by the revolution of the proletariat, and the marxists who followed him came to an easy conclusion: whatever else might have happened, as the revolution had not happened yet, this must still be capitalism.

The marxist analysis, like the neoliberal model, only describes a small part of the institutional structures, the process and the outcomes of economic activity. One major flaw lies in the assumptions made about how capital is accumulated. Thomas Piketty argues, in his monumental work on *Capital in the twenty-first century*,[10] that wealth is being concentrated in private hands, because capitalists demand a rate of return greater than the rate of growth. The complex structures of ownership and control mean that arguments based on the profit motive often fail to understand the behaviour and motivation of the many actors involved in the economy. Many businesses and corporations, and most large ones, are not owned by the people responsible for them. That is not to say that they are owned by a different elite, by aristocrats, or by entrepreneurs, or by anyone else. Many are not owned by human beings. The key weakness of Piketty's argument lies in a failure to recognise that so much capital is impersonal. Non-human constructs, like corporations and trusts, might fail, as private entrepreneurs can fail; but unlike private entrepreneurs, they never get bored, they never retire and they never die. Ultimately, if capital is concentrated, it will not be in the hands of private individuals.

The limited scope of the analysis helps to explain why Marx's predictions fell so far of the mark. It is true enough that the economic model of capitalism is unstable, as several major crashes have demonstrated, but a whole set of mechanisms have developed to respond to that instability, a direction of movement that Marx thought impossible. There is no conception of what might be achieved through voluntarism, mutualism, collective action or government. There are certainly some countries and some circumstances where poverty has

---

[10] T Piketty, 2014, *Capital in the twenty-first century*, Cambridge, MA: Harvard University Press.

worsened as formal economies have developed,[11] but over time and across the piece there have been marked improvements in the living standards of most people, in most places.

The economic system

The dominant view of the economy under capitalism, in both neoliberal and marxist models, is that it works by a set of common mechanisms. Goods are produced in order to be exchanged, the principal medium of exchange is monetary, and in consequence the production of goods is related directly to financial conditions. Those mechanisms, rather than the motivations or the institutions, are central to the idea that the economy can be seen as a whole system.

The economic system depends critically on exchange, and exchanges are generally conducted through the medium of money. That in turn is often described in terms of a 'market' – people take goods or labour to market, to sell them for money, which they can then exchange to get goods – but the 'market' is just another catch-all term for everything that happens. The key transition in the move to contemporary economies is usually characterised as a movement from agriculture to industry, or from rural to urban areas; both are part of what is happening, but neither captures the key element in this process. It is a move not just out of farming, but out of subsistence farming – a world where people have to do everything for themselves, growing their own food and making their own things. 'Industrialisation' itself, Kingsbury argues, is a dated term – many contemporary developments have been marked by a transition to post-industrial service industries.[12] The central process of development is a transition from subsistence to a formal, exchange-based economy. What happens as the formal economy develops – both within agriculture and beyond it – is that people specialise, doing one main thing instead of many. They get money, and they use that money to buy things.

Much of what is written about development begins with a simple distinction between people who are in the formal economy and those who are not. That makes some sense, because in societies where people are not part of the formal economy, poverty is liable to be

---

[11] G Estava, S Babones and P Babcicky, 2013, *The future of development*, Bristol: Policy Press; P Shafer, R Kanbur and R Sandbrook, 2019, *Immiserizing growth*, Oxford: Oxford University Press.

[12] D Kingsbury, 2012, Introduction, in D Kingsbury, J McKay, J Hunt, M McGillivray and M Clarke, *International development: issues and challenges*, Basingstoke: Macmillan, p 3.

endemic and unavoidable. Economic development, or the lack of it, has major implications for the position of people within a country: it shapes how and where they live. It determines what kind of income they will have – not just how much, but the way it comes and the shape it comes in. People need to get a livelihood, and in a formal economy, that generally means that they need an income. For most people, that means either that they need to work, or that they need to share resources with someone who works.

Integration in the economy is critical to people's living standards. That means, in the first instance, that inclusion in the economy depends primarily on the labour market. That can mean several things, however. For decades, work in a modern economy was seen as something that was predictable, regular and stable: either a salary (paid on an account) or wages (typically paid in cash). There was said to be a 'dual labour market'. This was always a simplification, but it was a useful shorthand. Part of the labour market was represented by people, the working poor, who were secure and well-paid, another part were people on poor conditions and permanently low incomes.

This is still true in some places. The reason for writing about it in the past tense is that, shorthand or not, it no longer works very well as a description in many others. There has been an increasing emphasis on encouraging 'flexible' labour markets, where people are encouraged to move freely between workplaces. With that trend a greater number of people have found themselves in precarious situation: their incomes and work contracts are insecure, and the nature and size of their incomes fluctuate rapidly. This is not a new phenomenon, because even in the days of the dual labour market there were always people with irregular incomes and patterns of job-holding, often in employment that was marginal to the economy, liable to shift between work and unemployment. That condition – described in terms of 'sub-employment'[13], and sometimes of 'precariousness' – has extended to a much wider range of people.[14] In developed economies, then, there are three main labour markets: secure, low paid, and marginalised. And to that we need to add a fourth stream, who are none of those: those are people who are likely to be 'disqualified',[15] largely excluded from the labour market, typically because of physical or mental illness, status, ethnicity or some other kinds of disadvantages. Exclusion does

---

[13] D Matza and H Miller, 1976, Poverty and proletariat, in R Merton, R Nisbet (eds) *Contemporary social problems*, 4th edn, New York: Harcourt Brace Jovanovich.

[14] G Standing, 2014, *The precariat*, London: Bloomsbury.

[15] S Paugam, 2004, *La disqualification sociale*, Paris: Presses Universitaires de France.

not commonly mean that people never work at all, but finding work is likely to be difficult, and work is as marginal for them as they are marginal for the labour market.

The distinctions between these different categories are somewhat blurred in practice. People who are marginal to an economy find themselves in unpredictable, precarious circumstances, moving between casual, temporary, ephemeral work, often undeclared or beneath the notice of the authorities.[16] That, too, is an aspect of poverty – understood not as permanently low resources (because the situation is impermanent) but rather, as Charles Booth once put it, 'living under a struggle to obtain the necessaries of life and make both ends meet.'[17] The same systems which might seem to be a way out of poverty can be, for others, part of the problem. We can see the problems of integration in a formal economy most clearly in the circumstances of people who are poor in developed economies, because those people are typically poor despite that nominal integration. In richer countries, some people will have no direct income of their own, being dependent on others, and others (particularly among older people) may be in receipt of benefits. It is not certain, however, that income from employment will be adequate, secure or sufficient to avoid harm if problems arise.

Market economies are often represented in developing countries as something much more sophisticated than market exchange, because that is the model of the developed economies. The second key element of the world economy is that there is a financial system, which makes it possible to sell not only what one produces or earns, but what one is going to produce or earn. Loans, credit, mortgages and so forth rely in principle on the debtor having future income or assets which will make it possible to pay off the loan. The providers of finance offer a wide range of services: allowing people to realise their future income, limiting risks and uncertainty (the principle of insurance, and arguably of futures trading) and making it possible to do things collectively, by pooling resources, that would not be possible for individuals. In some cases, financial institutions have an explicit social purpose. Building societies made it possible for people to pool their resources and help each other build homes;[18] mutual insurers have developed as non-profit-making membership societies; the Grameen

---

[16] Matza, Miller, 1976.

[17] C Booth, 1902, *Life and labour of the people in London*, vol 1, London: Macmillan, p 33.

[18] E Cleary, 1965, *The building society movement*, London: Elek.

Bank has grown by making it possible for groups of women working together to pool resources to start up small enterprises.[19] Those may not be representative of the financial sector, but they illustrate a more general point: finance depends on social and institutional structures more than it depends on the interactions of wealthy individuals. (There is a certain irony in that last point, because the economic theory on which much of the analysis of the finance industry has been captured by doctrinaire individualism.)

For many commentators, the critique of 'capitalism' has become inextricably bound up with the role of the financial system – in particular, 'casino capitalism' and the misbehaviour of bank executives, who have used these future-based structures to gamble with other people's money. There is a great deal of justice in that, but there are more fundamental concerns. The arcane processes by which property rights are determined and people's opportunities are set have been blamed for being part of the 'production of poverty'. The financial system poses problems for poor people and for poor countries. Poor people suffer from rules and practices which make debts more expensive for them than they are rich people, have the problems of gaining finance to help with housing, difficulty in raising funds for enterprise, lack of access to the facilities of modern banking. Poor countries have similar problems. One of the key reasons, Sumner suggests, that the governments of developing countries have been anxious to see themselves treated as 'middle-income' countries is that it directly affects their ability to raise finance, the range of financial options they have and the costs they have to meet.[20]

The third element of market economies is that there are conventions – defined and accepted ways of doing things. The rules of the game are complex, because so many of them are made at national level when the structures they relate to are often cross-national. As a general proposition, however, the structures of both market economies and of the financial system are regulated; there are widely shared norms, legal frameworks and systems of redress. Among these norms are laws relating to property ownership, contract, liability and limited liability and, crucially for the development of businesses, laws which permit incorporation and representation of collective interests as if an organisation was a person. The joint stock company with limited liability developed in the 19th century; the structure is an elaborate

---

[19] M Todaro, S Smith, 2015, *Economic development*, Boston: Pearson, pp 586–91.

[20] A Sumner, 2016, *Global poverty: deprivation, distribution and development since the Cold War*, Oxford: Oxford University Press, pp 23–4.

construct, but it is central to economic development in contemporary societies. It means that people can set up businesses without themselves becoming liable for debts that accrue if the business fails – a set of rules that implicitly shifts the burden of risk onto investors, customers and sub-contractors. Contrast the position of the poor. Debt can hobble the prospects of poor people; in extreme cases debt can enslave them. Redress and access to law are limited, and often denied. One disturbing, recurrent theme in *Voices of the Poor* is the role of legal authority. For poor people around the world, there are many failings of the institutions that ought to protect them. The abuse of power is commonplace.

The areas discussed so far – the formal market economy, access to finance, and protection and redress in transactions and exchange – have received a considerable amount of attention in attempts by international organisations to push economies towards development. All three of these areas have received considerable attention. The 'structural adjustment' policies of the 1980s and 1990s were heavily geared towards the construction of institutions and practices that would be consistent with the establishment of market transactions, finance and property rights. Structural adjustment was, by most reasonable tests, a failure.[21] More than thirty years on, it is impossible to say what the world would have looked like without structural adjustment – Bill Easterly has argued that there may ultimately have been long-term benefits[22] – but the implementation of policies was uneven at best,[23] and there were no clear benefits attributable to the policies when they were properly implemented. The effects of those policies were associated at the time with recession, unemployment and withdrawal of already limited public services; any beneficial developments since that time are most probably attributable to the myriad other factors – political, technological, cultural and social – which have been realised in the intervening period.

Poverty and the world economy

The idea that poverty can be attributed to 'capitalism' or the operation of the world economy takes several forms. It might be thought that

---

[21] See for example, H-J Chang, 2007, *Bad Samaritans*, London: Random House Business Books.

[22] W Easterly, 2018, In search of reforms for growth, https://t.co/U6a1EoIW9F, accessed 19.12.2019.

[23] World Bank, 1994, p 3.

poverty is produced by the world economy; that poverty reflects the distribution of economic power; that the operation of the world economy requires some degree of poverty in order to function; that poverty is a by-product of economic processes; or that the world economy operates to prevent people escaping poverty. Any combination of those positions is possible.

The view that poverty is produced by the world economy is often associated with marxism. The marxist model sees the concentration of capital, along with the processes of exploitation inherent in capitalist production, leading to progressive immiseration of the population. But the claim is not confined to traditional marxists: for Escobar, poverty and hunger are as much the product of a discourse of power as of material circumstances.[24] Mosse argues that 'impoverishment is inseparable from normal processes of capitalist economic development, especially where these result in dispossession, confiscation or privatisation of crucial livelihood resources, whether for colonial forest extraction, infrastructure development or 'new economic zones.'[25] Wherever there is misery, it is tempting to point the finger. If poverty reflects either the structure of capitalism or the exercise of its globalised power, misery should be increasing. Almost all the trends over the last twenty years, and probably the last forty years, show the opposite. Globally, the proportion of people in extreme poverty has been falling; several nations have seen massive improvements in living standards; poor people are less likely to die (an incontrovertible improvement).

For Feldman, relational poverty is a theory about the production of poverty through the exercise of power.[26] It is not difficult to link poverty to structures of power, because part of the pattern of relationships that define poverty rest on relative degrees of power – exploitation, the lack of community organisation, abuse by those in authority and the maintenance of disadvantage by birth, caste or gender. The exercise of power is sometimes taken to imply to the 'production of intended effects',[27] and there are commentators who have interpreted the treatment of poverty in terms of its service to the capitalist class:

---

[24] A Escobar, 1995, *Encountering development*, Princeton, NJ: Princeton University Press, Chapter 4.

[25] D Mosse, 2010, A relational approach to durable poverty, inequality and power, *The Journal of Development Studies*, 46(7): 1156–78, p 1171.

[26] G Feldman, 2018, Towards a relational approach to poverty in social work, *British Journal of Social Work*, doi: 10.1093/bjsw/bcy111 1–18.

[27] B Russell, 1960, *Power*, London: Unwin.

to buttress weak market controls and ensure the availability of marginal labour, an outcast class – the dependent poor – is created by the relief system. … Its degradation at the hands of relief officials serves to celebrate the value of all work.[28]

For Mosse, 'a relational view of poverty is one that asserts that "people are poor because of others … [They are] unable to control future events because others have more control over them".'[29] The quotation he is using is from a piece that was written for a different purpose – not an attempt to define poverty in terms of economic power, but to consider the impact of uncertainty on the relationships of poor people with other people.[30]

There is however some ground to cover before inequality, disadvantage and powerlessness can legitimately be attributed to the structure of economic power. It does not follow, because society is unequal, or because poverty may be produced by the deliberate actions of some people, that poverty is therefore being produced by the nature of the world economy; it may result from other processes. Women are disproportionately poor, not because of capitalism, but because they are disproportionately disadvantaged, mainly by men. People with disabilities are disproportionately poor because their circumstances are not adequately taken account of by people who do not share those disabilities. Poor people who lack power are often the victims of abuse, but the people who are abusing power – among them landowners, gangsters, hetmen, warlords, politicians and other local elites – do so regardless of the way that the economy works; some, arguably, take advantage of the lack of formal financial mechanisms that might undermine their influence. The extension of arguments about the exercise of power to the operation of the economic system calls for a long series of postulates about how all this can work – there has to be a common intention, a guiding hand, a process by which the exercise of power can be agreed, and a set of mechanisms to bring the policies into force. Contemporary critiques have moved away from that kind of instrumental view. For Foucault, 'Power is everywhere, not because it embraces everything, but because it comes from everywhere.'[31] Lukes suggests that where there are relations of dominance or hegemony,

---

[28] F Piven and R Cloward, 1972, *Regulating the poor*, London: Tavistock, p 165.

[29] Mosse, 2010, p 1158.

[30] G Wood, 2003, Staying secure, staying poor, *World Development*, 31(3): 455–71.

[31] M Foucault, 1976, *Histoire de la sexualité: la volonté de savoir*, Paris: Gallimard, p 122.

there is no need for direct instrumental mechanisms; people will defer to power because there they see no reason to challenge it.[32]

The view that the world economy needs people to be poor is somewhat less common than it once was. For markets to work, the argument runs, there have to be spurs or incentives to the right sort of behaviour. Arguments for 'incentivising' people to work often come down to the belief that people have to be rewarded for success and punished for failure, and that that is how things should be. Similarly, there needs to be 'creative destruction'; the economy works best if the best are allowed to flourish and the worst are destroyed. This is a process not unlike 'the survival of the fittest' – a phrase that came, not from Darwin, but from Herbert Spencer. Spencer argued that poverty is necessary for the economy to work:

> The poverty of the incapable, the distresses that came upon the imprudent, the starvation of the idle, and those shoulderings aside of the weak by the strong, which leaves so many 'in shallows and in miseries', are the decrees of a large, far-seeing benevolence.[33]

It is hard to say whether anyone believes this sort of thing nowadays, but the sermons of the neoliberal right-wing come close at times: inequality is good, the best must grow tall, poverty is a penalty for failure. There are several separable arguments here, but for present purposes only two need to be considered: whether inequality is functionally requisite, and if it is, whether the degree of inequality has to be so great as to imply the experience of poverty. The first question is contentious. It was suggested before that inequality might be seen as intrinsic to a market economy. It is intrinsic in the sense that the institutional arrangements of the market – where one person exchanges things, goods or services, for money – are unavoidably going to led to circumstances where some people get more and others get less; that is part of how the market works. Saying that inequality is functionally necessary goes further: it means that the inequality serves a purpose, and so that it has to be there for the purpose to be realised. If that is right, inequality has to be maintained; there is a limit to how

---

[32] S Lukes, 1978, Power and authority, in T Bottomore and R Nisbet (eds) *A history of sociological analysis*, London: Heinemann.

[33] H Spencer, 1851, *Social statics*, Chapter 25, Section 6, https://oll.libertyfund.org/titles/spencer-social-statics-1851/simple, accessed 19.12.2019.

far inequality can be mitigated, and even an argument to say that it should not be.

Relatively few people nowadays argue for inequality directly, in the sense of arguing (as Spencer argued) that disadvantage is a good thing; they are much more likely to object to attempts to remedy it, on the basis that this would limit freedom or exceed the legitimate role of government. Arguments for inequality are questionable on moral grounds, and there is some evidence to say they are mistaken about the practical effects. In moral terms, inequality has many undesirable aspects: denying resources to those most in need, limiting opportunities, encouraging stigma. In practical terms, there is no good reason to think that greater inequality leads to greater benefits for the population. *The Spirit Level* offers evidence that inequality has undesirable consequences, too; societies that are more unequal have more crime, more social problems and lower income than those which have less.[34] And it does not make a difference that inequality is inevitable; as Tawney comments, the impossibility of absolute cleanliness is no reason to roll around in a dungheap. [35]

In terms of the evidence, there is none to show that raising the standards of people who are disadvantaged makes the performance of the economy worse,[36] and there is some to the contrary. Hanlon and his colleagues argue that the effect of redistributing resources immediately and directly to the poor is not to undermine their incentives; it offers them choices, making it possible to escape from poverty.

> Transfers can create a virtuous development cycle at the household and community level – and nationally. Families with an assured, though small, income begin to take small risks by investing in their future: buying better seeds to try to increase farm production, purchasing goods that can be resold locally, or even spending more time looking for better jobs. In impoverished communities, it is hardly worth starting a business because none has money to buy. When they have a bit of extra income, most families spend the money locally, buying food, clothing and inputs. This stimulates the local economy, because local people sell more,

---

[34] R Wilkinson and K Pickett, 2009, *The spirit level*, London: Allen Lane.

[35] R Tawney, 1936, *Equality*, London: Allen and Unwin.

[36] A B Atkinson, 1995, The welfare state and economic performance, in *Incomes and the welfare state*, Cambridge: Cambridge University Press.

earn more, and buy more from their neighbours, creating the rising spiral.[37]

Most of the information available about statistical trends is open to question, and comparative analyses are vulnerable to inadequate data, biased selections and over-generalisation.[38] It is difficult to say what the connections are. It is at least possible to draw the conclusion that higher levels of inequality are not functionally necessary, because if they were, the performance of countries that are more equal, or those with higher levels of redistribution, would be impaired. That is not what happens. By and large, the world's most successful economies tend on the whole to have higher taxation, better health care, better support for poorer people, and more people engaged in government service than economies which are less successful.[39] That does not necessarily show that countries are richer because they do these things. It may be, quite simply, that richer countries have more to spend.

The fourth option, that poverty is a by-product of economic processes, is simpler and more plausible. The discussion in this chapter has pointed to three general characteristics of the world economy: the market economy, the financial system and property rights. They are all potentially exclusive, as well as inclusive. The market economy and the system of exchange depend on people having something to trade, and there are no guarantees that what people want to sell – their produce, or their labour – is something that someone else wants to buy. Finance, in turn, depends on the value of future labour or production. That implies two kinds of problem – debt, and the inability to incur debt.

It also makes sense to argue that poverty is produced by the generation of inequality, though the statistical evidence on this is not clear-cut.[40] Inequality is intrinsic to a market economy. Inequality means disadvantage, and people who have less money are necessarily disadvantaged relative to others. That is true because, in any competition for scarce resources – goods, land, food, access to privilege – people with more money can outbid them. Inequality implies that

---

[37] J Hanlon, A Barrientos and D Hulme, 2010, *Just give money to the poor*, Sterling VA: Kumarian Press, pp 6–7.

[38] P Spicker, 2018, The real dependent variable problem: the limitations of quantitative analysis in comparative policy studies, *Social Policy & Administration*, 52(1): 216–28.

[39] See P Spicker, 2017, *Arguments for welfare*, London: Rowman and Littlefield, Chapters 1 and 10.

[40] UNDP, 2019, *Global Multidimensional Poverty Index 2019: Illuminating inequality*, pp 13–14.

some people will not have access to the goods, amenities and activities that are available to others. That could be central to poverty; the point will be returned to in Chapter 4.

The view that remains is the suggestion that the world economy operates to prevent people escaping poverty. At one level, there is no need to explain why most people are poor; it is what happens when nothing else does. If there is no economic development, the people in the country that has failed to develop are liable to be poor. Even in developed economies, it is possible to identify people who are simply left behind – older people whose pension arrangements were made at a time when expectations were lower, workers who have been displaced by technological advances, young mothers who do not have the prospects of education or career that other women do. The accusation is sometimes made, however, that at times the world economy acts to hold people back, making it difficult for nations to develop. Poverty, Paul Collier argues, 'is not intrinsically a trap, otherwise we would all still be poor'.[41] His own analysis focuses on the pathology of poor countries, including issues of conflict, geography and poor governance, but the structure of the global economy also plays its part – for example, by pushing poorer countries to specialise in agricultural production or natural resources. Restrictive trade arrangements make it difficult for countries to develop their own industries. The process of structural adjustment, adopted by international organisations in the 1980s, imposed a liberal market structure on many countries which lacked the social and economic structure to offer protection to their citizens. Some other arguments about the restrictive practices of developed economies, for example on neo-colonialism or structural dependency, are considered later.

---

[41] P Collier, 2007, *The Bottom Billion*, Oxford: Oxford University Press, p 5.

Economic development

Development and the economy

The idea of 'economic development' is usually interpreted in terms of national economies, though it could also be seen as a characteristic of regions – geographical areas where there are distinct patterns of economic activity. At the simplest level, development is seen in terms of the establishment of a formal economy, and incremental growth in the value of what is produced – judged by the gross national product or (almost the same thing, in terms of the figures) the national income. Production, income and economic growth can happen only when there is a sufficient infrastructure, mechanisms for communication and exchange and engagement in trade. Much of the literature on growth and development is fixed on the narrow issues of income and wealth; development means much more than that. Consider, for example, the effect of living in a place where there is no connecting road; where electricity supplies are either unavailable, or at best intermittent; where there is no piped water supply; where standing water is not drained, or where people do not have basic sanitation. This usually goes under the general heading of 'infrastructure'; assessments of national income are liable to leave it out, but it makes a considerable difference to people's quality of life, and beyond that to the kinds of things it is possible for them to do. Hettige describes the impact of new roads in rural areas of the Philippines, Sri Lanka and Indonesia, transforming communications, trade and social relationships.[1] There is a social infrastructure to consider, too: identity papers, a postal address, the development of education systems, health care, and increasingly of social security benefits. Much of this is difficult to count; if it adds to estimates of national income, it is usually only considered in so far as it adds directly to economic transactions. A social arrangement offers people much more than ever appears in national accounts. The National Health Service in the UK is a paradigmatic example: every person has effectively the equivalent value of health insurance, and

---

[1] H Hettige, 2006, *When do rural roads benefit the poor and how?* Manila: Asian Development Bank, http://hdl.handle.net/11540/3323, accessed 11.10.2019.

while expenditure on health care delivery is counted, the value of the insurance is not.

The effect of development generates further economic engagement and further development. Rostow, in an influential account of the process, referred to this as 'take-off' – each nation has to achieve a sufficient momentum before its economy can fly.[2] Easterly is sceptical. He argues that 'most countries that escaped from extreme poverty did so with gradually accelerating growth', rather than a rapid, critical step-change.[3] Conversely, the development of other countries after 'take-off' may have faltered: Argentina was once one of the strongest economies in the world. Nevertheless, and despite differences in language and discourse, the idea that it is possible to have that kind of radical change that has been the primary aim of all kinds of governments in developing countries, regardless of political affiliation; it has been true of free-market systems, paternalists, social democrats and Stalinists. And there are governments that have done it – Chang points to the persuasive example of Korea, which was one of the poorest places in the world in the early 1960s and is now one of the richest.[4] Most generalisations are difficult to sustain. Banerjee and Duflo write:

> Economists (and other experts) seem to have very little to say about why some countries grow and others do not. Basket cases, such as Bangladesh and Cambodia, turn into small miracles. Poster children, such as Cote d'Ivoire, fall into the 'bottom billion'. In retrospect, it is always possible to construct a rationale for what happened in each place. But the truth is, we are largely incapable of predicting where growth will happen, and we don't understand very well why things suddenly fire up.[5]

Policy for economic development has often been concerned with extending integration into formal economies. This is supposed to be a 'rising tide': it raises all boats. As Mishra comments, it also sinks some,

---

[2] W Rostow, 1962, *The stages of economic growth*, Cambridge: Cambridge University Press.

[3] W Easterly, 2006, *The white man's burden*, Oxford: Oxford University Press, p 45.

[4] H-J Chang, 2007, *Bad Samaritans*, London: Random House Business Books, Chapter 1.

[5] A Banerjee and E Duflo, 2011, *Poor economics*, Penguin, p 267.

and dashes others on the rocks.[6] Untrammelled development leads to casualties – people who suffer from the dislocation, disrupted incomes, unemployment, slum conditions and environmental degradation that are characteristic of the early stages of industrialisation. Another, less obvious, limitation is that many poor people become marginal, rather than integrated – marginality is part of the experience of being poor.

There is no single economic relationship which is exclusively associated with poverty, nor even a distinct set of positions. People can be poor because they are insecure, low paid, or excluded from the formal economy. Even if these circumstances overlap, and the boundaries are often unclear, those are very different kinds of position. They expose people to very different kinds of circumstance, and indeed to different kinds of risk. They do have something in common, however, which is often related to risk: that is, vulnerability. Risk is the likelihood that something will go wrong. Vulnerability is the severity of harm that people will experience if things go wrong, which depends on the ability that people have to deal with the problems that occur. Rich entrepreneurs commonly have high risk and insecurity but limited vulnerability. Low-paid workers in a dual labour market tend to have low risk but high vulnerability. Part of the process of development, Streeten argues, is a trade-off of poverty for vulnerability:

> Diversified subsistence farmers may be poor but are not vulnerable. When they enter the market by selling specialised cash crops, or raising their earnings by incurring debts, or investing in risky ventures, their incomes rise, but they become vulnerable.[7]

The opposite of vulnerability is resilience – the capacity to deal with harms that arise.[8] The idea is widely used in studies of development to refer to the capacity of communities, systems and governments to deal with economic fluctuations. 'At its core,' the UNDP reports, 'resilience is about ensuring that state, community and global institutions work to empower and protect people.'[9] The same principle applies to the ability of a society to cope with natural disasters – there are more

---

[6] R Mishra, 1994, The study of poverty in North America, CROP/UNESCO symposium on Regional state-of-the-art reviews on poverty research, Paris.

[7] P Streeten, 1995, Comments on 'The framework of ILO action against poverty', in G Rodgers (ed) *The poverty agenda and the ILO*, Geneva: International Labour Office.

[8] R Chambers, 1989, Vulnerability, coping and policy, *IDS Bulletin*, 20(2): 1–7.

[9] UNDP, 2014, Human Development Report 2014, p 5.

deaths when they occur in poor countries.[10] In developed economies, the idea of resilience unfortunately seems to be used in a very different sense, emphasising the individual capacity and strength of character of poor people to cope with the slings and arrows of outrageous fortune. The problem of vulnerability is not there because poor people are not clever or tough enough to avoid them; the issue is that they do not have the protections that others have.

That means, of course, that a plan for economic development cannot be assumed to be the same thing as a plan to respond to poverty. The basic question that has to be asked about economic policies is: who will benefit? Roads, telecommunications, drainage and electricity supplies generally benefit everyone, even if they often benefit rich people more – people with a greater share often have more to gain. Housing, sanitation and water supplies tend to benefit poor people more, because richer people have been able to achieve a minimum standard before such policies are introduced. By contrast, banking, a stock market and shopping malls probably benefit the rich more. None of these consequences is certain – it depends on the context where the policies are applied, on the degree of exclusion and the opportunities that are created. Development is not always bad for the poor, but nor is it always good; policies should in principle seek to make some assessment of the distributive impact. In recent years, there has been an increasing emphasis in international agencies on the idea of 'inclusive growth'. The term is ambiguous: it might mean, Klasen argues, that there is an inclusive process – that growth is guided to bring people into the economic system; that it leads to a more favourable distribution to people on low incomes; or that it has inclusive outcomes, improving the situation of poor people both within and beyond the economic system itself.[11]

There are commentators who deny the validity of development as an objective – who think that 'development stinks'.[12] The 'post-development' critique rejects development in principle, partly on the basis that development represents much that is undesirable – capitalism, westernisation and unsustainable consumption – partly because it is unattainable, a 'deceitful mirage'.[13] The critique begins with a

[10] H Rosling, 2018, *Factfulness*, London: Hodder and Stoughton, Chapter 5.

[11] S Klasen, 2017, Measuring and monitoring inclusive growth in developing and advancing economies, in C Deeming and P Smyth (eds), *Reframing global social policy: social investment for sustainable and inclusive growth*, Bristol: Policy Press, Chapter 5.

[12] G Estava, cited in J Pieterse, 2000, After post-development, *Third World Quarterly*, 21(2): 175–91, p 176.

[13] M Rahnema and V Bawtree, 1997, *The post-development reader*, London: Zed, p x.

reasonable complaint: the discourse of development, Escobar argues, describes and analyses the process as if it were an abstract discussion of economic factors, and seems to have forgotten about the people who have to live with it.[14] But the representation of societies before development is marred by a sentimental romanticism, appealing to a world where people once were warm, happy and mutually supportive[15] – as if there were no examples of mutual aid or communal life in the developed world, and no oppressive practices in traditional societies.[16] There will be casualties – as there have been in every major process of industrialisation and movement towards a developed economy; but development also benefits the poor through a range of processes. Development increases people's capabilities – their options for doing things in different ways. It makes it possible to go beyond the limitations of traditional societies. Development, Sen argues, is about freedom – or at least, it can be as long as development is accompanied by some of the key protections that are available in most developed societies.[17]

Development shapes the patterns of life in a society. Some of the changes that come about through development are changes in social relationships, such as education and women's rights, but the process may be easier to explain with examples of technology. One example might be the washing machine. There are several necessary preconditions to meet before washing machines can even be thought of – water, electricity supply, space in the domestic environment, drains for waste water – and then there has to be the production of the machine itself. It is possible for there to be a different sort of social organisation, where people pay to have their laundry done instead – that is more common in the US – but the washing machine has become ubiquitous in many better-off societies, for a very good reason; it releases people, and in particular it has released women, from prolonged days of heavy domestic labour. 96% of British households have a washing machine[18] – a degree of consensus and uniformity that seems hard to imagine before the event. Another example might be the mobile phone. Changes in telephony might not have had the

[14] A Escobar, 1995, *Encountering development*, Princeton, NJ: Princeton University Press, Chapters 2 and 3.

[15] See for example, M Rahnema and V Bawtree (eds), 1977, *The post-development reader*, London: Zed, especially Part 1.

[16] A Ziai, 2004, The ambivalence of post-development, *Third World Quarterly*, 25(6): 1045–60.

[17] A Sen, 2001, *Development as freedom*, Oxford: Oxford University Press.

[18] Office of National Statistics, 2010, *Family spending: 2010 edition*, Table A50.

transformative effect in developed countries that they are currently having in developing ones, because developed countries already had access to communications; but it is difficult to overstate their impact in Africa on information, trade and access to resources in countries where until recently people's prospects and networks were overwhelmingly confined by their physical location.[19] That, too, illustrates a general principle: development makes it possible for people to gain money and access to markets, and so access to goods, exchange and services they could not otherwise realise.

These examples point again to the ways in which the nature and character of social relationships change with changing conditions – as well as the way in which resources and relationships are intertwined. Where there is development, capabilities change – for example, for communications, for transport, for social contact. People who are poor lack the capabilities that other people have, and that affects the people they interact with, their opportunities, their scope for human development. One of the implications of that process is that the conventional approaches to linking resources with deprivation don't work. Klasen and Villalobos report a growing divergence over time between income-based measures of poverty on one hand, and deprivation on the other, as assessed by the UN Multidimensional Poverty Index. Their data come from Chile, but they speculate that this is likely to be a more general phenomenon;[20] the divergence reflects changes in urbanisation, educational provision and the composition of households. Development changes relationships.

There are many societies in transition, where development has been only partial, where poverty can be understood as a lack of integration with development. But there are others where development has taken root, where relationships need to be understood in a different context, and the character of poverty changes accordingly. This is sometimes referred to as the 'new poverty', but there is nothing new about it – it was visible in the mediaeval cities of the Reformation, the society of the Industrial Revolution and the urban societies of many developing countries. If poverty is understood as relative deprivation – not having the means to share the patterns of life common in a society – then there is nothing here that implicitly avoids disadvantage; a proportionate

---

[19] S Radelet, 2010, *Emerging Africa?* Baltimore, Maryland: Center for Global Development; and see UNDP, 2019, Human Development Report 2019, New York: UNDP, Chapter 6.
[20] S Klasen and C Villalobos, 2019, *Diverging identification of the poor: a non-random process*, Oxford: Oxford Poverty and Human Development Initiative.

increase may still leave people poor. If poverty is about dependency, exclusion or the abuse of authority then an increase in income alone will not change it. If poverty is a problem of economic position, then the position of poor people is still at the bottom.

Growth

Growth, a World Bank paper claims, is generally good for the poor.[21] The empirical evidence they review doesn't really show that; it does show, more or less, that on average poor people get a proportionate share of income, which is less than everyone else, and the relative nature of income leaves them as vulnerable to exclusion as they were before. Later data have suggested that the gains made by the richest 1% have been disproportionate, and that they have captured 27% of income growth since 1980.[22] Within these general trends, Shaffer and his colleagues note that there is considerable variation in the extent to which poor people do gain. In a number of cases there was no reduction in poverty after growth, and in 39 out of 159 countries the bottom fifth of the income distribution had less income than before.[23] Fukuda-Parr comments that while some strategies for poverty reduction in poor countries do pay attention to whether poorer people benefit from growth (Tanzania, Uganda, Vietnam), others simply assume that growth is beneficial (Yemen, Nicaragua, Madagascar) or even, in the case of Malawi, that food production is a protection against hunger.[24] Sen and Drèze show clearly that it is not.[25]

'Growth', however, means two distinct things at the same time. On one hand, it refers to the process of development, the creation of national resources and the establishment of an economic base. At the same time, growth is also an engine for economic activity, production and distribution of resources. Although development is about more than economics, the relationship between development and the growth of income and resources is relatively straightforward:

---

[21] D Dollar and A Kraay, 2000, *Growth is good for the poor*, http://documents. worldbank.org/curated/en/419351468782165950/Growth-is-good-for-the-poor, accessed 11.10.2019.

[22] UNDP, 2019, Human development report 2019, New York: UNDP, pp 110–2.

[23] P Shafer, R Kanbur and R Sandbrook, 2019, *Immiserizing growth*, Oxford: Oxford University Press, pp 40–1.

[24] S Fukuda-Parr, 2008, *Are Internationally Agreed Development Goals (IADGs) being implemented in national development strategies and aid programmes?* New York: New School, pp 8–9.

[25] A Sen and J Drèze, 1989, *Hunger and public action*, Oxford: Oxford University Press.

there is a clear and direct link between the development of a formal economy and the experience of growth. In relation to the position of people who are poor, the benefits of growth are fairly evident; as they become integrated into the patterns of a formal economy, they get the opportunity to exchange labour for money, and goods, and so assets. It would be foolish to claim that there are not problems or casualties from the process of economic growth; but it would be equally foolish to suppose that there are no compensating benefits. It cannot be denied that development does, overall, make an important difference to the lives of many people, but not all forms of development are equivalent. For Collier, 'most developing countries are clearly heading for success', but for others – 58 relatively small countries, responsible for a billion people – development is failing. When he looks at the reasons for that failure, he finds that no common explanation holds – the countries do not have a single shared experience, but a series of problems.[26] Underdevelopment and poverty go hand in hand, and life in underdeveloped countries can be short; but things are improving. 25 years ago, there were 14 countries which had more than 200 deaths among every 1000 children under five, and 17 more had rates between 150 and 200 per 1000. Now the worst rate in the world is Somalia with 122, and only five countries have more than 100 deaths per 1000.[27]

Many of the critiques of economic growth in developed countries are based on the premise that there ought, at some point, to be enough; that there is something wrong with an engine of development that cannot stop, or pause, or even slow down without having negative effects; and that because the incessant pressure to grow must eventually hit limits to growth, it is doomed to failure. Malthus predicted, more than two hundred years ago, that we would run out of resources.[28] He was wrong. The new Malthusians think there are too many people in the world and that overpopulation and limits on resources will combine to condemn the surplus population to poverty.[29] They are making the same mistakes as Malthus, and they do not have the excuse of not having the evidence in front of them. Population does not increase

[26] P Collier, 2007, *The bottom billion*, Oxford: Oxford University Press, pp 5–8.

[27] UNICEF, 2019, *The state of the world's children 2019*, https://www.unicef.org/reports/state-of-worlds-children-2019, accessed 16.10.2019.

[28] T Malthus, 1798, *Essay on the principle of population*, www.gutenberg.org/files/4239/4239-h/4239-h.htm, accessed 19.12.2019.

[29] D H Meadows, D L Meadows, J Randers and W W Behrens, 1972, *The limits to growth*, London: Earth Island; D H Meadows, D L Meadows and J Randers, 1992, *Beyond the limits*, London: Earthscan.

exponentially. The key influences on fertility are infant mortality rates and the rights of women,[30] and as they improve, fertility falls. The position on resources is just as misconceived. Natural resources are finite, but they are never actually exhausted: as they become scarcer they become more expensive and difficult to get, and substitutes are used instead. (That is why we have not run out of coal, and mines are being closed up with the coal left in the ground.) Denying resources and development to poor countries, so that richer countries can maintain their existing privileges, is economic nonsense. It is also morally outrageous.

It is probably true, as income increases, that growth yields fewer direct benefits. An increase of personal income by $1000 a year would more than double the resources and entitlements of many people throughout the world; in the richer OECD countries, the same sum typically represents 2–3%, the growth in one or two years. However, monetary values are relational, and not all that increase would carry a clear benefit. Some part of the impact of growth is inflation – a reduction in the value of money – which occurs because people with more money can bid up the prices of scarce commodities, like land. Higher income does not necessarily imply higher consumption. Fred Hirsch argued that there are 'social limits to growth'.[31]

Another aspect of growth is more difficult to come to terms with: growth is necessary to keep some parts of the economy going at all. The industries which make development possible need to be able to sell their production. We cannot have distribution networks without transport, transport without transportation and infrastructure, transportation and infrastructure without the industries to make them. The 'primary producing' industries make commodities from which other things can be made – metals, energy, concrete and so forth; many 'service industries' offer services to other industries, making it possible for specialised firms to obtain finance, essential information or expertise without having to create their own capacity to do the job. And in turn, the incomes and services needed by each of these activities creates further demand for others to provide for them.

Tony Crosland also made a case that growth was fundamental to redistribution and to protection of the poorest. His argument was stark. Without growth, further redistribution is only possible by taking away money from people who have it. With growth, it is possible to

[30] T Hewitt, I Smith, 1992, Is the world overpopulated? in T Allen and A Thomas (eds) *Poverty and development in the 1990s*, Oxford: Oxford University Press.

[31] F Hirsch, 1976, *Social limits to growth*, Cambridge, MA: Harvard University Press.

redistribute the increase, so that everyone gains something. Crosland argued that redistribution where there was no growth would be politically impossible.[32] He may well have been right about that, and if he was, arguments against growth effectively become arguments against redistribution.

Human development

The importance of income can be exaggerated: even doubling income from two to four dollars a day is uncertain to transform lives in itself, and much poverty is now found in countries which have seen substantial increases in national income.[33] More important is the general impact of development on social and economic relationships. Poverty is relational; so, in principle, is development. Where development works for the poor — as it certainly can — it does it by changing the economic and social relationships that they experience. That implies, in turn, that policies for promoting growth may or may not offer enhanced opportunities and capabilities for poor people — it depends on what happens during the process. Development is not just about money. It is about the way that people live — their physical conditions, to be sure, but also about their housing, education, living in communities, communications, employment, information, the people they interact with, the things they can buy, and so on. A focus on economics alone is unlikely to capture all the issues that affect poor people. Formal economies evidently have implications for social relationships. They tend to commodify goods, services and labour, translating things into terms which allow monetary exchange. However, substantial parts of the productive process are removed from the world in which commodities are traded and exchanged. Examples are personal relationships, domestic labour, parenting, and large parts of leisure activities — in other words, a great deal of the most important things in life. The study of social policy is concerned mainly with how people live their lives, and while involvement in the economy is clearly important, it is only part of a much wider whole.

Amartya Sen comments: 'Growth is about GDP or GNP, and is not about human beings as such, it's about commodities. So development

---

[32] C A R Crosland, 1974, *Socialism now*, London: Jonathan Cape, p 74.

[33] A Sumner, 2016, *Global poverty: deprivation, distribution and development since the Cold War*, Oxford: Oxford University Press.

translates that into things connected with human life.'[34] Human development was defined in the first Human Development report as 'a process of enlarging people's choices. The most critical of these wide-ranging choices are to live a long and healthy life, to be educated and to have access to resources needed for a decent standard of living. Additional choices include political freedom, guaranteed human rights and personal self-respect'.[35] Development, Sen argues, is a form of freedom; that is not putting the thing too high. Hardly any aspect of life is untouched.

The tests we use – income, growth, the labour market – do not really capture the difference. Amartya Sen, who helped Mahbub ul Haq develop the Human Development Index, has said this about it:

> I told Mahbub, "Look, you are a sophisticated enough guy to know that to capture complex reality in one number is just vulgar, like GDP." And he called me back later and said, "Amartya, you're quite right. The Human Development Index will be vulgar. I want you to help me to do an index which is just as vulgar as GDP, except it will stand for better things."[36]

It is difficult to marshal evidence without being reductionist whatever we do, so we may as well make a virtue of necessity. The best kept figures are on infant mortality and child health. Infant mortality is hardly a 'measure' of poverty, but it is an excellent indicator of it; it also tells us something about the welfare of children, the health of mothers, the infrastructure of health care and the resources of the societies where they live. The figures are still based on based on estimates – expert assessments, which have to balance uncertain knowledge with practical experience. The Child Mortality Report, a joint production of UNICEF, the UN, the World Health Organization and the UN, explains the methods: a combination of records, surveys, estimation and high-level statistical compromises to even out unexplained fluctuations.[37] Table 3.1 is taken from the 2019 UNICEF report,

---

[34] A Sen, 2012, Human development in the post-2015 era, www.in.undp.org/content/dam/india/docs/human-development/Amarty%20Sen%20Lecture_%20Human-Development-in-the-Post-2015-era.pdf, accessed 19.12.2019.

[35] UNDP, *Human development report 1990*, New York: Oxford University Press, p 2.

[36] Sen, 2012.

[37] UN Inter-Agency Group for Child Mortality Estimation, 2017, *Levels and trends in child mortality*, New York: UNICEF.

Table 3.1: Under-5 mortality – the countries with the highest rates

	Under 5 mortality per 1,000 children		Malnutrition – moderate and severe (%)		GNI per capita (2018, adjusted for PPP $)
	1990	2018	Stunting	Wasting	
Somalia	181	122	25	15	n.a.
Nigeria	213	120	44	11	5,700
Chad	211	119	40	13	1,920
Central African Republic	174	116	40	8	870
Sierra Leone	262	105	38	9	1,520
South Sudan	183	99	31	24	1,550
Mali	254	98	30	13	2,230
Benin	178	93	32	5	2,400
DR Congo	184	88	43	8	900
Lesotho	91	88	33	3	3,610
Equatorial Guinea	157	85	26	3	18,170
Cote d'Ivoire	151	92	30	8	3,163

Source: UNICEF, 2019

The state of the world's children.[38] The figures are not perfect – they are largely based on patchy survey evidence that has to be moderated and supplemented by expert opinion, and the estimates have not been very stable from year to year – but they stand as the best guesses available.

The first two columns show trends in child mortality. The improvements in recent years are marked and strong – a direct riposte to those who claim that growth immiserises people, or that it forces increasing numbers of people into poverty. The next two are estimates of malnutrition, included here as a way of adding further dimensions to what we can tell about children's health. Stunting is being under the normal height for one's age, which reflects past malnutrition or ill health; wasting is being underweight for one's height, which happens when food is short. The number of underweight children has been falling in general, but in sub-Saharan Africa the other tests have shown an increase in malnutrition since 1990. The figures are open to challenge, because agencies can only weigh and measure the children they get to see, and age is not always certain.

As a general rule, we should always treat figures like this as indicators – pointers or warning lights – rather than unassailable facts; it is impossible to be exact in countries where communications are poor,

---

[38] UNICEF, 2019; World Bank, 2019, World Development Indicators, Table WV.1.

records are uncertain and contact is interrupted by civil strife. Infant deaths can happen for reasons other than poverty – these are evidence of poverty, not precise measures. But the indicators have to be taken seriously, both in their own right and as pointers to other problems. It is not surprising that war-torn Somalia, which has had no effective government for several years, has a high infant mortality. However, when we see a country like Nigeria on the list – and the relatively high death rates in some other countries with higher incomes, such as Angola or Equatorial Guinea – the figures raise questions. Higher figures in higher-income countries suggest serious inequalities or inadequate public facilities. It is often evident in such countries that despite the total national wealth, a substantial proportion of their populations live on very limited income, not being integrated into the growing formal economy.

That said, the trends in recent years have been remarkably encouraging. All of these countries have seen major falls in child mortality over the course of the last 25 years. Some of the best performing countries in the developing world have seen a drop of more than three quarters – for example, Bangladesh, down from 144 to 30, or Cambodia, down from 116 to 28. Some countries, notably China, have seen substantial economic growth as well as a major fall in child mortality, while others such as Rwanda and Nepal have achieved the improvement despite impossibly low incomes. *The Economist* has called this 'the best story in development'.[39]

---

[39] *The Economist*, 2012, The best story in development, www.economist.com/node/21555571, accessed 19.12.2019.

4

Inequality

A major part of the discussion of the relational aspects of poverty has been the discussion of inequalities, and there have been several points in the argument so far which have referred to inequality rather than poverty. Inequality refers to social disadvantage.[1] Most of us have some things about us that distinguish us from other people – age, gender or ethnicity are examples – but difference alone does not imply that people are unequal. Disadvantage might reflect difference, but it implies much more: it implies that rights, opportunities or resources are available to some and denied to others. When we say that people are unequal, we mean not that they are different, but that some of them are disadvantaged. In the same way, an argument for equality is not an argument for the obliteration of differences, but for the removal of disadvantage.

Inequality is fundamentally a relational concept, and several key forms of relational disadvantage have provided the main focus for its discussion in sociology. The most important are class, status and power. Class refers primarily to economic position. In marxist terms, class is defined by people's relationship to the means of production; in a Weberian sense, it refers to people with a common economic position or set of circumstances.[2] Status is seen variously as referring to the structure of social identity, a form of social honour, as a set of roles; for Weber, status 'is in the main conditioned as well as expressed through a specific style of life'.[3] Relationships of power are more difficult to summarise: while many writers treat power in a political sense, as the ability to change or influence others, Foucault treats power as many-sided, changing the way that people behave in relation to each other.[4] The position of poor people is not necessarily one where they are wholly powerless, but often they may find themselves embedded in

---

[1] See P Spicker, 2006, *Liberty, equality, fraternity*, Bristol: Policy Press, Part 2.

[2] H H Gerth, C W Mills, 1948, *From Max Weber*, London: RKP.

[3] M Weber, 1967, The development of caste, in R Bendix and S M Lipset (eds), *Class, status and power*, London: Routledge and Kegan Paul, (2nd edn) pp 31–2.

[4] M Foucault, 1976, *Histoire de la sexualité: la volonté de savoir*, Paris: Gallimard.

vertical power structures where they are beholden to patrons, political clientelism and local elites.[5]

Class, status and power are manifested in relation to social divisions and differences: common inequalities are found in relation to poverty, race or ethnicity, and gender. The link between gender, low status and poverty is strong enough to mean that it is now treated routinely as part of anti-poverty policy in developing countries. Women are denied rights, resources and redress. The situation in developed countries tends to be better, but not so much better that poverty is not predominantly experienced by women – a problem that has been called the 'feminisation of poverty'.[6] (The main problem with that term is that it seems to imply that it is a state of becoming, newly in the process of happening; it isn't.)

People can potentially be disadvantaged in lots of ways, however, and disadvantage and poverty interact, often to such an extent that it is difficult to tell them apart. Take, for example, the position of people with physical disabilities. Physical health is always important, but it becomes even more important when one's body, strength or appearance is the only power that people have to draw on.[7] There are disadvantages, too, above and beyond the problems that disabilities cause people who suffer them. There are the problems of prejudice and discrimination: the reactions of other people. There are the problems of low social status, and cumulative loss of opportunity. There are the difficulties caused because the world is geared to people without the same disabilities – the physical design of housing, amenities, transport and the built environment. There are economic costs, and the likelihood of reduced income. Disability is a reason for disadvantage in itself, but the pattern of disadvantage overlaps with poverty.

Another reason for inequality, once the most prominent form, is inequality from birth, or 'ascribed status'. People are considered, in many societies, to be born into a position of disadvantage. In societies where caste is still influential, it affects what jobs people can do, and who they can marry. Membership of some minority ethnic groups, such as the Roma in Europe, suffer a combination of

---

[5] D Satterthwaite and D Mitlin, 2014, *Reducing urban poverty in the global South*, London: Routledge, pp 61–5.

[6] I Garfinkel and S McLanahan, 1988, The feminisation of poverty, in D Tomaskovic-Devey (ed) *Poverty and social welfare in the United States*, Boulder: Westview Press; J Lewis and D Piachaud, 1992, Women and poverty in the twentieth century, in C Glendinning and J Millar, *Women and Poverty in Britain in the 1990s*, London: Harvester Wheatsheaf.

[7] D Narayan, R Chambers, M Shah and P Petesch, 2000, *Voices of the poor: crying out for change*, Oxford: World Bank/Oxford University Press.

extreme discrimination with major problems of health, education and income. Even in societies which see themselves as more equal, coming from a poor background – trailer camps, shanties, slums – can be a disadvantage for life.

There are, of course, many other circumstances which lead to disadvantage. The Equality Act in the UK lists a range of other categories besides those already mentioned: age, gender reassignment, marriage and civil partnership, race, religion, and sexual orientation.[8] The Belgian federal law on equalities has some different items on the list: language, political orientation, health status and future health status, genetic disorders, social origins and 'fortune' (referring, as I understand it, to means, wealth, or at least the appearance of it);[9] that is as near as this construction of inequalities gets to poverty. Each of the lists points to the deficiencies in the other. The UK law does not directly recognise some of the ancient sources of prejudice – birth, class, heritage and money; Belgian law is weaker on issues of identity. These inequalities are diverse, complex, and often interlinked.

Poverty and inequality

There are many aspects of inequality which are not simply equivalent to poverty, and there are calls for equality – the removal of disadvantage – which are quite distinct from responses to poverty. The most basic form of equality is the equality of persons: the right of everyone to be treated with dignity and respect, regardless of their status. Then there is the equality of rights, such as human rights and equality before the law. Third, there is the equality of citizenship, where people have the status of members of the political community. Fourth, there is access to the conditions of civilisation – the ability to live with sufficient resources and amenities to avoid undermining a person's dignity. At the fullest, there is equality of welfare – an attempt to ensure that people have access to the conditions and standards of life which are required in the society where people live.[10]

Despite the differences, there is undeniably some overlap between the concepts. Poverty often seems to threaten the status of persons, and an inequality of persons can condemn people and groups of people to

---

[8] UK Public General Acts, Equality Act 2010, https://www.legislation.gov.uk/ukpga/2010/15/contents, accessed 29.8.19.

[9] E Bribosia, I Rorive, 2018, *Country report non-discrimination*, Belgium, Brussels: European Commission, pp 74–5.

[10] P Spicker, 2006, *Liberty, equality, fraternity*, Bristol: Policy Press.

poverty. Women, people in minority ethnic or tribal groups, or people with disabilities are all vulnerable to poverty; the problems of inferior status are likely to be reflected in disadvantage in many ways. In the same way, the disadvantage of non-citizens – for example, the position of migrant workers – is something that is associated with poverty rather than a condition that is equivalent to it. However, it is only in the last two senses of equality that the ideas of poverty and equality really seem to flow directly into each other. If people do not have access to the conditions of society – if they are denied access to housing, health care, education, or the financial resources available to others – they will be poor. If they are disadvantaged in their access to basic standards of living which are expected in society, they will be poor.

It would not be true to say that all disadvantage leads to poverty. The inequalities of gender are pervasive in many other aspects of social interaction, and there are clear examples of gender-based disadvantage even among sections of the population who are relatively privileged – such as the 'glass ceiling', which limits the opportunities for promotion of female professionals. At the same time, poverty and inequality are closely connected. Wherever there is poverty, there is social disadvantage – there may be places where everyone seems to be poor, but usually it takes very little effort to identify status differentials, or to locate better-off people to whom the poor people in that community have some relationship. (Shanty towns, for example, grow because people have to live somewhere; but how they live is shaped by a social structure, an economic context and limited access to land.) In circumstances where well-being is impaired, but there is no clear element of social disadvantage – for example, because the deprivation is the outcome of war, natural disaster or disease – the situation is not necessarily thought of in terms of poverty (though that has to be subject to the general reservation, that poverty makes those situations much worse). Coming at the issue from the perspective of inequality, the link between poverty and inequality is just as strong: while some examples of inequality are about different things, and there are circumstances where richer people also suffer disadvantages, there is a tendency for inequality to be translated into the denial of well-being, and wherever the denial of well-being is attributable to social disadvantage it might fairly be described in terms of poverty.

Poverty and inequality are both relational terms. Inequality is a broader term than poverty, because the character of the relationships and range of disadvantages it refers to might be of a different level or a different kind. But poverty is a form of disadvantage, and that means that poverty is a form of inequality.

Unequal resources

Discussions about the inequality of resources have tended to concentrate on the distribution of income. The reasoning behind this seems straightforward: if a large number of people have limited resources, it is likely that they will be poor, and the more unequal the distribution of resources, the more likely that is to be true. Wherever there is an unequal distribution of resources, there will be differences in power, in lifestyle and in entitlement. The focus in the literature on income, rather than resources in a more general sense, is partly a reflection of the general availability of income data, but also a recognition that income is more closely related to consumption than nominal wealth. There are large reservations to make about this position. The links between general income inequality and other indicators of poverty are not straightforward. The differences between different countries are pronounced, the statistical associations are weak, and the data are open to challenge. Other important elements of inequality such as gender are not adequately reflected in the approach.

One common indicator of poverty compares the income of poor people to the median income in a society – the most commonly used threshold, now referred to in the European Union as being about the 'risk' of poverty, is 60% of median income. The median is the mid-point of the income distribution, a place generally occupied by lower-paid workers (not by middle-income workers, because there are other non-workers below all the others). When someone's income is a long way below that mid-point, they cannot afford things that other people have. This is intended to capture the 'economic distance' of a poor person from the rest of society. O'Higgins and Jenkins explain:

> there is an inescapable connection between poverty and inequality: certain degrees or dimensions of inequality ... will lead to people being below the minimum standards acceptable in that society. ... This does not mean that there will always be poverty when there is inequality: only if the inequality implies an economic distance beyond the critical level.[11]

---

[11] M O'Higgins, S Jenkins, 1990, Poverty in the EC: 1975, 1980, 1985, in R Teekens, B van Praag (eds) *Analysing poverty in the European Community* (Eurostat News Special Edition 1–1990), Luxembourg: European Communities, p 207.

Using the median implies by definition that no more than 50% of the population can be poor. The test is based on income, not assets or command over resources; it is difficult to relate to individual circumstances, especially for complex households and people with fluctuating incomes; and it compares poor people not to others who have a secure lifestyle, but to the lower end of the earning distribution. However, it does not mean (as some politicians and journalists seem to suppose) that more people are defined as poor if more people become rich. Comparing people to the median means only that people on very low incomes are compared with others on incomes that are not quite so low. (From UK figures, it appears to be true nevertheless that there is a correlation between income poverty measured in these terms and inequality in the higher parts of the income distribution.[12])

The 60% test is a test of dispersion – it is perfectly possible, if income at the lower end is not too widely dispersed, for everyone to be closer to the median. Several criticisms might be made of the standard.[13] The median is often, in social terms, a fairly low income – it typically falls in the lower part of the earnings distribution, and often it is characterised by people on relatively insecure incomes. The 60% standard is only a rough guide, like many tests in this field – it was arrived at partly because researchers offered a range of thresholds at 40%, 50% and 60%. The higher figure was agreed at the Laeken Council. (The UK government had miscalculated the average, using the mean instead if the median, and needed to cover its embarrassment. Because the standard was arbitrary in any case, there was no serious opposition to the proposal.) The test has been subject to a range of questionable statistical calculations, trying to equivalise income between different households and in some cases leaving out housing costs altogether. Despite all the problems, it does capture something important: that people who are significantly disadvantaged in financial terms are likely to be poor by other tests. The correspondence between the two is imperfect: Bradshaw and Finch apply different tests, and while they overlap, they are certainly not interchangeable.[14]

In developing countries, the most frequently available figures are the Gini coefficient and the income share of the bottom fifth of the

---

[12] A McKnight, M Duque and M Rucci, 2017, *Double trouble: a review of the relationship between UK poverty and economic inequality*, London: Oxfam/LSE.

[13] P Spicker, 2012, Why refer to poverty as a proportion of median income? *Journal of Poverty and Social Justice*, 20(2): 165–77.

[14] J Bradshaw and N Finch, 2003, Overlaps in dimensions of poverty, *Journal of Social Policy*, 32(4): 513–25.

population. The Gini coefficient is a summary indicator, based on the cumulative share of income the least well off to the best off. It's widely used, but the same number might represent a range of patterns of inequality. Perhaps surprisingly, there is no clear relationship between the Gini coefficient and the specific deprivations recorded in the Multidimensional Poverty Index.[15] There are simply too many factors at play to identify consistent patterns.

A simpler indicator is the 'quintile ratio', which shows the share of the poorest fifth relative to the richest fifth.[16] In the United Kingdom, the quintile ratio is 7.2 – that is, the richest fifth get more than seven times as much as the poorest. Some very poor countries have relatively low ratios, below 5.5 – Niger, Mali, Burundi, Afghanistan, Pakistan. As incomes increase, countries are likely to have very high ratios: in some African countries (Lesotho, Zambia, Namibia, South Africa) the ratio is greater than 15, and in some South American countries (Brazil, Colombia, Bolivia, Honduras) it is greater than 20. As a general proposition, these examples seem to support the hypothesis of the 'Kuznets curve': countries get more unequal as they develop, but as access to resources spreads, they become more equal again. But there are many exceptions: the Central African Republic has a desperately low national income and a quintile ratio of 18, while Indonesia has been growing rapidly with a ratio of 6.3. It becomes more difficult to hold to the Kuznets curve when some of the details are considered. Some of these countries are part of the way to development, and there is a marked difference between urban and rural communities: but that could be said of India, which has a ratio of 5, in much the same terms as it is said of Nigeria with a ratio of 12.2. (Those two countries currently have very similar average incomes.) Mexico and Brazil also have similar per capita incomes, and have been cited as examples of emerging economies, but Mexico has a ratio of 10.7 while Brazil's is 20.6.

These are middle-income countries. One of the most striking trends in recent years, Sumner argues, is that the problems of poverty have become more visible and concentrated, not in the poorest countries, but in countries that are well on the way to development. 'The causes of much of global poverty', he argues,

---

[15] UNDP, 2019, Global Multidimensional Poverty Index 2019: Illuminating inequality, pp 13–14.
[16] UNDP, 2013, Income quintile ratio, http://hdr.undp.org/en/content/income-quintile-ratio, accessed 10.12.2019

have become less about the lack of resources and more about questions of national inequality, and issues of social policy, patterns of economic growth and economic development and the form of late capitalism pursued.[17]

The implication of the more extreme inequalities in these countries might be that poor people have been left behind; but it might equally mean that they are unable to command resources because richer people have them instead. It is difficult to generalise. Social scientists usually want to offer general insights into economic and social processes; the differences in the examples point to the problems of trying to work that way. Every country is shaped by a wide range of factors – their history, their experiences, their economy, their relationship with their neighbours, and so on – and that means that every country is, to some extent, a special case all on its own. It is always possible, of course, to look at specific data and then to try to offer some kind of retrospective narrative, investing the figures with meaning; that is the curse of comparative studies. But the underlying flaw in any generalisation is that inequalities and economic distance reflect much more than material goods or services. The information we have on inequality does not tell us what form the inequality takes, how the inequality is expressed, or why countries differ so markedly in the degree of inequality they suffer from. The discussion of inequality is not just a matter of resources; it takes us into the area where social, economic and political relationships dominate.

Responses to inequality

There is a wide range of different approaches to inequality.[18] The most basic is equal treatment: the idea that people should be treated equally, without bias, prejudice or favour, on the basis of characteristics like birth or race. The second is equality of opportunity – the opportunity to compete on equal terms. The third is equality of provision – securing that, where public provision is made, people are not disadvantaged in their access to it. Fourth is equality of basic security, ensuring minimum standards in essential areas such as housing, health care or income which make it possible to function in society. The strongest demand for equality is for equality of outcome – not uniformity for

---

[17] A Sumner, 2016, *Global poverty: deprivation, distribution and development since the Cold War*, Oxford: Oxford University Press.

[18] P Spicker, 2006, *Liberty, equality, fraternity*, Bristol: Policy Press.

everyone, but the removal of disadvantage. The Universal Declaration of Human Rights declares that everyone has a right to 'a standard of living adequate for the health and well-being of himself and his family, including food, clothing, housing and medical care and necessary social services'.[19] That goes well beyond basic security.

As we move along this spectrum, the policies and approaches which are implied may seem to converge more and more directly with policies against poverty. Each of the concepts may help to mitigate poverty; by the time we get to the fourth stage, basic security, it is already difficult to tell approaches to poverty and inequality apart.

However, things are not so simple. The problem is not just that there are competing views of inequality, but that inequalities are also understood in several dimensions. Rae points to a distinction between concepts of equality that are focused on individuals, blocs or segments of society. 'Individual-regarding' inequality is straightforward enough: one person is compared with another, 'Bloc-regarding' inequality compares social categories – women with men, minority ethnic groups with the majority, disability with able-bodied, and so on. 'Segments' compare people within social categories – poor children with other children, for example, or young adults with and without educational qualifications. It is possible for a policy to be egalitarian in one sense and inegalitarian in others – for example, in policies intended to give women access to positions of privilege, or to redistribute resources to an older person at the expense of a low-paid worker.[20] And that makes it difficult to be certain that egalitarian policies are pro-poor, even if the intentions are good.

The most direct responses to economic inequality are either to stop it before it happens, or to try to compensate for inequalities after they have appeared. Stopping it before it happens sounds appealing, and it is probably less liable to political resistance, but it is complex. Limiting the scope of inequality in economic resources generally depends on engaging people extensively in economic activity – typically, on having development, growth and a high level of secure, stable, well-paid employment, which tends to be in the public sector because only the public sector guarantees such employment without depending on economic demand or the vicissitudes of the market.

The redistribution of resources is a basic part of the activity of government – there is redistribution wherever the people who pay for a service are not the same as people who benefit. In some cases

---

[19] United Nations, 1948, Universal declaration of human rights, Article 21.
[20] D Rae, 1981, *Equalities*, Cambridge, MA: Harvard University Press.

the benefits are received by broad categories of the population, such as older people, or urban dwellers, or certain regions, or industries, and redistribution sometimes goes to the better off rather than to people who are poorer. The main forms of redistribution for the benefit of poorer people are either direct transfers (such as income maintenance benefits), or public spending on projects and services that benefit poorer people along with others, including schools, houses and sanitation. Direct transfers are challenging, because they involve taking money away from some people to move to others, and most people will struggle to hold on to what they have; the poorer the country, the more difficult it becomes to redistribute resources. Hoy and Sumner think that far more could be done by way of redistribution in developing countries, and they may be right;[21] but their confidence that a range of different policies could eradicate three quarters of global poverty depends in part on the adoption of different priorities for policy, and partly on the administration of effective systems for redistribution. These are difficult to manage in practice, because of the fundamental problems of identifying, selecting and targeting specific recipients to produce the maximum effect. For Tawney, the basic strategy of equality had to be different:

> the pooling of its surplus resources by means of taxation, and the use of the funds thus obtained to make accessible to all, irrespective of their income, occupation or social position, the conditions of civilisation which, in the absence of such measures, can only be enjoyed by the rich.[22]

There has to be an infrastructure of public services that guarantees basic security and conditions for as many people as possible.

[21] C Hoy and A Sumner, 2017, *Gasoline, guns and giveaways*, Washington DC: Center for Global Development, https://www.cgdev.org/sites/default/files/gasoline-guns-and-giveaways-end-three-quarters-global-poverty-0.pdf, accessed 19.12.2019.
[22] R Tawney, 1931, *Equality*, London: Allen and Unwin, p 122.

5

Exclusion

As the policy communities dealing with poverty have come to be aware of the relational elements of poverty, the discourse they engage in – the terms in which poverty is discussed – has had to be adapted to allow the issues to be addressed. One of the most prominent elements in this discourse has been a focus on exclusion and inclusion. People are poor, Townsend argued, if 'Their resources are so seriously below those commanded by the average individual or family that they are, in effect, excluded from ordinary living patterns, customs and activities.'[1] There are two key issues there which take us beyond the starting point of a lack of resources. One is the emphasis on participation in society: part of the experience of poverty is that living in society depends on interactions with other people. The other is the idea of exclusion: that people's social relationships lead to them being denied the option of living the way that other people live. Exclusion and impaired participation in society are integral to the experience of poverty. For the United Nations, 'social exclusion describes a state in which individuals are unable to participate fully in economic, social, political and cultural life, as well as the process leading to and sustaining such a state.'[2] Bhalla and Lapeyre observe that while other ideas of poverty have typically focused on issues of distribution, the idea of exclusion shifts the focus towards relationships.[3]

Levitas and her colleagues have developed a concept of social exclusion as a multidimensional set of issues, taking into account resources, quality of life and participation in society. The issues include:

- Resources
  - Material/economic resources
  - Access to public and private services
  - Social resources

---

[1] P Townsend, 1979, *Poverty in the United Kingdom*, Harmondsworth: Penguin, p 31.
[2] UN DESA, 2016, *Leaving no one behind*, ST/ESA/362, New York: United Nations, p 18.
[3] A Bhalla and F Lapeyre, 1999, *Poverty and exclusion in a global world*, Basingstoke: Macmillan.

- Participation
  - Economic participation
  - Social participation
  - Culture, education and skills
- Political and civic participation
- Quality of life
  - Health and well-being
  - Living environment
  - Crime, harm and criminalisation[4]

As ever, most of the issues under consideration in that list are relational (and that includes resources); it is difficult to distinguish this from a relational concept of poverty.

Poverty and stigma

There is a long association between poverty and the idea of 'stigma' – a sense of shame, humiliation and rejection. Historically, both the attribution of stigma and the application of deliberate policies to make poor people ashamed of their poverty were associated with the English Poor Law, where the 'stigma of pauperism' was often defended as a valuable deterrent to dependent poverty.[5] However, the association of poverty with stigma is much more wide-ranging than that specific history might suggest. The problems of degradation, prejudice and low status are problems for poor people everywhere;[6] they are a major part of why poverty ought to be understood in terms of relationships.

The discussion of stigma in the academic literature usually genuflects in the direction of Goffman's sociological account of stigma. Goffman juggles with a series of inconsistent explanations: that a stigma is an attribute possessed by the stigmatised person, an attribute that is *not* possessed by the stigmatised person, a 'shameful differentness', a stereotype in the minds of other people or caste, or some kind of mélange of all of these.[7] The roots of the rejection of people who are poor can be attributed to prejudice, to power, but they are overlain by other stigmatising labels – the accusations that poor people are physically or mentally different, that they have a different culture,

[4] R Levitas, C Pantazis, E Fahmy, D Gordon and D Patsios, 2007, *The multi-dimensional analysis of social exclusion*, Bristol: University of Bristol.

[5] P Spicker, 1984, *Stigma and social welfare*, Beckenham: Croom Helm, pp 15–19.

[6] R Walker (ed), 2014, *The shame of poverty*, Oxford: Oxford University Press.

[7] E Goffman, 1963, *Stigma*, Harmondsworth: Penguin, pp 12–21.

Figure 5.1: Stigma and social rejection

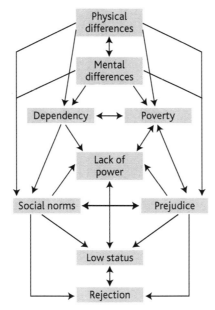

Source: Spicker, 1984, p 175

that they are lazy, immoral, dishonest or – a theme that recurs all too frequently – that they are dirty. In my own studies of stigma, I found that it was possible to describe links between all kinds of differentness, and patterns of social rejection.[8]

Irrational and random as they may seem, the connections between different types of stigma are made rather too often to be dismissed simply as stereotypes. The accusations seem to be multi-directional – they are made towards people who have a disability, people from minority ethnic groups, unmarried mothers or people who are unemployed, as they are towards people who are poor – and people in stigmatised groups become vulnerable to poverty, even as people who are poor are misclassified into stigmatised groups, so that it becomes impossible to distinguish what is cause and what is effect. Lister refers to the process as 'Othering' – people who are poor become Something Else.[9] Stigmatisation touches on a deep set of processes in human society, beyond rationality, often beyond discourse.

---

[8] Spicker, 1984, p 175.

[9] R Lister, 2004, *Poverty*, Cambridge: Polity Press.

The concept of exclusion

The idea of exclusion has grown legs and wings, and that makes it difficult to pin down any precise, consistent usage of the term. The idea has its origins in French social policy, itself strongly influenced (despite the republican emphasis on anti-clerical thought) by Catholic social teaching. Solidarity, or mutual aid and responsibility, is seen in Catholic teaching as a fundamental principle in society, and people are bound together in complex, often overlapping, networks of solidarity. Developing after the 1830s, the principle of solidarity became part of the discourse of French politics, culminating in the political movement for 'solidarism' in the 1890s.[10] (Many texts attribute the idea of solidarity, mistakenly, to Durkheim. Durkheim's work was written more than fifty years after the idea took hold, and he uses the term in his own distinctive way.) The *Code de sécurité sociale* declares that it is based on the principle of solidarity, and much of the purpose of French social policy – especially the foundation of the *régime général* – was intended to 'generalise' or extend these networks to people who would not otherwise be covered.[11] When the idea of exclusion was introduced in the 1970s, it was used quite directly to refer to the people who had been left out of the process.[12] The idea of insertion, or social inclusion, became prominent in subsequent social policies, and when later the UK government raised objections to the European Union's consideration of poverty, the French-speaking directorate of the Commission switched seamlessly to discussion of exclusion instead.[13]

Exclusion is used to refer partly to people who are left out of systems of support – such as people with disabilities, young people or migrants, who have not been able to earn rights through contribution. But it is also used to refer to people who are shut out – Roma, single homeless people, people leaving care – and those who are pushed out, including ex-prisoners, people with AIDS, and minority ethnic groups. Those examples mainly come from developed countries, but there are similar processes at work in developing countries, too. Robert Chambers argues powerfully for considering women in the rural areas of developing countries as an excluded population: 'Poor and rural women are a poor and deprived class within a class. ... Rural

---

[10] P Spicker, 2006, *Liberty, equality, fraternity*, Bristol: Policy Press, Chapter 5.

[11] J-J Dupeyroux, 1989, *Droit de la sécurité sociale*, Paris: Dalloz, p 286.

[12] R Lenoir, 1984, *Les exclus: un français sur dix*, Paris: Editions du Seuil.

[13] S Tiemann, 1993, Opinion on social exclusion, OJ 93/C 352/13.

single women, female heads of households and widows include many of the most wretched and unseen people in the world.'[14]

There are many sorts of exclusion: the exclusion of people from different tribes or religions, the exploitation of people from remote and rural areas, and the rejection of mental illness. (The last point is worth a brief digression. Foucault imagined that the transition to modern society led to rejection and incarceration of people with mental illness; this is hopelessly off the mark.[15] The traditional responses to mental illness include burning, beating and exorcism.[16] There are still places where people who manifest mental illness are likely to be held in chains, or, as a reflection of modern technology, given electric shocks – one of my former students was working with these issues in East Africa.) It is also important here to recognise the role of importance of the lack of power of the poor. The problems of exploitation, the diversion of resources to those with power, exposure to corruption and lack of bargaining power are a significant part of the experience of poverty.[17]

Some problems of social relationships are implicit in the discussion of integration in the formal economy. Poor people are liable to be excluded – left out, shut out or pushed out. That overlaps with the problems of vulnerability discussed earlier, because exclusion from networks of social support and solidarity work to exacerbate vulnerability, but clearly exclusion from the economy is a major issue in its own right, and it is often associated with exclusion in other forms – the inability to participate in society, and the inability to gain access to the conditions of life that others have. Hickey and Du Toit point to a further problem: the issue of 'adverse incorporation', where people are included only on unfavourable terms. In so far as poverty is constituted by a system of social relationships, those terms may mean that poor people are locked into poverty.[18]

Although labour markets are clearly the largest part of the source of people's links with the formal economy, there are some large exceptions. In nearly all the developed countries, we excuse older people from the labour market by providing them with a pension.

[14] R Chambers, 1983, *Rural development*, London: Longman, p 19.

[15] M Foucault, 1961/1965, *Madness and civilisation*, London: Tavistock; K Jones, 1993, *Asylums and after*, London: Athlone Press.

[16] J R Hanks, L M Hanks, 1948, The physically handicapped in certain non-occidental societies, *Journal of Social Issues*, 4(4): 11–20.

[17] Chambers, 1983.

[18] S Hickey and A Du Toit, 2007, *Adverse incorporation, social exclusion and chronic poverty*, Manchester: Institute for Development Policy and Management.

There are elaborate arrangements in many places that aim to persuade people that they are getting back money they had laid out while they are working, but this is typically done with smoke and mirrors; the truth is that people who are working generally pay for pensions now, and when they retire their pension will depend on people who are working then. (These are sometimes referred to as 'pay as you go', solidaristic or dynamised pensions; regardless of the administrative arrangements, the upshot in each case is the same, that the working population supports older people.)

The same arguments extend, more or less, to people who are younger and not working. It is possible to pretend that younger people in need are able to pay for their upkeep through social insurance, redistribution through a person's life cycle or 'income smoothing', but the blunt fact is that people who have an income generally support other people who do not. One of the great myths about these arrangements is that they are the construct of a welfare state which imposes taxation on part of the population to pay for another part. We know what happens in countries where the state does not do this, and it is not what many critics of the welfare state imagine: people who can afford it have typically entered voluntary social arrangements, rather than relying on market-based commercial systems. In much of Europe, the origins of provision for pensions, unemployment, disability and long-term sickness lie in 'solidarity' and mutual assistance, often developed around the workplace.[19] Governments came to these arrangements very belatedly, usually with the intention either of extending provision for those who were excluded or in order to shore up existing arrangements that otherwise might be insufficiently financed. In France, the major government intervention came after World War II, by which time nearly half the population was covered by complex alternative forms of social protection. Unemployment insurance in several northern European states is still substantially voluntary,[20] though elements of compulsion tend to be used to protect the most vulnerable workers.

The idea of exclusion has been used to focus on a range of issues that are concerned with relationships, social dynamics, and social obligations. Some experiences of exclusion are referred to in other parts of this book – for example, exclusion from participation in the formal economy, and the denial of rights. It is difficult to approach the

---

[19] P Baldwin, 1990, *The politics of social solidarity*, Cambridge: Cambridge University Press.

[20] J Clasen and E Viebrock, 2008, Voluntary unemployment insurance and trade union membership, *Journal of Social Policy* 37(3): 433–52.

issues systematically, because exclusion is concerned as much with the things that do not happen as with things that do; opportunities that are not realised, systems that do not work, support that is not given. Some of those issues relate to ordinary aspects of social life, that other people might routinely look for – such as employment, education or housing. Some relate to systems of institutional protection, including property rights, legal systems, and the safeguarding of personal security, And then there are further issues about the relationships of poor people to the structure of authority – the provision of basic services, corruption and abuse by those in authority. Popular representations of poverty often tend to focus on privation – the shortage of essentials like food, clothing, fuel or shelter. By contrast, many of the themes raised by poor people in *Voices of the Poor* are about social relationships – isolation, powerlessness, gender and the problem of government.[21] The experience of poverty is as likely to be identified in terms of exclusion as it is by lack of resources. In the absence of an accepted discourse about relational issues, the language of exclusion has often been used to fill in the gaps.

In Chapter 4, I argued for a fairly strong overlap between the idea of poverty and certain aspects of inequality. The same happens in the relationship between poverty and exclusion. Exclusion is a broad concept in its own right, referring to many situations where people might be left out, shut out or pushed out of society. There are forms of exclusion which are not about poverty: the stigmas of physical difference, the lack of provision for migrants, the moral rejection of people such as drug users groups, might easily lead to poverty, but they are not evidence of poverty in themselves.[22] Conversely, it can be argued that there are relationships which do not necessarily imply exclusion, but may well imply poverty – the inferior economic and social status of women, of domestic servants or of certain low status occupations. Having said that, there is a great deal that has been said or written about exclusion which might well apply to poverty. The European Union initially justified the focus in these terms:

> When we talk about social exclusion we are acknowledging that the problem is no longer simply one of inequity between the top and bottom of the social scale (up/down) but also one of the distance within society between those

---

[21] D Narayan, R Chambers, M Shah and P Petesch, 2000, *Voices of the poor: crying out for change*, Oxford: World Bank/Oxford University Press.

[22] P Spicker, 1984, *Stigma and social welfare*, Beckenham: Croom Helm.

who are active members and those who are forced towards the fringes (in/out). We are also highlighting the effects of the way society is developing and the concomitant risk of social disintegration and, finally, we are affirming that, for both the persons concerned and the society itself, this is a process of change and not a set of fixed and static situations.[23]

Bailey and his colleagues write, in similar vein:

First, in contrast to the narrower focus upon material resources in poverty research, social exclusion is said to refer to a process of being 'shut out' from, or denied access to, social, economic, cultural, and political systems, and to an enforced inability to participate in widely accepted social norms which can arise from a variety of sources. Second, social exclusion is typically viewed as a dynamic process rather than as a static condition. Third, social exclusion is a relational concept, and not simply a material state, characterised by powerlessness, denial of rights, diminished citizenship and disrespect.[24]

This could all have been said about poverty; the idea that a relational focus has to be justified in terms of an entirely different concept points to something wrong at the heart of traditional poverty research. Exclusion has become a way of talking about all the really important things about poverty that otherwise get left out. For Amartya Sen, 'the real importance of the idea of social exclusion lies in emphasizing the role of relational features in the deprivation of capability and thus in the experience of poverty.'[25]

The indicators that have been developed to examine social exclusion in Europe are, for the most part, indicators of poverty;[26] and sometimes they are better indicators of poverty than the narrow focus on economics and low income that has bedevilled poverty research. There

---

[23] Commission of the European Communities, 1993, Medium term action programme to control exclusion and promote solidarity, COM(93): 435, p 43.

[24] N Bailey, E Fahmy and J Bradshaw, 2017, The multidimensional analysis of social exclusion, in G Bramley and N Bailey (eds), *Poverty and social exclusion in the UK*, vol 2, Bristol: Policy Press, p 312.

[25] A Sen, 2000, *Social exclusion: concept, application and scrutiny*, Manila: Asian Development Bank, p 6.

[26] For example, A B Atkinson and E Marlier, 2010, *Analysing and measuring social inclusion in a global context*, New York: United Nations.

is a growing trend to talk in terms of 'poverty-and-social-exclusion'; the joint focus serves to make sure that central issues of relationships, participation and social resources are appropriately considered.[27] It also means that much of the work needed to translate a relational perspective into operational and empirically well-founded indicators has already been done.

Voice and empowerment

Participation in society depends on a wide range of relationships. Citizenship and participation in the political community has been seen as especially important, because it is the means through which rights can be realised; but it is also part of being able to realise the aspiration of sharing in the lifestyle and conditions that others in a society expect. At the level of the individual, empowerment is promoted through rights, especially legal rights, developing social skills, and 'normalisation' or the development of personal autonomy. In social groups, the strategies include voice or the reporting and transmission of opinions, participation, community education and community development. The importance of this kind of network has sometimes been translated into a concept of 'social capital', which is a way of describing the value and advantage gained by working through social groups.[28] The term has licensed economists to bend their theories around some of the non-material, intangible relationships that make a difference to people's lives.[29]

Concepts of voice and empowerment have been profoundly influential in the consideration of anti-poverty policy. In the main, it reflects a sense that poverty is marked by powerlessness, and that it is essential to redress the balance. One of the slogans recently attached to health care captures the simple appeal of that principle: 'no decision about me, without me'. At the same time, there has also been an element of pragmatism in the extension of democratic governance. Poverty presents so many problems, for the people who experience it and for the governments who have to respond to the circumstances, that it can be difficult to know where to start. If it was just about legitimacy, voting should serve; but the process of voice and

---

[27] For example, G Bramley and N Bailey (eds), 2017, *Poverty and social exclusion in the UK, Volume 2: the dimensions of disadvantage*, Bristol: Policy Press.

[28] R Putnam, 2000, *Bowling alone*, New York: Simon & Schuster, Chapter 19.

[29] G Svendsen and J Sørensen, 2006, The socioeconomic power of social capital, *International Journal of Sociology and Social Policy*, 26(9/10): pp 411–29.

participation in decision-making does more than just to legitimate policy. It improves the quality of information, it makes governments more responsive, it identifies the issues that matter most to the people who are affected by them.

This book is focusing on the national scale, and the scope for these measures to national policies tends to be limited. Some parts of these responses are individual; some are done at the level of the group or the community. Discussions of political participation at the national level tend to focus on the limited mechanism of the popular vote. The forms of participation and empowerment that have transformed the lives of poor people at the levels of neighbourhoods and communities are not really visible at this level. It is tempting to think that perhaps they could be, but it would call for an extensive reconfiguration of the patterns through which voice, political participation and accountability are expressed at national levels.

Responding to exclusion

Exclusion, like poverty itself, can seem so wide-ranging and broadly defined that it becomes almost impossible to see how to respond. However, the terminology is underlain by a powerful interpretative model, and the responses can be framed in terms of that model. The starting point is the converse of exclusion – solidarity. If exclusion is defined by lack of solidarity, solidarity is evidently the way to counter it.

Solidarity has important limitations. It is not necessarily experienced by everyone: the idea is exclusive as well as inclusive. It is not dichotomous; between inclusion and exclusion, there are many complex states, where solidarities can be stronger, weaker, more or less developed. It is not presumptively equal; the relationships of solidarity that people have are personal, particular and special to them. That also means that solidarity is not enough to protect people; in some cases, solidarities can bind people into relationships that are oppressive or exploitative, such as relationships of caste and gender disadvantage.

The first, most basic strategy for exclusion is generalisation. That idea comes from France: it refers to the progressive, incremental, outward extension of solidaristic networks and relationships.[30] The process can be done in several ways: bringing people into the formal economy, improving communications through infrastructure development, extending the scope of social protection. It is implicit in the idea of

---

[30] J J Dupeyroux, 1989, *Droit de la sécurité sociale*, Paris: Dalloz, p 286.

generalisation is that it is a process, rather than a solution; the object is to include more people than before, not to establish comprehensive or universal services. That is compatible with a strategy based on general rights, but they are not the same. The soldaristic approach is likely to look different in practice – pragmatic, incremental, bringing in people in groups and categories rather than either universally or one by one. This was the strategy of the French government post-war, and arguably (though there has been some loss of direction in recent years) it is guiding the policy of the European Union.[31] The main limitation of generalisation is that it cannot be enough; there are just not enough routes in for people who are marginalised or excluded. That implies the need for further steps.

The next strategy might be seen as a part of generalisation, but it goes further; it is the strengthening of solidarity through the development of supplementary provisions. One of the many confusions about the discourse of 'inclusion' and 'exclusion' in the literature is the assumption that the terms are dichotomous – that people must be one thing or the other. Many people are 'marginal'. They are not excluded completely; but they are part of fewer, weaker networks than others, which makes them less supported, less integrated and more vulnerable. The literature on 'social capital' recognises the differences in the capacity of different social networks; building social capital is rarely about creating it where none exists, but it is about strengthening, supporting, facilitating and empowering such networks.

The third strategy is *'insertion'*, or the integration of excluded people into networks of solidarity – the term is usually translated as 'inclusion', but of course all the other strategies are examples of inclusion, too. The term developed in France, initially being used for people with disability and young people, and then being extended to cover millions of people who were excluded in a wide range of senses. Insertion in the *Revenu Minimum d'Insertion*, now replaced by the *Revenu de solidarité active*, was based on two processes. The first was a contract between the individual and the local agency (the *Commission locale d'insertion*), negotiated with a social worker, intended both to offer opportunities and to bind people to undertake actions that would enhance their inclusion – a mixture of responsibilities and privileges. The second process, often neglected in political discussions of the benefits, was that the CLI in turn made a series of contracts with providers in order to ensure that there were real opportunities

---

[31] P Spicker, 1997, Exclusion, *Journal of Common Market Studies*, 35(1): 133–43.

and openings available for claimants to use.[32] The fundamental design recognised inclusion as a social process, not just an individual one.

Exclusion is an important part of the experience of poverty, and despite the limitations, developing social inclusion has proved to be one of the most powerful methods of countering the associated problems. The World Bank has argued for the extension and expansion of systems of social protection, but those systems are widely based on national policies – the politics of membership, rather than the language of general rights, though the UN has subsequently extended the idea of exclusion to imply that no-one should be left behind.[33] Most of the strategies discussed in this chapter – generalisation, insertion and citizenship – have been developed at the level of national governments. The European Union has expressed particular interest in generalising solidarity, because it has the potential to extend across national boundaries. There is much to be said for the aspirations of internationalists, and there is reason to be concerned at the way that the politics of membership has marginalised migrants and minority groups; but the truth of the matter is that policies for solidarity, mutual support and social protection are overwhelmingly delivered within nations, and often they are delivered by them. If we want to limit the scope of social exclusion, national policies are still the way to go.

---

[32] P Vanlerenberghe (chair), 1992. RMI: Le pari de l'insertion, Paris: la documentation française.

[33] UN DESA, 2016, *Leaving no one behind*, ST/ESA/362, New York: United Nations, p 18.

6

Poverty and rights

The language of rights and legal redress is still relatively marginal in social scientific work on poverty, but it has become a major part of the discourse about the subject in development studies and in international organisations. Amartya Sen's seminal work on poverty emphasised the importance of people's entitlements. Where there have been famines, he argues, the problem has not been that there is not enough food; rather it has been that people are not entitled to eat the food that is there. Famines are likely to be about distribution, rather than shortage as such.[1] 'Entitlement' usually means much the same thing as 'rights', but when people talk about rights, there is a tendency to think of them as something based in the legal system, often deriving from the authority of government. Sen's concept of entitlement is much more broadly based than that. People become entitled because they are able to command goods. As development proceeds, they are likely to do that through the medium of money, and they get money through engagement in the formal economy.

The word 'likely' is of some importance here, because the general statement about money is only part of the picture. In the context of a developed formal economy, many things (and certainly most of those goods and services which have a monetary value) are parcelled out this way. Someone, somewhere will have to pay out some money to get resources, goods or a service. But it is not necessarily the case that the person who buys resources will be the person who has command over them: it may be a spouse, a parent, a head of household, an organisation, even a community. That makes it difficult at times to determine who has access to what. Feminists have made the case that women in some non-poor households may effectively be poor because they are denied use of key resources, including food.[2] The key question is whether people have entitlements – in some societies they do, in others they have none – and so whether they can be said to have command over resources.

---

[1] A Sen, 1981, *Poverty and famines: an essay on entitlement and deprivation*, Oxford: Clarendon Press.

[2] J Millar and C Glendinning, 1989, Gender and poverty, *Journal of Social Policy*, 18(3): 363–81.

Rights against poverty

Rights are implicitly relational; they are norms or rules which govern social relationships.[3] The nature of these rules varies, but what is special about them is that, whether or not they affect the behaviour of the people who hold the rights, they affect the way that others behave towards them. Many rights imply correlative duties, and the relationship between rights and the behaviour of others is sometimes misrepresented in the argument that rights and duties are necessarily correlated.[4] There are rights, however, which imply no direct obligation on others; freedom does not mean that others should act in a particular way, but only that they should refrain from acting in certain circumstances. Hohfield distinguishes four categories of rights: claim-rights, immunities, powers and liberties.[5] Claim-rights are rights which imply duties on other people; many rights to the receipt of social services generally fall into this category. Liberties prevent actions by other people. Powers are a restricted form of liberty, which is allowed to some people to do things which others cannot; a driving licence is an example. Immunities are also a form of liberty, which make people exempt from obligations which apply to others; an example is a tax relief, though this might also be seen as a claim-right.

Claim-rights tend to be more prominent in the discussion of poverty, but liberties are often asserted with even more force. The basic claim-rights most often referred to in discussions of poverty are claims for social security – that is, poor relief or income maintenance; rights to housing, in the sense both of access to decent housing and avoidance of deprivation; access to health care; and the right to be educated. The basic liberties which are sought include protection from crime; protection from unsafe or unhealthy environments; the avoidance of discrimination; and legal security, in the protection of citizens from arrest or legal harassment, and the avoidance of injustice. Some rights hover ambiguously between categories: the right to raise a family may be seen either as a claim for support or as a presumption against intervention, while the right to work is sometimes represented as a claim-right to be provided with work, and sometimes as a liberty to pursue work in the marketplace.

---

[3] P Spicker, 1988, *Principles of social welfare*, London: Routledge, p 58.

[4] S Benn and R Peters, 1959, *Social principles and the democratic state*, London: Allen and Unwin, Chapter 4.

[5] L Hohfield, 1920, *Some fundamental legal conceptions as applied in judicial reasoning*, New Haven: Yale University Press.

Rights are commonly classified as particular or general rights. People have a particular right if someone has undertaken a personal obligation towards them (for example, as the result of a promise, a contract, or an injurious action). In a formal economy, people build up networks of economic rights and obligations, and their command over resources is based not so much on the recognition of universal principles, or even the grant of specific rights related to citizenship, but income and assets drawn from a range of sources. The benefit systems of many developed countries are based on particular rights – rights which derive, not from the actions of government or the state, but on systems of solidarity based on professional affiliation, work record or membership of voluntary associations. Pensions and medical care are especially likely to depend on this kind of solidaristic arrangement. Particular rights have been at least as important as general rights in protecting the circumstances of the poor; in many countries, among them Germany, the United States and the welfare states of Northern Europe, they are arguably more important.

There is a problem here. Enshrining the system of entitlement in terms of rights and citizenship can make it difficult for newcomers – and particularly for poor newcomers – to gain access to the amenities and resources that other people have. When poor people come to the cities in newly developing countries, they typically have one of two options: they can squat, building a shack or shanty on unoccupied land, or they can rent. Where people squat, the conditions are often dire, but over time they 'consolidate',[6] gradually improving their conditions. In societies where all the land is parcelled out, this is not an option. In countries where landholding is more firmly established, such as India, poor people are more likely to be charged rent for basic living space – or have to live on the street. Entitlements can cause problems as well as solving them.

The growing emphasis on general rights can be seen as a way of trying to counteract this tendency. People have general rights if those rights apply to everyone else in similar circumstances (for example, as children, old people, or mentally ill people). Because so many poor people lack command over resources, and any developed network of particular rights, it is understandable if discussions of the rights of the poor tend to be framed in generalised or universal terms. That should ensure that every poor person is offered the protection that only some will otherwise enjoy. General rights take two main forms. Some are dependent on personal circumstances (the circumstances in

---

[6] J Perlman, 1992, *The myth of marginality*, Berkeley, CA: University of California Press.

which people have become poor, like old age, disability and sickness), which properly speaking are 'contingent general rights', and general rights which are available to anyone in the category, which are usually referred to as 'universal' rights. Some contingent general rights – this can be shortened to 'contingent rights', for convenience – are intended to define the categories of people who are eligible: for example, old people, children, disabled people and so on. In some cases, such as protection for older people, this has been an effective strategy for inclusion; a similar case can be made in relation to people with learning disabilities.[7] Others are intended to exclude those who are ineligible: so, the first Old Age Pensions in Britain excluded people who had been dependent on the Poor Law, and current means-tested provision excludes people who otherwise fit the criteria for benefit but are not available for full-time work. The primary difference lies in the presumption of entitlement, which is important in practice; the key question is whether a person has to prove entitlement or whether another party has to prove non-entitlement.

The discussion of universal rights is sometimes framed in terms of social citizenship. For T H Marshall, was 'a status bestowed on those who are full members of a community. All those who possess the status are equal with respect to the rights and duties with which the status is endowed.'[8] Various writers have seen the development of citizenship as a promising route for extending and securing the rights of vulnerable people.[9] An emphasis on citizenship offers nation states a focus for social inclusion – a means of identifying members, a set of rules about who gets helped, a system of rights and responsibilities. If citizenship is understood as membership of a political community, the process of identifying members, defining rights and establishing networks of solidarity all seem to work as an inclusive strategy. The relative isolation and social disqualification of migrants, asylum seekers and members of minority ethnic groups seems to reinforce the identification. The recent efforts of European states to identify the characteristics of citizens more clearly, and to test prospective entrants, can be seen as steps in this direction[10] – if one looks at them in a favourable light. There is, however, a conceptual barrier – yet

---

[7] P Spicker, 1990, Mental handicap and citizenship, *Journal of Applied Philosophy*, 7(2): 139–51.

[8] T H Marshall, 1982, *The right to welfare*, London: Heinemann.

[9] For example, R Lister, 1990, *The exclusive society*, London: Child Poverty Action Group.

[10] S Wallace Goodman, 2014, *Immigration and membership politics in Western Europe*, Cambridge: Cambridge University Press.

another instance where the solution presents problems of its own. Built in to the idea of membership, there is a sense that there will be borders, boundaries and limits to solidarity. A citizen is a member of a club: membership brings privileges, but those privileges are not open to everyone. It is commonplace, for example, for migrants to be denied the same rights that others have. In any system which relies on particular rights, migrants are unlikely to have built up the rights that others will have; but in systems that depend more on general rights, such as the United Kingdom, there tend to be time restrictions, minimum residency requirements, and special rules for non-citizens such as asylum seekers. If people are being defined as members of an in-group, others must be defined as members of an out-group.

Poverty and human rights

This has led to an increasing emphasis on universal human rights, rather than the more restricted rights of citizenship. In relation to social security, the United Nations has argued that the international covenants imply a wide range of services, including health care, and social protection in the event of unemployment, disability, maternity, sickness, old age, bereavement and industrial injury.[11] In relation to poverty, the UN has issued guidance which describes extreme poverty as a violation of human rights. The *Guiding Principles on Extreme Poverty and Human Rights* begin with an understanding of poverty as 'a multidimensional phenomenon that encompasses a lack of both income and the basic capabilities to live in dignity'.[12] States have duties, for example:

- to protect people in poverty from stigmatisation, and to 'prohibit public authorities, whether national or local, from stigmatizing or discriminating against persons living in poverty';
- to enhance the involvement of women in decision-making;
- to give poor people rights of redress;
- to ensure that persons living in poverty have access to at least the minimum essential food that is nutritionally adequate and safe, basic shelter, housing and sanitation;

---

[11] United Nations, 2007, General comment no. 19: the right to social security, in UN, 2008, *Human rights instruments*, vol 1, HRI/GEN/1/Rev.9, pp 152–71.

[12] United Nations, 2012, Guiding principles on extreme poverty and human rights, www. ohchr.org/Documents/Publications/OHCHR_ExtremePovertyandHumanRights_ EN.pdf, accessed 19.12.2019.

- to 'repeal or reform any laws that criminalize life-sustaining activities in public places, such as sleeping, begging, eating or performing personal hygiene activities';
- to provide legal aid for criminal and civil cases; and
- to ensure that all workers are paid a wage sufficient to enable them and their family to have access to an adequate standard of living.[13]

The claim that poverty violates human rights depends on an argument that the issues are universal – they apply to all humans, everywhere. However, many of the rights we have – and many of the rights that people have to welfare provision – are particular: they are not for everyone, but for certain people at certain times. Pensions, for example, are commonly based in a sort of contract, where the level of the pension depends on the contributions a person has made over a period of years. Rights to housing and employment usually fall into similar categories. Other rights are based on citizenship – membership of particular political community; health care and education are of this kind. Rights of citizenship are 'thicker', in the sense of being more detailed; human rights are 'thinner', but more generally applicable.

The problem with human rights is that it is not always clear who they are held against, or who has the duty or the responsibility to do anything about them. The Guiding Principles 'are premised on the understanding that eradicating extreme poverty is not only a moral duty but also a legal obligation under existing international human rights law'. 'International human rights law' may not be law as we understand it, but it offers more than fine words and moral posturing. Campbell suggests that classifying poverty as a violation of human rights has a series of implications. It implies monitoring and surveillance of actors who are creating poverty. It implies modification of national laws to hinder the production of poverty, possibly including criminal sanctions. It could be used to justify global measures. It invites courts, rather than governments, to adjudicate on the issues. And it exposes states in violation of the norms to be subject to sanctions by other countries.[14]

The economic and social rights identified by human rights law are to some degree justiciable – that is, they can be raised in the courts of states that are signatories to the conventions. One of the most important decisions in this field is the Velasquez Rodriguez Case,

---

[13] United Nations, 2012, pp 5–6, 6, 11, 15, 17, 19 and 27.

[14] T Campbell, 2007, Poverty as a violation of human rights, in T Pogge (ed), *Freedom from poverty as a human right*, Oxford: Oxford University Press, pp 56–7.

decided by the Inter-American Court of Human Rights in 1988. The Court held that states can be held responsible if they fail to respond to violations of human rights. 'Where the acts of private parties that violate the Convention are not seriously investigated, those parties are aided in a sense by the government, thereby making the State responsible on the international plane.'[15] UN conventions on human rights explain that:

> the Covenant norms must be recognized in appropriate ways within the domestic legal order, appropriate means of redress, or remedies, must be available to any aggrieved individual or group, and appropriate means of ensuring governmental accountability must be put in place.[16]

The International Commission of Jurists gives lots of examples of court decisions in different countries which uphold human rights in these general terms,[17] but many of the examples are forced. It may be true that the actions of some governments protect human rights as well as offering services to their population, but it does not follow that they are motivated by or have any regard to ideas about human rights in doing so. Most provisions are based in the constitutional principles of the state where they are applied, which shows only that such laws can be enforced if they are passed. For example, the German courts do not need to refer to UN conventions to justify the defence of an 'existential minimum'; they do so by reference to federal Germany's basic law. Some, but relatively few, judicial decisions have been based in reference to the norms recommended in international conventions.[18] The most convincing examples come from trans-national judicial review bodies – the European Court of Human Rights, the Inter-American Court of Human Rights and the African Commission on Human Rights and People's Rights – because those are the bodies most likely to refer specifically to international conventions. It may be more important that, regardless of whether or not the legal judgements refer directly

---

[15] Velasquez Rodriguez Case, Judgment of July 29, 1988, Inter-Am.Ct.H.R. (Ser. C) No. 4, www1.umn.edu/humanrts/iachr/b_11_12d.htm, accessed 9.12.2019.

[16] UN Committee on Economic, Social and Cultural Rights, 1998, General comment no. 9: the domestic application of the Covenant, in United Nations, 2008, Human rights instruments, vol 1, HRI/GEN/1/Rev.9, p 45.

[17] International Commission of Jurists, 2008, *Courts and the legal enforcement of economic social and cultural rights*, Geneva: ICJ.

[18] International Commission of Jurists, 2008, pp 33–4.

to human rights instruments, the way that laws are understood may be recast in terms that are compatible with international conventions. Those conventions also have has the advantage of empowering international organisations to work in this field.

The rights of communities

There is a curious omission in this discussion of rights – my thanks are due to Camilo Perez-Bustillo for pointing it out to me. There is an implicit assumption in the material reviewed so far that rights are held by individual human beings. Some are not. In moral terms, rights might be held by groups of people – local communities, indigenous populations, families. In legal terms, the position is usually more restrictive, but an institution can own property, or a business can hold rights under a contract. An incorporated business is a legal person – that is part of what being 'incorporated' means. That does invite the question whether groups of people might not also be able to exercise rights on the same terms.

A 'group' of people is not the same thing as a category. A social group is defined not just by a common identity, but by relationships between members, and the capacity to form relationship with others outside the group; a group is capable of taking collective action. When we talk about the rights of women, or rights for people with disabilities, we generally mean to refer to people with some common characteristics, and the rights that are being referred to are the rights they hold as individuals. The rights of a community, of a minority group, or indigenous peoples are a different kind of right, based on the group. It is the group that has the rights, such as the rights to hold property or be entitled to take redress. This construction could be important for a discussion of nations, because there are circumstances when the rights that might be open to discussion are rights for the nation as a whole – rights to self-government, to compensation, to a homeland. As with individuals, some of those rights may be particular – rights obtained under contracts or agreements – and some may be general rights established by government. It is not clear that human rights and international obligations can be thought of in the same way, but there is at least a case to be made – some groups and communities have common interests, and there are international agreements established in these terms.

The United Nations adopted its Declaration of the Rights of Indigenous Peoples in 2007. Many of the rights expressed, such as rights not to be subject to violence or discrimination, could be seen as individual human rights too. Beyond that, the Declaration promises rights to maintain a culture, to protection of religious traditions and maintenance of minority languages. It states, among many other things, that

> States shall provide effective mechanisms for prevention of, and redress for:
> (a) Any action which has the aim or effect of depriving them of their integrity as distinct peoples, or of their cultural values or ethnic identities;
> (b) Any action which has the aim or effect of dispossessing them of their lands, territories or resources;
> (c) Any form of forced population transfer which has the aim or effect of violating or undermining any of their rights;
> (d) Any form of forced assimilation or integration;
> (e) Any form of propaganda designed to promote or incite racial or ethnic discrimination directed against them.'[19]

The Declaration is not binding on member states, and several countries, most notably Canada, have expressed reservations about whether it is compatible with the established rights in their legal system. (Those reservations were shared by the US, New Zealand and Australia; the government of Australia has subsequently signified its agreement.)

The idea that there may be collective rights has yet to make any substantial headway, and for as long as that is true the scope for applying the idea to poverty is likely to be limited. At the same time, it is all too visible that there are communities, tribes and nations in deprived circumstances, and that a lack of recognition or self-governance can prejudice their ability to develop economically, politically and socially. The subject may not be a significant element in discussions of rights and poverty now, but it is hard to imagine that it will not come to be so in future years.

Delivering rights in practice

Rights that are held only in principle are not enough. One option is to offer different kinds of support to the different groups. This depends on a principle of selectivity – correctly identifying which is which,

---

[19] United Nations, 2007, Declaration of the Rights of Indigenous Peoples, www.un.org/esa/socdev/unpfii/documents/DRIPS_en.pdf, accessed 19.12.2019.

and responding according to circumstances and need. That approach has been taken in the UK through a series of 'tapered' benefits, which offer supplementary income to lower-paid workers, gradually withdrawn as income increases. There are many problems with selectivity. It inevitably creates difficulties in identifying boundaries, and in maintaining equity of treatment as people fall on either side of them. If benefits are being withdrawn as income increases, there is the problem of the 'poverty trap' – withdrawing benefits at a high marginal rate of deduction could mean that people will be little or no better off with an increase in earnings. Selectivity is unavoidably complicated – difficult to administer, and difficult to understand. And to this it is necessary to add another, potentially catastrophic complication: the position of people with precarious incomes. If incomes fluctuate unpredictably – not untypically, doubling or halving in a relatively short period of time – the problems are amplified. The UK Tax Credit Scheme, a complex set of benefits based on tapers, was described by the Ombudsman as being fundamentally unsuited to the needs of low-income families.[20] The cold blast of reality did not, regrettably, prevent the next government from extending the principles more generally.

It is possible to offer support in different forms. Many systems define cross-cutting categories of potential recipient – pensioners, people with disabilities, people with young children, and so on. There has been a widespread movement in many developing countries to offer conditional cash transfers; the conditions, such as sending children to school, help to make the measures politically acceptable. The programmes are selective; they rely on (rather inefficient) tests to exclude people who are not eligible. The selection in most cases has two stages; the selection of a poor area, and then the use of a 'proxy means test' – in the absence of good information about income, the proxies use key indicators that predict deprivation in that society. These tests are easier and cheaper to run than full tests of income, and the information about whether people have basic assets is likely to be more stable. However, the process is very approximate, and it can seem arbitrary.[21] The World Bank has found that 'it is hard to add new beneficiaries in the short term and hard to remove them from the

---

[20] Parliamentary and Health Service Ombudsman, 2007, Tax credits – getting it wrong? HC 1010, p 5.

[21] Australian Aid, 2011, Targeting the poorest: an assessment of the proxy means test methodology, https://www.unicef.org/socialpolicy/files/targeting-poorest.pdf, accessed 19.12.2019.

program rosters when a crisis has passed.'[22] It should be acknowledged that even if the process is not accurate nor reliable, it does inject funds into very poor areas, and that has led to appreciable improvements in the lives of the people who receive it – though that might be partially offset by the losses of those who don't.[23]

In relation to people with precarious incomes or circumstances, the most practical routes are those which are universal – related to a broad category, or not conditional at all. There is a common misconception that universality is expensive, because generous and unconditional provision could be; but it cannot be assumed that provision will be generous. In practice, the leading models for universal provision – such as the UK National Health Service – have been famously austere. In 1993, the World Health Organization proposed the development of Basic Health Care Packages (sometimes known as Essential Health Packages, Minimal Health Packages or other variations on the theme): simple, basic, limited care offered on a minimal budget to populations in general.[24] The BHCP is provided universally – testing people for eligibility is complex, burdensome and often self-defeating. The services offered are minimal. BHCPs have not made provision for chronic illness, old age, or high-tech Western medicine – these things are expensive, and there are alternatives which have bigger impacts. They have focused instead on a range of more limited interventions – dealing with maternal mortality, basic health promotion and infant mortality. This approach is much cheaper, and much easier to administer, than the complex and costly adjustment to personal need that is characteristic of most medical care in the developed world. It is always difficult to pick out cause and effect from a myriad of interacting factors, but on the face of the matter, the effects of BHCPs have been spectacular, with major reductions in maternal and infant mortality. Infant mortality has fallen by a quarter in many countries and in the best cases by rather more.

The arguments for universality have been crystallised in some writing by a focus on Universal Basic Income. Unlike universal health care, unconditional basic income has not been fully tried, and many of the comments about how people will ultimately behave are speculative

---

[22] World Bank, 2009, https://openknowledge.worldbank.org/bitstream/handle/10 986/2597/476030PUB0Cond101Official0Use0Only1.pdf, p 197.

[23] D Filmer, J Friedman, E Kandpal and J Onishi, 2018, *General equilibrium effects of targeted cash transfers*, Washington DC: World Bank Group.

[24] World Bank, 1993, *World development report 1993: investing in health*, Washington DC: World Bank.

or utopian. The attraction of the policy is that it offers a generally applicable, rights-based approach. UBI has three elements. The first is that it is a guaranteed cash income. Income is not the only way of directing resources to people – health care, education and water supply are often better delivered on a communal basis outwith the economic market – but it is evidently important. The results of studies on cash assistance, including conditional cash transfers, show strong links between the cash and people's welfare, including improvements in nutrition, sanitation, education, health, benefits and economic engagement. It is possible, of course, to extend people's entitlements and resources in other ways, without cash assistance – it can be done by fostering employment and economic growth – but it cannot be done comprehensively.

That leads to the second component, which is that UBI offers the assistance universally. People get incomes in many ways – engagement in the economy, employment, public employment and membership of households where someone else has an income. If the issue was only about providing people with an income, it might be possible to do this on a residual basis – passing over people who have an income, and focusing on those who do not. That is not as easy as it sounds, because the process of selection is always complex, difficult and liable to error. Benefits go to some people who should not have them and do not go to others who should. Means-testing to find out people's income is intrusive, difficult to operate effectively and generates perverse incentives. Universality fills in the gaps, not just for those who pass the tests, but for everyone else.

The key objection to universality in this form has always been that it is potentially wasteful: Pen comments that universality is 'like filling the sky with shot to hit a single duck'[25]. But even in the better-off societies, there are more ducks than anyone can reasonably take aim at – as precarious employment has grown, so has the possibility or likelihood that people will suffer low income at different points in their lives, and while the proportion of people who are actually on low incomes at any one time may be somewhere between a quarter and an eighth of the population, those figures do not preclude the possibility that most people even in the more advanced economies will suffer poverty within a period of a few years. As we shift the focus to poorer countries, the numbers of people suffering from low income or the risk of it increases, and the case for universality becomes stronger still.

---

[25] J Pen, 1974, *Income distribution*, Harmondsworth: Penguin, p 377.

The third element is possibly the most controversial: that Universal Basic Income should be unconditional. Cash transfers have often had moderate conditions attached, for example about seeking health advice or ensuring that children attend school; that probably reflects public scepticism and political resistance to helping the undeserving. It is not clear from the evidence that the conditions have much direct effect, but any condition must imply some people will be left out. Hanlon and his colleagues argue that the real advantage of conditional cash transfers doesn't have much to do with the conditions, or with the process of selectivity. The greatest gain comes from offering cash to poor people, because – contrary to the prejudice that people will stop working if they have a small income[26] – the cash makes it possible for people directly to improve their lives. 'Cash transfers work. To reduce poverty and promote development just give money to the poor.'[27]

---

[26] For example, C Murray, 1984, *Losing ground*, New York: Basic Books.

[27] J Hanlon, A Barrientos and D Hulme, 2010, *Just give money to the poor*, Sterling, VA: Kumarian Press, p 179.

7

Poverty and social policy

If poverty is a matter of resources, then the primary, central response to the situation is to make resources available, either directly by making goods and services available to people, or indirectly by equipping people with the skills and opportunities they need to gain access to those things. I have made a case that poverty needs to be seen in very different terms, as a set of relational issues, including inequality, the lack of rights and exclusion. If poverty is a matter of relationships, then the response to poverty depends on measures that will alter the nature of those relationships: addressing inequalities, promoting security, voice, empowerment, inclusion and rights.

Policies that address resources, and policies that address relationships, are not mutually exclusive – it is possible to do all of them at the same time. At times they overlap with each other, such as the arguments for greater social security or a guaranteed income. However, they are certainly very different, and the proponents of each tend to be sceptical of the power of the alternatives to address the fundamental issues that they are addressing. The positions are not easy to disentangle, but at the same time there is often extensive evidence from practice, and it should be possible to clarify at least some of the interconnections.

Consider, first, the impact of resources and income on economic and social relationships. The lack of income, many commentators argue, acts to exclude people from normal social activities; it makes it impossible for participate in normal social life. Townsend made that point central to his understanding of poverty.[1] If resources are the central issue, poverty can be reduced if people have more resources; and the most direct response to the lack of resources is to provide them.

There are those who would argue that offering direct financial support creates a relationship of dependency, and so of poverty;[2] there is an exchange of status for financial support.[3] The development of retirement pensions has led, Walker argues, to the 'structural

---

[1] P Townsend, 1979, *Poverty in the United Kingdom*, Harmondsworth: Penguin.

[2] G Simmel, 1908/1965, The poor, *Social Problems*, 13(2): 118–39.

[3] R Pinker, 1971, *Social theory and social policy*, London: Heinemann.

dependency' of older people,[4] but pensions are widely accepted as legitimate. In this context, it is difficult to see much conflict between a relational and a resource-based perspective. Both are concerned with the ability of people to participate in society. A relational perspective implies a little more pessimism about the transformative potential of extra income, because that is not going to be enough to eradicate poverty; but both perspectives are fully consistent with arguments to increase resources.

There are also arguments to increase resources indirectly – for example, the idea that the best route out of poverty is through work.[5] This is not altogether convincing, partly because it has been used as an attempt to shift the burden of escaping poverty onto the poor, but mainly because work in itself is no guarantee of adequate resources. In the UK, pushing people into work has not led to a reduction in poverty; it has only led to an increase in the proportion of people who are working in insecure jobs on low incomes. There is a further problem which comes from trying to individualise a general proposition. It may be true that people in work are less likely to be poor, but it doesn't follow that entering work will have that effect on the next person into it, any more than encouraging people to focus on their marriage prospects would. It all depends on the job, as marriage depends on who you marry.

There is still, nevertheless, a relational argument for emphasising work, family or education. These are all ways of advancing people's integration with social networks; consequently they have the potential to make a substantial impact on poverty, too, and a lower likelihood of low income, while not certain, is indicative of that. Relational policies – such as social inclusion, voice or empowerment – do not have a simple, one-to-one correspondence with the resources, income or deprivation experienced by poor people. Even so, it is possible to see a broad pattern of improvement. Where people have (for example) pensions, health care, education, adequate housing, work opportunities, greater gender equality and personal security, their lives tend to be better, and it is likely that their resources too will improve.

A striking feature of the way that these arguments have been played out in practice is the way in which policy makers have set out to achieve one of the objectives of anti-poverty policy by adopting

---

[4] A Walker, 1980, The social creation of poverty and dependency in old age, *Journal of Social Policy*, 9(1): 49–75.

[5] For example, S Indrawati, 2016, Jobs: the fastest road out of poverty, https://blogs. worldbank.org/voices/jobs-fastest-road-out-poverty, accessed 19.12.2019.

measures that are mainly justified by another. Many of the advocates of a basic income have made the case, not so much that basic income is a direct response to deprivation and the lack of resources, but that basic income can be transformative, changing the ways in which people relate to each others.[6] Conversely, many people who have claimed to be centrally concerned with poverty have tried to address, not the availability of income or finance, but issues in educational inequality, health care, gender, race or disability.

From a relational perspective, these prescriptions are not quite as off-beam as they may at first appear. If the focus was genuinely concentrated on low income, resources and economic position, the relationship of any of these factors to poverty might seem tangential. For example, the association of poverty with 'race' is highly questionable. The language used in Britain and the US about minority ethnic groups tends to associate poverty with visible groups – people of South Asian origin in the case of the UK, African Americans in the US. Both the language and the attribution of poverty status are misleading; the situation disguises a considerable degree of diversity both between and within the experience of different ethnic groups. It is true that people in disadvantaged groups are more likely than others to be on low incomes, but 'more likely' does not mean 'likely'; only a minority of people in these categories suffer disadvantage. That does not mean, however, that describing these minority groups as 'poor' is never appropriate. The relational issues in poverty – issues about social relationships, disadvantage, community organisation, the use and abuse of authority, rights, representation and empowerment – apply to these groups with some force. People use the language of poverty to talk about this because it is the strongest moral language they have to refer to social relations and situations which are unacceptable.

Policies for poverty

Poverty takes many forms, and there are many possible responses to the problems. Unsurprisingly, then, there is no single or standard approach; but the argument of this part has focused on a range of relational understandings of poverty. Each seems, in its own light, to call for a distinct response.

---

[6] See K Widerquist, J Noguera, Y Vanderborght, J Wispelaere (eds), 2013, *Basic income*, Oxford: Wiley-Blackwell; A Downes and S Lansley (eds), 2018, *It's basic income*, Bristol: Policy Press.

Table 7.1: Responses to poverty

	Problems	The way out	Key policies
Economic position	Economic marginality Low incomes Precarious wages Vulnerability	Development Growth	Economic inclusion Social protection
Material need	Lack of resources	Entitlement Resources	Poor relief Rights Redistribution
Social relationships	Exclusion	Participation in society	Empowerment

There are dangers in taking these prescriptions too literally. People who think they understand poverty are liable to be misguided; the problems are complex, and any claim that is based in a single cause or a specific element is pretty much certain to be wrong. Sometimes the easy solutions are dangerous. Relatively straightforward measures, such as industrialisation, job creation or physical infrastructure, have costs as well as benefits, losers as well as gainers.

Some problems are 'wicked'. They are ill-defined and unclear. They are complex: just when we think we have got hold of the problem, we find we have only got part of it. They change as things develop, refusing to stand still while they are being dealt with, so that a response that starts out looking appropriate gradually seems to miss the point. They seem to be impossible to control. Rittel and Webber identify several characteristics of wicked problems. Wicked problems cannot be definitively formulated, or tied down. (Dealing with poverty is their first example.) It is difficult to tell if the problem is solved, and they have no 'stopping rule' – it is not possible to say when the job is done. Solutions are not right or wrong, but better or worse. Their list goes on, and some of the things they say are not true of poverty – for example, that it is not possible with a wicked problem to learn by trial and error, or that every problem is unique.[7] For present purposes, that doesn't matter much – it's in the nature of the beast that generalisations don't work too well. The many understandings of poverty are inter-related, they overlap with each other, they are liable to be confused or lumped together; but they do lead in different directions, and sometimes a policy to deal with one can contradict a policy that is intended to deal with another.

---

[7] H Rittel and M Webber, 1973, Dilemmas in a general theory of planning, *Policy Sciences*, 4(2), 155–69.

Accepting that poverty is a wicked issue – complex, multidimensional, unclear and changeable – has three main implications. First, we do not necessarily know, and cannot assume, what the problems are. However, tackling complex problems has to start somewhere. One of the central insights offered by the emphasis on poverty as a multidimensional issue has been to emphasise the importance of the understanding, experience and voice of the people who suffer it, as a way of clarifying issues and developing priorities.

Second, poverty is dynamic. The problems are not going to sit there waiting for someone to solve them, so that they can be picked off one by one; new problems and issues are arising all the time. Some people will stop being poor; others will become poor. One of the reasons why the people responsible for urban regeneration opt to spend money on improving housing schemes is that the houses don't disappear after they've been improved; but programmes dealing with unemployment, deprived children, families or poor communities have a way of changing the targets, personnel, relationships and people they are responding to.

Third, if we are not dealing with a set, specific problem, or even a defined process, it can be hard to work out what sort of response should be made. Benefits, labour laws, public services might make a difference – but any intervention addresses only a part of a constellation of problems, and leaves further issues to address. Worse, it is not always clear what is an improvement, and what is not. The international organisations, especially the World Bank, are rather keen on evaluating effects using pilots, control trials and precise data management to judge the contribution that specific approaches make. There are methodological objections to that, which will be returned to later, but at a broader level, this kind of approach is self-defeating. Some policies have unintended effects. Some – such as industrialisation, economic growth, contracts for employment – change the situation where they are being applied.

Preventing poverty is particularly difficult. Most attempts to deal with the 'root causes' of poverty – through education, through breaking the cycle of deprivation, through promoting work – have proved to be misconceived. They had to be, because complex, multidimensional, relational issues cannot possibly be addressed through a main single policy. That does not need to be a counsel of despair, because there are other things that can be done. One is to deal with problems directly. The essential reason for providing basic health care, sanitation, decent housing, gender equality, good education or child care is that people need these things now, not that it will stop them from being poor in the future. (That might still be true, but it doesn't make sense to suppose it will be.) Another is to reduce people's vulnerability – the extent to which, if bad things happen, they will be harmed by it. Insurance, social protection and public services are ways of doing this.

This is not an argument for avoiding the issues. Policies, as the idea of 'wicked problems' implies, are never going to work comprehensively and exhaustively, but they can address some parts of problems; they can do better or worse. When Jeffrey Sachs argues for 'quick wins',[8] he is not pointing to policies that will resolve the problems of poverty, or address the full range the problems; he is trying to make a difference. It is possible to do very much more, but the spirit of that approach is the right one; the more that can be done effectively, the better things will be.

---

[8] J Sachs, 2005, *The end of poverty*, New York: Penguin.

PART II

Rich and poor countries

8

Poverty in national perspective

Poverty can be understood in many ways, at many levels. Milanovic discusses three different ways of looking at the world.[1] The first, 'Concept 1', treats all nations as equivalent, counting for one and no more than one. Some countries have caught up with others, but the distance between the top and the bottom, and between higher- and lower-income countries, is as big as ever. The second, 'Concept 2', weights countries according to the size of their population. Using that as the test, the relationship between rich and poor seems to be fairly stable. The third approach, 'Concept 3', disregards nationality. A recent Human Development Report comments that 'even though the global population increased from 5 billion to 7.5 billion between 1990 and 2017, the number of people in low human development fell from 3 billion to 926 million'.[2]

Table 8.1 shows some basic indicators of human development in different regions of the world.[3] There are useful insights to be gleaned from this kind of information – the impoverished condition of sub-Saharan Africa, the narrowing of the gap for many other countries, the realisation that life expectancy can be improved even if income is relatively low. But this approach conceals as much as it reveals. Averaging damps down the size of effects – there are considerable differences between parts of Europe, and Central Asia is different again.

For all kinds of reason, these figures are not to be trusted. Most of the elements that make up the indices are questionable; the figures that are used tend to be the easiest ones to collect, but even then the evidential base is often unreliable, with expert assessments varying year by year. All of these figures ought to be seen as indicators – signs or pointers – rather than true, indisputable 'facts'. Life expectancy figures reflect three related but different issues: infant mortality, adult health and personal security. Schooling is important for everyone, but it is also a relative good – the benefits of schooling depend a lot

---

[1] B Milanovic, 2009, Globalisation and inequality, in N Yeates and C Holden (eds), *The global social policy reader*, Bristol: Policy Press, Chapter 2.5.

[2] United Nations Development Programme, 2018, *Human development statistical update*, New York: UNDP, cover.

[3] UNDP, 2018.

Table 8.1: Human development in the regions of the world, 2018

	Human Development Index	Life expectancy at birth	Mean years of schooling	Gross National Income per capita
Arab states	0.703	71.9	7.1	15,721
East Asia and the Pacific	0.741	75.3	7.9	14,611
Europe and Central Asia	0.779	74.2	10.2	15,498
Latin America and the Caribbean	0.759	75.4	8.6	13,857
South Asia	0.642	69.7	6.5	6,794
Sub-Saharan Africa	0.541	61.2	5.7	3,443
Least developed countries	0.528	65.0	4.8	2,630
World	0.731	72.6	8.4	15,745

Source: UNDP, 2019, Human Development Report 2019, NY: UNDP, p 303.

on what happens to everyone else. Gross National Income per capita (GNI pc) looks to be the most precise of the three sets of figures, but is often an approximation – it is difficult to measure, especially where people are not engaged in a formal economy.[4] GNI is not a certain proof that welfare is increasing. It only counts monetary transactions; two countries which have different kinds of arrangement for social care or education may well have different GNIs as a consequence. It counts bad things as well as good ones: for example, GNI increases both with illicit drug use and with the anti-addiction measures that have to be introduced to stop it – 'bads' and 'anti-bads'.[5] A child who leaves school to sell things on the street is adding to GNI.[6] We use figures about national income not because they are beyond argument, but because they are generally the best we have available. They are indicators, not measures, of welfare. Indicators can be helpful as a way of knowing whether things are bad, or whether they are getting better or worse, but none of them is certain.

Understanding poverty in global terms might well be thought to lean to concepts 2 or 3 – reducing the emphasis on states, or even taking the state out of consideration. But the statistics in the table are based on national data, not individual indicators. We work out what

---

[4] See *The Economist*, 2014, How Nigeria's economy grew by 89% overnight, www.economist.com/blogs/economist-explains/2014/04/economist-explains-2, accessed 19.12.2019.

[5] N Hicks and P Streeten, 1979, Indicators of development: the search for a basic needs yardstick, *World Development*, 7(6): 567–80.

[6] M Todaro and S Smith, 2011, *Economic development*, Harlow: Pearson.

is happening in a region by clumping together information from the countries in it. We do not have information about poor individuals throughout the world. Even if we did, it would not necessarily be helpful to present the information as if it was about individuals – the 'world' average offers at best a measuring rod, not a figure that tells us what conditions might be like for any real person.

Many of the patterns of poverty considered in this book cut across nations. Some of the issues are personal, at the level of individuals, families and communities. Some, notably those in economics, are trans-national – they apply across boundaries and territories; the responses, including solidarity and universal rights, are no less global issues. Many of the arguments about global poverty are concerned with global issues and trends – 'capitalism', globalisation, structural dependency and neo-colonialism, the Washington consensus and the role of international organisations among them. But equally, there are other issues which make little sense if we divorce them from the context of the countries where they take place – particularly issues of government and politics, but it is no less true of national economies, or of social structures in particular countries. Focusing on countries – 'methodological nationalism' – has its limitations, but it offers important insights into the process and structures of poverty – both in the relationships of poor people to political authority, and in the relationship between poor countries and richer ones.

In practice, most of the information available about poverty deals with the issues not as a set of global phenomena, but in terms of countries and regions. In so far as poverty can be discussed in general terms, the literatures on developed and developing countries have much in common. Both are concerned with the fine details of everyday life, with the complex processes that lead to poverty, and with a wide range of experiences. When it comes to considering issues affecting specific countries, however, treatments of richer and poorer countries start to look very different. Social policy in the developed world tends to be seen in terms of the specific context of the country in question: writing from Britain or the US, for example, depends heavily on the institutional structures of those countries, and it can be parochial. There is rather less emphasis on the governmental framework in the discussion of developing countries, and rather more on international issues. That probably reflects, in fairness, the reality that in poor countries, the state and conventional politics are rarely as important as the politicians think they are, and that there may be many other institutional players, including international organisations, NGOs and multinational companies.

Methodological nationalism

Looking at 'countries' at all calls for some justification. Why, it might reasonably be asked, are nations or countries a relevant category for consideration – any more relevant, say, than a township or a community, an ethnic group (such as ethnically Chinese people living in Malaysia) or a geographic region (such as West Africa)? There are some strong arguments for considering poverty in a national perspective. One is conceptual. If poverty is understood in terms of social relationships, we have to take account of the context in which those relationships are formed; and, for a whole set of good reasons, that context is commonly translated into the boundaries of a state. That happens partly because those boundaries themselves reflect networks of interaction and discourse; partly because the boundaries of states are supposed to reflect societies, and a political community; partly because states have imposed rules, for example about language, commerce and employment, which lead to greater commonality; and partly because states apply policies and laws in common across disparate nations and social groups, so that relationships are developed within a national framework. Methodological nationalism cannot account for everything in social policy, but states define the world in which such policies operate.

Another part of the case is empirical. The analyses we rely on in social science are sometimes national, sometimes sub-national, sometimes cross-national, but they are hardly ever truly international. In medical research, it's common for studies to focus on patients with specific conditions recruited across of scores of hospitals in different countries, treating them as if they were all part of the same sample. This simply can't be done in studies that depend on social relationships, and while it is sometimes possible to construct a meta-analysis – a study that combines the results of different studies in different places – there is always the risk that specific conditions in specific places will distort the results of any combined study. It is something of a commonplace in the literature on development that the inclusion or exclusion of China or India might simply overwhelm the impact of findings from other, smaller countries.

Probably the most important argument, however, relates to policy. Most policies are conceived, and measures against poverty are taken, at the level of the 'country' or the state. Social policy is all about responses – what can be done; and what can be done is generally speaking done at the level of the state, which is (almost by definition) the primary policy unit in any specific place.

A country or state is, for most purposes, a territorial unit, but it is more than that. Most countries are seen, somewhat inexactly, as 'nation states'. There are countries where several nations have been combined together into one state – the United Kingdom, Belgium and Switzerland are examples – and others where the authority of the state runs in disparate territories which have no direct physical connection with each other (five French overseas territories, located in the Caribbean, South America and the Indian Ocean, are treated legally as part of France and so of the European Union). There are others where a nation, a community with a common culture, language and history is ruled by several different governments. The growth of nationalism led in the 19th and 20th centuries to the creation of many nation states, where the territory the state governs is identified recognisably with a particular political community. The identification of nations and states is imperfect, but a reference to 'states' would usually be taken to be about something different to 'nations' – the characteristics of the states which govern people in different places, rather than the situation of those who are governed. A nation might be thought of as an 'imagined' community, but for present purposes, it should also be thought of as a political community – a defined citizenry with a common system of government. The arguments for a national focus have several practical justifications, but they are also moral. The point of considering issues like poverty is to change things, and as soon as we begin to consider the means by which change can be brought about, we move towards a consideration, not just of the poverty of individuals, families and households, but a world in which there are communities, societies and political institutions.

The nation as a territorial entity

Contemporary nations are generally associated with countries, particular territories and particular populations. That alignment raises a series of issues that need to be considered in a national context – where it makes sense to treat the wealth or poverty of the country as a whole. First, nations have a physical geography: they live and operate in specific locations. Hulme and his colleagues, looking at the causes of chronic poverty in developing countries, identify a series of related problems:

- low-quality natural resources;
- environmental degradation;
- disasters (flood, drought, earthquake and so on);

- remoteness and lack of access; and
- propensity for disease – such as the problems of hot, humid countries in the tropics.[7]

They describe these issues in terms of the 'environment'. Debates about the environment tend to degenerate into speculation about distant futures; these points are about something much more real and immediate – the things that countries are experiencing now. Physical geography is not destiny, however. Australia and New Zealand are remote; Italy and Japan are subject to natural disasters; Sri Lanka and Cuba have shown what effective health services can do for poor populations, while parts of Glasgow have mortality rates comparable to developing countries. Some of the world's poorest countries are rich in natural resources – and there is an argument to say that an abundance of natural resources can be a curse, bringing with it a class of entrepreneur oriented towards extracting resources rather than human development.[8]

The second category of national issues is the physical infrastructure – the legacy of roads, schools, sanitation, communications, energy supplies and so forth – necessary both to the economy and to social development. The poverty or wealth of a country is built up over time.

A third broad set of national issues concern the economy. It pleases many economists to suppose that outcomes might be governed by 'rational choice' – that people do what they have incentives to do. For Mancur Olson, that meant that the success or failure of poor countries was likely to be determined by the structure of incentives determined by different governments, and good or bad governments made the difference as to whether or not poor countries grew or floundered.[9] In one sense, a national economy is an artificial construct – there is not one set of activities that define an economy, the borders are fuzzy and intangible, the actions that take place are based on a myriad of considerations. Some critics are dismissive of collective concepts, and on that basis they would reject the idea that macroeconomic ideas have any real validity.[10] But if we were to apply the same test to other

[7] D Hulme, K Moore and D Shepherd, 2001, *Chronic poverty: meanings and analytical frameworks*, Manchester: University of Manchester.

[8] P Collier, 2007, The bottom billion, Oxford: Oxford University Press, Chapter 3.

[9] M Olson, 2014, Big bills left on the sidewalk, in M Seligson and J Passé-Smith (eds), *Development and underdevelopment*, Boulder, CO: Rienner, Chapter 26.

[10] For example, F Hayek, cited in D Green, 1987, *The new right*, Brighton: Wheatsheaf Books, p 148.

collective entities – a bank, a university, a legal system – we would end in much the same place; holding to these concepts consistently depends on a long series of conventional understandings. For much of the last hundred years, however – and in particular, since the arguments made by Keynes – it has been possible to think of the national economy as if it was effectively a unit, and to seek to manage the fortunes of a whole economy by manipulating a range of economic tools and levers, including fiscal policy, monetary policy, direct state intervention and foreign trade. Mosley argues that a combination of political institutions and fiscal policy have together the capacity to overcome the natural resources trap, primarily by institutions that protect the position of multiple actors, safeguarding economic competition and ensuring exchange rates that favour exporters.[11]

This kind of country-centred analysis can be extended to other fields, and a fourth category concerns the characteristics of that population: its vital statistics (births, fertility, mortality, migration), the dependency ratio (the number of workers relative to the number of non-workers), human capital (education and skills) and health. Social policies can in some cases alter those characteristics – not, in most cases, by applying the same rules to everyone (China's one-child policy was an example, but it is very unusual), but by seeking to affect aggregates and averages through a combination of partial policies, incentives, subsidies, regulations and legal interventions.

The fifth main category concerns national institutions – government, law and the state. Problems with authority are part of the problems of poverty, and difficulties associated with voice and empowerment are major elements in the experience of poor people. The problems of poor countries are often exacerbated by inadequate governance, limited information, low skills and corruption. Acemoglu and Robinson make the case for a country-centred focus much more strongly. There are good reasons, they argue, why poverty and wealth are visible at national borders – the reasons why Mexico is not like the United States, why South Korea is not like North Korea, why Poland is not like Germany. They write: 'While economic institutions are critical for determining whether a country is poor or prosperous, it is politics and political institutions that determine what economic institutions a country has.'[12]

---

[11] P Mosley, 2017, *Fiscal policy and the natural resources curse*, London: Routledge.

[12] D Acemoglu and J Robinson, 2012, *Why nations fail*, London: Profile Books, p 43.

The limits of methodological nationalism

There was a time when nearly all economic and political analysis would have been done in national terms. The approach to macroeconomics which dominated thinking after World War II was rooted in that kind of perspective. It has become unfashionable, partly because of globalisation – nations and states seem to be much more fluid and less well-defined than once they were – and partly because of the resurgence of neoliberal ideas about the economy, politics and society. There is still a strong element of country-by-country analysis in comparative social policy, because social policy focuses on the governments as policy units, but there are important methodological weaknesses in that literature: attempts to apply uniform principles across different circumstances and conditions, for example in analysis of 'welfare régimes', are inconsistent with what we know about policy development.[13]

Most of the processes referred to in Part 1 happen within nations – they are about the ways in which poverty is developed, expressed and experienced in the context of specific countries. Aspects of those processes are distinctively part of the experience of the countries where they occur. If we want to understand the experience of poverty in Nigeria, for example, we really ought to know something about its colonial legacy, the civil war, the use of its natural resources, its experience of development, the ownership and distribution of assets within the country, and religious and tribal divides. That sounds fairly specific and particular, but the same sorts of questions can be raised, in different ways, in many places which have had a very different history. Most of these points cannot be understood in terms of the experience of a single country. Colonialism, ownership and the distribution of resources are as much about the relationship between countries as they are about processes within them. The poverty of nations is not, then, always understood in terms of nations alone.

Yeates and Holden criticise the limitations of 'methodological nationalism – an inability to think outside the constraints of the "nation state".'[14] The nation state is not of course the only locus. Modern societies are increasingly likely to be ruled through a complex system of multi-level governance, including local, regional and international governors. The efforts of international NGOs are often focused on the

---

[13] P Spicker, 2018, The real dependent variable problem: the limitations of quantitative analysis in comparative policy studies, *Social Policy & Administration*, 52(1): 216–28.

[14] N Yeates and C Holden, 2009, *The global social policy reader*, Bristol: Policy Press, p 77.

township or community. There is no point in arguing that a national perspective is the only way of looking at issues, or even that it is generally the best place to start – that depends on the issues being considered. However, a national perspective says something distinctive about the allocation of resources. The distinctions between different countries are large ones, and the differences between nations matter. Beyond that, if we want to identify, understand and respond to poverty, countries or nation states have a crucial role in determining the way those things are done. That is true partly because people who live next to each other tend to share some common problems, but it is more true because key policies are made at the level of the state, and dealing with information at that level makes it possible to compare and contrast the effects of differences in circumstances and policies. Hoy and Sumner argue that most of the low-income poverty in the world – fully three quarters – could be relieved at the level of the nation state, if only their priorities were different.[15] Focusing on states in this way is the basis of much work in comparative social policy. There are lots of problems in comparative work of that sort, and the results need to be treated with caution, but a breakdown state by state, rather than a global figure, makes it possible to examine what the options are for policies to make things better.

There are limits to what can be done through a focus on countries. Social science depends heavily on a process of generalisation – identifying underlying relationships which are then taken to apply more widely, and making it possible to predict what the effect of new approaches and policies might be. Many of the projects sponsored by international organisations try to set up experimental situations, where the social context can be 'bracketed off' and the impact of identifiable variables can be tested. Often this is done by identifying a specific variable, holding other factors constant and seeing how the variable relates to others. The same techniques are widely used in medical science.

There are serious problems in using this approach in comparative studies – problems relating to evidence, to methodology and to theory. The evidential problems are there, not just because the basic data are hard to find, but because the data do not support the kind of analysis being applied to them. Cross-national comparisons treat every country as a policy unit; that is how it is becomes possible to compare,

---

[15] C Hoy and A Sumner, 2017, *Gasoline, guns and giveaways*, Washington DC: Center for Global Development, https://www.cgdev.org/sites/default/files/gasoline-guns-and-giveaways-end-three-quarters-global-poverty-0.pdf, accessed 19.12.2019.

say, the United States of America with the Netherlands.[16] Applying 'Concept 1' depends on this; so, arguably, does 'Concept 2'. There are lots of studies that rely on data from about 20–30 countries, and that is just not enough to justify the use of the statistical methods that are typically used.[17] If we were looking at data about individual humans, we would know that even if we recognise that people are internally complex, and even if we took multiple readings over time, findings based on 20 or 25 subjects are difficult to generalise from. When we are looking at developed economies, that sort of figure is the norm. Many comparative researchers cheat: they get hold of multiple data points from a handful of countries and treat them as if they had hundreds of independent points of data, when the data cannot be treated as independent and in fact they still only have a few subjects. The data are not good enough to support many of the generalisations that economists and social scientists want to make.

The methodological objections reflect the complexity of the issues being studied. Most of the problems that social scientists deal with are, in their nature, multi-faceted, and there is always a possibility that there is something about the circumstances or some combination of factors that has not properly been considered. In principle, the influence of key measures is identified quantitatively by disentangling the influence of key variables from other influences. Many of the projects sponsored by international organisations try to set up experimental situations, where the social context can be 'bracketed off' and the impact of identifiable variables can be tested. Typically this takes the form either of 'natural experiments' or Randomised Control Trials.[18] Banerji and Duflo advocate a greater use of RCTs, but their own examples show cases where this fails. In one study they mention, it appeared that textbooks did not help education; that was misleading. In another, the evaluation was supposed to identify the influence of contraception on family size; it overlooked the importance for parental decisions of the prospects of children surviving to adulthood.[19] Experiments and RCTs work by screening out extraneous information; the gaps that are left are only to be expected.

---

[16] For example, R Goodin, B Headey, R Muffels and H-J Dirven, 2000, *The real worlds of welfare capitalism*, Cambridge: Cambridge University Press.

[17] For example, M Bryan, S Jenkins, 2015, Multilevel modelling of country effects: a cautionary tale, *European Sociological Review*, 32(1): 3–22.

[18] For example, W Easterly, 2006, *The white man's burden*, Oxford: Oxford University Press, pp 326–8; A Banerji and E Duflo, 2011, *Poor economics*, London: Penguin, pp 14–15.

[19] Banerjee and Duflo, 2011, Part 1.

Some of the objections reflect the difficulty of doing good research in less than ideal conditions. The basic data are poor; the mathematical assumptions are routinely compromised. There is an immediate bias in pilot studies to try to show success, and many initially promising results have been shown not to be replicated when programmes are rolled out. People may act differently when they are being monitored in research programmes – that insight, the 'Hawthorne Effect', is one of the standard axioms of social science research.[20] Most studies which declare confidently that they have found the cause of something are found out later to be wrong. The best analyses are generally qualified, tentative and tend to focus on relatively small effects.

Much more fundamentally, however, the study of poverty does not lend itself to a focus on distinct variables. The methodological objection to control trials is explained most clearly by Pawson and Tilley.[21] The problems are multidimensional; it is hard to tell which factor of many is really making the difference. Taking variables in isolation depends on the idea that it is possible to bracket off a particular approach, identifying its influence without being misled by all the other information that defines a country – historical, economic, social, geographical, administrative and political. The effect of a control trial is to cut out, or bracket off, the social and economic context where the policy is being introduced. In other words, the process deliberately excludes everything we ought to take account of. It is helpful to know that something has had an effect in a particular context – and often more helpful still to know what does not – but the process of a control trial does not offer a secure basis for any scientific generalisation. Every insight has to be qualified with reservations and the possibility that things might work out differently. The largest problem, then, is theoretical. Poverty is a relational concept, and any attempt to cut it away from the relationships that make it up is doomed to failure.

[20] R Olson, J Verley, L Santos and C Salas, 2004, What we teach students about the Hawthorne studies, *The Industrial-Organizational Psychologist*, 41(3): 23–39.
[21] H Pawson and N Tilley, 1997, *Realistic evaluation*, London: Sage.

9

Poverty and the state

The relationship between population, territory and government is not always crisp and clear: some states have territorial claims beyond their existing borders, and some maintain relationships with their citizens wherever they may be. (For example, citizens of the United States are expected to pay tax although they are not resident in the country; the Republic of Ireland acknowledges claims for citizenship on the basis of family connections from some people who have never lived there.) The citizens of every state can be thought of as a political community, linked by their common relationship to the country's political and legal institutions. Often this political community is identified with a nation, but the idea of the nation embraces a range of possible communities.

In its 'thickest', most developed sense, a nation is a political community with a common history, identity and culture. Relatively few states fit that model closely. Most countries in the world, Béland and Lecours argue, are actually multinational – the 'nation state', although it presents nation and territory as if they were the same, inevitably has to accommodate people from a range of backgrounds.[1] Governance operates at several levels. This has implications for the definition of the political community; localism and sub-state nationalism can imply a weakening of national solidarity. Decentralisation is often presented as a way to enhance the power and resources of the regional communities, but Prud'homme suggests that it can, paradoxically, have the opposite effect, particularly in developing countries where the regional disparities are strongest. Decentralised government leads to less redistribution between rich and poor regions of a country, and that in turn implies a greater concentration of resources in the richer areas.[2]

The definition of the political community (and of the nation) is important for social welfare, because among other things it defines a framework for the responsibilities that people have to each other – both for the groups that are part of that community, and for the people who are outside it. The process is both inclusive and exclusive. It is

---

[1] D Béland, A Lecours, 2008, *Nationalism and social policy*, Oxford: Oxford University Press, Chapter 1.

[2] R Prud'homme, 1995, The dangers of decentralization, *The World Bank Research Observer*, 10(2): 201–20.

inclusive because it asserts the nature of the community that is being provided for. Harris writes:

> As long as the nation state is the main framework – and it is hard to think about political community outside its frame – for solidarity, sovereignty and the exercise of political ideologies, nationalism, often by violent means, furnishes the political unit and its system with legitimacy. ... the nation state remains the main protector of cultural and physical security of people as well as the main distributor of cultural rewards and material resources.[3]

It is exclusive because, as part of the same process, it also defines the people for whom governments are not responsible. Most countries distinguish the status of citizens from the position of migrants.

There is some ambivalence, within this model, towards poorer people. On one hand, poor people are commonly held to be citizens, with the rights and responsibilities shared by every member of the political community. On the other, the very nature of poverty tends to imply limited participation, stigma and exclusion. A common part of the experience of poverty is a lack of power. Part, too, is the ascription of an inferior status, often associated with class, gender, ethnicity and nationality.

There is a sense in which the problems of the people are liable to become the problems of their government, regardless of the reasons for those problems. That is not true in every case – there is a distinction, however arbitrary it may be, to be made between personal problems, such as grief, and social problems like mental health – but it is not unusual for one type of problem to be redefined as another. Poverty has not always been thought of as a social problem. (In Victorian London, Southwood Smith arranged tours for dignitaries to try to persuade them that it was; and Charles Booth's early researches were undertaken to disprove what he thought were the exaggerated claims of the socialists.) It is not uncommon for politicians nowadays either to deny that there is poverty (accepting it would imply a need to do something about it) or to blame the poor for their own condition (which excuses others from moral responsibility). Wherever the issues of poverty are recognised, however – and that is true of most countries in the world – they become a part of the agenda of government. The

---

[3] E Harris, 2009, *Nationalism: theories and cases*, Edinburgh: Edinburgh University Press, p 35.

themes and issues raised by poor people in *Voices of the Poor*[4] – such as precarious livelihoods, insecurity and vulnerability, lack of entitlement, and disempowering institutions – are all generally thought of as part of the remit of a contemporary government. Where they are not, they are still a violation of human rights, and most governments have come to accept that they have at least a duty to protect their citizens from them. Modern governments are likely to be engaged with issues of poverty because that is what governments do.

Democracy

The place to start for many contemporary discussions of the role of government is with the principle of democracy. Democracy can seem, at times, to mean all things to all people; nearly every nation state claims to be democratic, but they do not all mean the same thing by it. For some, democracy is government 'for the people': democracy is a normative term, characterised by values such as the sovereignty of the people, or the people's will, government by popular consent, or the protection of people's interests. For others, democracy is prescriptive, a guide to how decisions ought to be made: government by discussion,[5] accountability or participation. Joshua Cohen has argued for a 'deliberative' model, arguing for cooperation, equality and social inclusion.[6] And then there are interpretations that emphasise democracy as a set of institutional arrangements – voting, representation, a free press and competition between political parties.

Many of the arguments around democracy are arguments about process: democracy is usually presented as a system concerned with how decisions are made, rather than what the decisions are. But democracy is not just about institutions, elections or voice; nor is it a simple question of process or method. In the course of the last thirty years or so, many countries have been created or newly established. The traditional explanations of national formation, such as defence or the assertion of a national culture, have played a role, but that is not enough to explain why these countries have wanted to mirror the structures and behaviours of the West. Democracy is believed to have tangible, substantive benefits; it is the road to prosperity.

---

[4] D Narayan, R Chambers, M Shah and P Petesch, 2000, *Voices of the poor*, Oxford: World Bank/Oxford University Press.

[5] E Barker, 1961, *Principles of social and political theory*, Oxford: Oxford University Press.

[6] J Cohen, 1997, Deliberation and democratic legitimacy, in R Goodin and P Pettit (eds) *Contemporary political philosophy*, Oxford: Blackwell.

At first sight, the links may seem tenuous. Viewed as a normative ideal, democracy does little directly to guarantee economic development. The principles associated with democratic government, such as open communications and freedom of association, have been helpful to economic development, but the same kind of development has also happened in more restrictive societies. There may, arguably, be a connection between democracy and other structures, such as the development of banking and conventional systems of share ownership, but that is not clear; besides, these elements were strongly emphasised in the process of 'structural adjustment', and the results were mixed at best.[7] There is nothing in the conventional structures of democracy – institutions such as voting, a free press, representative legislatures or independent courts – that either guarantees economic success or makes it certain that poor people will be protected.

There does seem however to be at least one finding that is general and consistent. Amartya Sen argues: 'in the terrible history of famines in the world, no substantial famine has ever occurred in any independent and democratic country with a relatively free press. We cannot find exceptions to this rule …'[8] Sen's generalisation is open to argument – some countries that have suffered famine may well still claim to be democratic[9] – but there is something there that needs to be taken into account. For Sen, the explanation lies partly in the character of political processes that demand attention from politicians and decision makers,[10] but mainly through the development of entitlements. Poverty and famines are produced through lack of entitlement – not because of shortage as such, but because poor people are denied access to the goods, resources and services that are already there.[11] Democracies create entitlements, and entitlements – a combination of social, economic and political rights – make it possible for people to avoid poverty. As is so often the case, it can be hard to disentangle people's material circumstances from their relational status – but there is no need to do so; it is all part of poverty.

---

[7] For example, H-J Chang, 2007, *Bad Samaritans*, London, Random House Business Books.

[8] A Sen, 1999, The value of democracy, *Development Outreach*, 1(1) 5–10: 8, http://documents.worldbank.org/curated/en/286031468314683319/Development-outreach-1-1-governance-and-the-market-economy, accessed 19.12.2019.

[9] See M Woo-Cumings, 2002, The political ecology of famine, https://www.adb.org/sites/default/files/publication/157182/adbi-rp31.pdf, accessed 19.12.2019.

[10] Sen, 1999.

[11] A Sen and J Drèze, 1989, *Hunger and public action*, Oxford: Oxford University Press.

The combination of political institutions, personal rights and accountable governments is most commonly represented in terms of the 'liberal' democracies. The idea of liberal democracy tends, however, to underestimate the strength of a further set of principles, related to social rights and citizenship. Social rights did not necessarily develop along with democratic governments; Marshall's assertion, that political and civil rights develop before social and economic ones, is highly questionable.[12] At the same time, the extension of social rights is still work in progress. The social rights which are associated with democracies are often particular and tied to specific interest groups; many governments that would consider themselves democratic have only belatedly started to extend social rights to parts of their populations that were previously excluded.

The role of government

For many commentators, the first duty of a government is the maintenance of order; Nozick, for example, suggests that the most basic function of government is to be the 'Dominant Protection Agency', and that a minimal, 'night-watchman' state is the most extensive that can be justified.[13] Legal systems are often associated, in the popular mind, with criminal sanctions, but these are only a small part of the overall function of law. For government to function legitimately, it needs much more than a system of sanctions or penalties. The real first task of any government is to establish the rule of law – the framework within which people's interactions take place. This covers, not just in the regulation of criminal activity, but areas such as property holding, trade, contracts, tort and family law. Law provides the framework in which key elements of our lives are structured: personal relationships, housing, economic transactions and employment among them.

The authority of government to do this might be attributed to general principles, such as the welfare of the people, but at root all such authority depends more on a set of conventions than on any generic moral foundation. Governments offer a system of rules, ultimately backed by force but limited in its effect if there is not already a high degree of compliance from the population that is being served. The rule of law is identified through systems for the authorisation, recognition and change of laws, mechanisms for adjudication and redress, and the principles by which behaviours are regulated and disputes settled. The

---

[12] T Marshall, 1981, *The right to welfare*, London: Heinemann.

[13] R Nozick, 1974, *Anarchy, state and utopia*, Oxford: Blackwell.

rule of law is fundamental to effective governance, and governance in these terms is strongly associated with human development.[14]

Because so much of the literature about poverty is based on economic resources, the lack of basic rights and entitlements is often interpreted in terms of the structure of property rights in general and land-holding in particular. The absence of regulation of daily life tends, understandably, to be translated into a more general concern with people who are disadvantaged as a result – especially the rights of women and of children. Those are broader topics than the question of poverty alone, but it is worth for the moment carving out a slice from those big issues, and considering the implications of the lack of legal protection. The lack of protection means, for women, weak property rights, subservient treatment in the home, a lack of protection against violence, and an absence of the sort of structures that have made substantive welfare provisions possible in developed countries. For children, it includes all of those factors, along with problems of child labour, neglect and abandonment. Some parts of the weakness of legal structures in poor countries reflect the lack of an adequate, supportive framework – the absence of redress, the failure of law enforcement (often exacerbated by corruption), and the lack of routine administrative structures that are able to manage the regular tasks of government, such as providing basic documentation and records, certification and licensing. Without those things, it is difficult to ensure that children get health care and education, that resources go to the right places, that taxes are gathered, that environmental and physical dangers are controlled, and so on.

Developed legal systems differ markedly, but they have something in common: a set of meta-rules about how decisions are made. Hart calls these the 'secondary rules': the rules of recognition, so that we can tell what is law and what is not; rules of change, so that laws can be altered; and rules of adjudication, so that it is possible to apply and develop the law through application in specific circumstances.[15] The 'rule of law' is central to modern government, and particularly to contemporary understandings of democracy. Governments which proceed arbitrarily, which ignore or override the rights of citizens, or which fail to offer redress when rules are broken, are bad governments. Governments which follow predictable rules are

---

[14] M Trebilcock and M Prado, 2011, *What makes poor countries poor?* Cheltenham: Edward Elgar.

[15] H L A Hart, 1961, *The concept of law*, Oxford: Oxford University Press.

not necessarily good governments, but if they are bad, it will be for other reasons.

For governments to establish a role, they need to have determined areas where government may act, areas where it may not, and the processes and methods it will use to do things. Part of this will be determined through basic law or a constitution, but a larger part is based on practice and usage. The United Kingdom developed services during the Victorian age of laissez-faire in relation to public utilities, public health, hospitals and education. There tends to be a presumption in the US that the Constitution exists to prevent government from developing new areas of intervention, but despite that the federal government has been able over time to establish roles in relation to social security, health care, employment services, social inclusion and community work. Most governments have adapted pragmatically to such demands.

The World Bank, in the 1997 *World Development Report*, suggested a basic scheme for identifying the role of the state.[16] It offers a somewhat limited interpretation, falling short of the generalised role of governments adopted in most developed countries, because it does not allow for an adaptive, pragmatic approach; and it does not include, either, many of the things that governments aim to do, such as trying to change behaviour through incentive or subsidy, preventing undesirable social outcomes, or promoting social cohesion and culture. The scheme represents, nevertheless, an acceptance that governments can and should accept responsibility for people's conditions and circumstances within their territory.

Governments did not always see their role in these terms. The first state provisions for welfare were probably those made by city-states in Northern Europe;[17] there was some imitation in England under the Tudors, and eventually the system was codified into a national Poor Law. The Poor Laws lasted, in one form or another, for 350 years, and that experience, coupled with imitation of the model in other places, has led writers in Britain and America to focus on the state as a provider of last resort – a 'residual' model of welfare. However, locating the responsibility in the state was not by any means the general pattern. Many other countries did little directly in relation to poverty. Systems of mutual support were developed by a range of actors, including employers, trades unions, voluntary and mutual aid societies. Governments came late to the party. Bismarck's Germany was

[16] World Bank, 1997, *World development report 1997: the state in a changing world*, Washington DC: World Bank, p 27.

[17] See P Spicker, 2010, *The origins of modern welfare*, Oxford: Peter Lang.

Table 9.1: World Bank – functions of the state

	Addressing market failure				Improving equity
Minimal functions	*Providing pure public goods:* • Defence • Law and order • Property rights • Macroeconomic management • Public health				*Protecting the poor:* • Anti-poverty programmes • Disaster relief
Intermediate functions	*Addressing externalities:* • Basic education • Environmental protection	*Regulating monopoly:* • Utility regulation • Antitrust policy	*Overcoming imperfect information:* • Insurance (health, life, pensions) • Financial regulation • Consumer protection		*Providing social insurance:* • Redistributive pensions • Family allowances • Unemployment insurance
Activist functions	*Coordinating private activity:* • Fostering markets • Cluster initiatives				*Redistribution:* • Asset redistribution

Source: World Bank, 1997, p 27

one of the first countries to try to establish a role for government in such arrangements; equally, Bismarck was one of the first government leaders to realise that governments were running behind. In the course of the 20th century, many other governments did something similar, seeking either to supplement and extend mutualist provision, or alternatively trying to take them over.

These policies seemed extraordinary in the early 20th century, but as time went on they came to be general and – despite continued political resistance – unexceptional. There have been several common pressures. Democracy has grown around the world: it is marked both by the combination of mechanisms to give citizens a voice in government, and a general perception that governments are there to serve the interests of their populations. At the same time, several governments which are not democratic have moved in similar directions – China is an example, but the former communist bloc also had extensive systems of support. Governments find themselves under considerable pressure, once they set foot on the path. Provision made for people in the last resort cannot stop at the last resort; there are continuing problems of policing the boundaries, and constant pressure to extend. It needs to be recognised, too, that there has also been a growing commitment among politicians and governments themselves. Provision has often developed on a voluntary basis: when compulsion has been introduced, as it was in Scandinavian countries in the 1990s, and as it has recently been in the US for health insurance or the UK for workplace pensions, it has typically been used to secure or extend provision for people who would otherwise be excluded.

Governments and poverty

Governments interpret obligations to respond to poverty in different ways. For some, the central task is the pursuit of development and economic growth. Poverty is not the central issue, but there is a general supposition that the effect of growth will be to raise the position of the poor, as it raises the position of others. There are governments which accept partial responsibility for aspects of social protection – for example, for basic health care provision or child protection – but do not extend this to all poor people. Then there are governments which accept a residual responsibility for the poorest – there have been cases where governments have started to do this belatedly, in the hope of generalising protection to those otherwise left out, but it is just as possible to start the other way around.

The common element in these very different approaches is that governments are accepting the principle that they are in some sense responsible for the quality of people's lives – that is, for their welfare. If governments have a responsibility to meet the needs, aspirations or rights of their citizens, then the issues of poverty affecting individuals, households, communities and areas should be tackled at a national level as well. It seems fairly clear that governments of all stamps and hues are effectively presented with a series of problems and issues, to greater or lesser degrees, and need to formulate responses to those problems effectively. When the issues are considered only at the national level – a deliberately narrow perspective – the fields of activity are still enough to mean that even governments with the feeblest commitment to the welfare of their citizens are still likely to be engaged in issues directly related to poverty.

It is important to recognise, too, that some of the most effective measures against poverty are not necessarily conceived or executed in those terms. For example, the development of health services, and related measures for public health, can be construed in many ways. The extension of health insurance to China's previously excluded peoples – it now covers 94% of rural and 87% of its migrant populations – has been represented as a matter of equity and social justice.[18] Health care

---

[18] K Dalen, 2018, *Reflections on recent welfare reform in China*, Bergen: CROP.

might be seen as social security, as welfare, or perhaps simply as part of what governments do. Discussions of welfare are likely to be translated into the provision of particular kinds of service: public services for all, such as roads, water supplies, sanitation and drainage, and social services such as social security, health and education. There are good reasons for that. If welfare is to mean anything to the people that governments serve, the generalised discussion of economic prosperity has to provide tangible benefits. It may be surprising, though, that acceptance of these issues as government responsibilities should be quite so general as it appears to be.

Policies are developed through a process of interpretation, negotiation, and translation into practical terms. There are lots of problems that people have which governments do not treat as their business. Whenever governments get involved in the issues of poverty, the issues are likely to be redefined to fit the remit. This is not because those governments have necessarily any intention to undermine efforts to deal with poverty, or because they are imposing an ideological view – though that may happen, of course – but because politics is all about doing what is possible, and governments can only function sensibly in terms of their own authority. There are practical limits to what governments can do about what happens in employment contracts, or between men and women in the home, or what they can do directly about people's health. So, regardless of good or bad intentions, poverty or welfare has to be developed in terms that can be acted on, and unavoidably that means that what is actually dealt with gets trimmed to shape.

The constraints on government

The responses that governments make to poverty are heavily constrained in many ways. One set of constraints lies in legal authority. In a constitutional government, authority derives from a basic law; in the UK, which has no written constitution, it is based in parliamentary sovereignty; but in any case, the principle of the rule of law means that there has to be some way by which the authority of government is recognised and acted on. Writing from the perspective of the UK, it seems strange to argue that governments might not have the authority to act against poverty. That is true partly because the UK tradition is pragmatic, and partly because the British state has been involved in responses to poverty for nearly five hundred years. In the US, by contrast, the federal government was largely denied such power; when Franklin Roosevelt ushered in the creation of social security, it was immediately responded to by legal action in an (unsuccessful) attempt to declare it unconstitutional – and defended by a threat to change the rules.

Some other constraints are imposed by administrative capacity. It is all very well to say, as some Western governments do, that we should top up the incomes of poor people; to do that, we have to be able to identify who is poor and who is not. Means-testing is horrendously complicated. Incomes come from multiple sources; they are not stable; people's household and family circumstances change while they are being measured. That, of course, is an observation from a relatively rich developed country which has a wealth of official records, papers and established processes to make the management of information easier. Try to do as much in a country where births are not necessarily registered; where people do not routinely have papers, or social security numbers, or other means of official identification; where dwellings do not have a system of addresses; where there is no practical routine system for passing communications between government offices and citizens; where people do not have financial records or access to banking. That picture is less accurate than it used to be – the spread of mobile communications across Africa has made it much more possible to contact people, to distribute goods, to get help. But it is still true that, for many governments, trying to identify poor people individually would be beyond their scope. There is a faction within the World Bank that remains firmly convinced that 'targeting' the poor by means-testing must be more efficient and effective than less discriminating or universal approaches: 'the policy has been found to reduce national poverty at almost twice the rate of a universal approach.'[19] That, Stephen Kidd has argued in a blistering response, is magical thinking, or fantasy, based on a 'patently silly assumption of perfect targeting'. In practice, he argues, a universal pensions scheme performs better in terms of coverage, transfer value and poverty reduction.[20] (His main example is the transitional economy of Georgia. The same World Bank report attributes Georgia's relatively high poverty reduction to the higher coverage and higher value of the benefits it offers.[21]) Other universal alternatives, which have had

---

[19] World Bank, 2018, *The state of safety nets 2018*, Washington DC: World Bank, p 83.

[20] S Kidd, 2018, A magical use of evidence, https://www.developmentpathways. co.uk/blog/a-magical-use-of-evidence-the-world-banks-state-of-social-safety-nets-2018-report/, accessed 10.10.2019.

[21] World Bank, 2018, pp 62–3.

creditable outcomes, include Basic Health Care Packages (promoted by the World Bank[22]) and Universal Primary Education.

Another set of constraints is one which virtually all governments complain about: the cost. Saying that poor people cost money is not very helpful in itself, because the costs can take very different forms. One option, possibly the first that many think of, is a transfer payment – a process of taking money away from richer people and giving it to the poor. In economic terms, this is not really 'spending' at all – it is largely neutral, because there is the same amount of money in a national economy after a transfer as before it. The scope for doing it, however, is limited, because while rich people may have a lot more money, the nature of inequality tends to mean that there are not very many rich people, and there are an awful lot of poor ones. A different kind of cost is incurred by the provision of facilities and services to benefit the poor – creating a basic structure of services, such as roads, drains, schools and medical centres. And another option is to benefit the whole population, in the belief that this will benefit the poor as well.[23]

Discussions of costs are often interpreted solely in terms of finance – whether governments can raise money, what interest they have to pay, and so on. Discussions of cost are a shorthand for something still more important, which is a discussion not only of finance but of capacity. Governments in poor countries can find it difficult to raise taxes.[24] They may be able to do other things – mobilise labour, take over primary resources such as land or minerals, set up infant industries, and so forth. These approaches may have worked for China (though interpretations differ); they have not worked for most of sub-Saharan Africa.

Governments are as capable of doing harm as they are of doing good. There have been times when governments have been seen as able to do anything they chose – an impression reinforced by a long history of arbitrary dictators, military strongmen and kleptocrats throughout the Third World. There have also been, however, strong ideological justifications given for the exercise of dictatorial power: the high point of this model was Stalinism, which seemed to promise

---

[22] World Bank, 1993, *World development report 1993: investing in health*, Washington DC: World Bank.

[23] D Dollar and A Kraay, 2002, Growth is good for the poor, *Journal of Economic Growth*, 7(3): 195–225.

[24] P Mosley, B Chiripanhura, J Grugel and B Thirkell-White, 2012, *The Politics of Poverty Reduction*, Oxford: Oxford University Press, Chapter 5.

that an all-powerful central government might be able to bring about economic development through centralised direction.[25] The combination of Stalinism with nationalism was powerfully influential in developing countries.[26] For example, Kwame Nkrumah in Ghana claimed to reject Stalinism, but he shared the belief that government could direct economic development through socialism in one country;[27] the same approach was reflected in many African countries. Contemporary governments have learned to be more humble. They do not have the authority to do anything they please; they do not have the capacity. They may be one actor among many – others typically include international organisations, donor countries offering foreign aid, NGOs, multinational countries and – of course – the people who live in the country. Governments have had to learn to proceed through negotiation, partnership and planning.

---

[25] A Nove, 1964, *Was Stalin really necessary?* London: George Allen and Unwin.

[26] W Duncan, 1988, Ideology and nationalism in attracting Third World leaders to communism, *World Affairs*, 151(3): 105–16.

[27] A Mazrui, 1976, *Nkrumah: the Leninist czar*, Transition, 75/76: 106–26.

10

Poverty in rich countries

Many commentators have been persuaded by Peter Townsend's argument that the nature and character of poverty differs according to the society where it occurs.[1] The idea of relative deprivation has been interpreted in different ways. For Runciman, it was a sense of deprivation that people experienced because they did not have the goods, amenities and services that other people around them did have.[2] Relative deprivation may mean that deprivation is a reflection of inequality – that people are unable to command resources, like land, housing, education and opportunities, because others with more resources have been able to secure the goods to the exclusion of the poor. Deprivation may be relative because it is socially constructed – because circumstances such as homelessness or food distribution depend on the rules that apply in particular societies.

Poverty in developed countries has some features which are much like poverty in poor countries, and others which are quite unlike. On one hand, there are groups of people who have to face similar privations in rich and poor countries: homeless people who sleep rough and are not allowed into covered areas, people who are malnourished, people who cannot afford medical care. A recent report for the Rowntree Foundation in the UK, supposedly about 'destitution' (though that term means something different), estimated that more than half a million people in the UK had gone without at least two essentials in the previous month – shelter, food, heat, light, clothing or basic toiletries.[3] There is an evident difference in scale and proportion between rich and poor countries – there is simply more material deprivation in the global South. On the other hand, the character of the experiences that people undergo seem qualitatively different. Life is different when people have electricity supplies, road transport, water to the home, and postal services. But the reason why poverty looks and feels different in less developed countries is not that the meaning of poverty is different, or even that the norms being

---

[1] P Townsend, 1979, *Poverty in the United Kingdom*, Harmondsworth: Penguin, p 31.

[2] W Runciman, 1972, *Relative deprivation and social justice*, Harmondsworth: Penguin.

[3] S Fitzpatrick, G Bramley, F Sosenko, J Blenkinsopp, S Johnsen, M Littlewood, G Netto and B Watts, 2016, *Destitution in the UK*, York: Joseph Rowntree Foundation.

•

applied are shifting; it is that the issues relate to a distinct social system. Development is not a matter only of economics; it represents a much broader and deeper change in human relationships. Development depends on the establishment and growth of a web of interactions, exchanges and relationships. There are marked differences between countries, but that should not be surprising. Poverty is so diverse that developed countries are not necessarily like each other, either.

From a relational perspective, the similarities between countries are stronger, and many common themes emerge. In developed economies, there are still problems of economic insecurity, precariousness and the struggle to maintain a livelihood. There are the problems of ill health and disability. There are problems of inequality: educational disadvantage, exclusion from access, and inferior public services. There is a lack of rights, limited influence either individually or collectively, and the abuse of authority. These are the problems of poverty, and they occur in richer countries as they occur in poorer ones.

How is it, one might wonder, that poverty continues to exist in rich countries? If poverty is understood as a state of being, even a socially constructed state of being, that does seem to be a puzzle. Some explanations are pathological; they attribute the persistence of poverty to the problems of poor people themselves. There is no shortage of commentators who think that the persistence of poverty needs to be explained in terms of the character, deficiencies, behaviour or culture of the poor. There are many varieties of pathological explanation. Some are individualised: Charles Murray thinks that poverty is a rational choice when benefits are available.[4] Many members of the general public attribute poverty to laziness or lack of will power.[5] Some pathological explanations are based in families, genetics and breeding. Social policies after the beginning of the 20th century were guided by eugenics and a belief that poor people were 'degenerate',[6] and after that was discredited the language switched to a discussion of 'problem' families. In Britain, we hear continually about 'troubled' families who have been unemployed for three generations (if there are, researchers haven't been able to find them).[7] And there are arguments

---

[4] C Murray, 1984, *Losing ground*, New York: Basic Books.

[5] Eurostat, 2010, *Combating poverty and social exclusion*, Luxembourg: European Union, p 13.

[6] See D Pick, 1989, *Faces of degeneration*, Cambridge: Cambridge University Press; E Carlson, 2001, *The unfit*, New York: Cold Spring Harbor Laboratory Press.

[7] R Macdonald, T Shildrick and A Furlong, 2014, In search of 'intergenerational cultures of worklessness': hunting the yeti and shooting zombies, *Critical Social Policy*, 34(2): 199–200.

that poverty is based in a sub-culture – expressed for example as a 'culture of poverty', a 'dependency culture' or an 'underclass'. The language keeps changing, because the arguments have been exploded time and again. Of course poor people live differently, and behave differently – that's part of what poverty means. It doesn't follow that they've chosen to do so, or that they should be blamed for their lives.

If poverty is not a state of being, but a set of relationships, the persistence of poverty in rich countries is much less of a mystery. In some ways, poor people in rich countries gain from the wealth of people around them: roads, schools, drainage, water supply. In other ways, they can lose because other people are wealthy: examples are advanced education, employment and career opportunities. As we move away from the focus on material deprivation, the distinctions made between poverty in different countries start to look less clear and less certain. There are larger numbers of people in developing countries who are not part of a formal economy, but in all kinds of economies there are people who are marginal, insecure and vulnerable. When it comes to social relationships, there are issues of persistent disadvantage, for example through gender and disability, social isolation and obstacles to participation in the wider society. The relational elements of poverty are experienced in rich countries as they are in poor ones.

The main alternatives to pathological explanations are structural – explanations which describe poverty in terms of the structure of social, economic and political relationships. Some reference to the social structure is often assumed in the consideration of relational poverty; it is hard to understand why relationships take the form they take, or work in the way they do, unless some kind of structural account is offered. The social structure leads to relationships of disadvantage, and those relationships are intrinsic to the concept of poverty. At the simplest level, poverty reflects patterns of inequality. Beyond that, the effect of economic marginality, a lack of rights or exclusion is all too likely to produce the circumstances of poverty. All the processes which are considered in the first part of this book continue to apply in countries after development. It is not surprising that poverty persists; it would be more surprising if the problems of poverty were not experienced in richer countries.

Money and markets

Debates about poverty in developed countries tend to concentrate on money. That is true partly because that is where the research and evidence has tended to focus, but more so for a much better reason: many of the key issues of material deprivation have been settled in other ways, and the areas that remain to be dealt with are areas conventionally dealt with through the mechanism of the market. On one hand, take the critical issue of surface drainage. Where there is none, standing water poses risks to health, offers a breeding ground for mosquitoes and parasites, and often poses problems like sanitation or flood risks. In most Western countries, these problems are no longer an issue – they have been dealt with – and while they occur, for example in discussions of disaster relief, they are no longer part of the routine discourse of poverty. On the other hand, consider a contrasting issue: the availability of energy, typically through an electricity supply. The infrastructure generally exists in a developed economy, but access to it and the use of electricity by people in a household depends on their ability to pay. The same pattern repeats across a wide range of essential goods and services – food, housing, water, cooking facilities, transport, and so on. When Sen writes about lack of 'entitlements', that principle is typically translated into commodities. In developed societies, that is translated further into the ability to pay. The key distinction between those who have access and those who do not is whether or not they can afford it.

This is often reduced in the literature to a simple question: do poor people have enough money? The question is unanswerable in general terms, partly because money is only directly relevant within the confines of market distribution, and partly because the value of money is relative. Inequalities matter. There is a widespread view in economics and political theory that if some people get to be better off financially, it should not negatively affect other people's welfare. That idea is built in to one of the standard assumptions of micro-economic theory, 'Pareto optimality': that welfare is increased if one person is better off and no-one has anything taken away.[8] This can easily be violated by measures that favour the poor, and Martin Ravallion proposes a modified version: 'any poverty measure should at least satisfy a weaker version of the Pareto principle, namely that social welfare cannot fall if anyone experiences a welfare gain and must rise if any poor person gains.'[9] Even that modified principle poses problems. Both approaches are individualistic; they take it for granted that the question of who gains and who loses can be judged discretely for

[8] For example, R Sugden, 1981, *The political economy of public choice*, Oxford: Martin Robertson, p 3.
[9] M Ravallion, 2016, *The economics of poverty*, Oxford: Oxford University Press, p 117.

each person, and it cannot be. Economics is all about the allocation of resources under conditions of scarcity. The price of scarce items is a function of the demand, and the demand is a function of available resources. It is in the nature of markets that people who are able and willing to pay more for things than other people are more likely to get them – and that, because the price of goods reflects demand, those things will also be harder to get for people with fewer resources. Some goods are 'positional': the value of certain commodities, such as education or living space, is based in the social position that the commodities give access to.[10] The problem is seen most clearly in the use of land and access to housing. The rich can use their resources to shut out the poor. That is what happens in gated communities. It happens in whole towns, where squatter settlements are bulldozed or homeless people are moved on by the police. Where people are poor, they are not able to get access to land in their own right, and that means typically that they have to move to other places, or squat, or rent property from someone who owns it. If they can do none of these things, they may have to live on the streets. The Pareto principle is self-contradictory. If some people gain disproportionately, other people will be worse off.

Money operates in a context where goods and services are provided in a market. The advocates of 'free markets' make large claims for the capacity of markets to provide. In many cases those claims have been justified – but not in all. Food, clothing and domestic goods are widely available in developed market societies, and that availability is attributable to market distribution. But the market is one of the strongest and clearest circumstances where the solution is part of the problem. The standard critique of markets is based on 'market failure', where the market is unable to operate as it should because of the character of the goods provided or the systems through which it might be distributed.[11] Examples of market failure include collective goods, like roads and parks; problems generated by local monopolies, for example in water supply; and imperfect information or the inability to choose, such as may be found in emergency medical treatment.

---

[10] F Hirsch, 1976, *Social limits to growth*, Cambridge, MA: Harvard University Press.
[11] For example, S Connolly and A Munro, 2006, Economics of the public sector, Hemel Hempstead: Pearson, Chapter 9; HM Treasury, n.d., Green Book, at https:// assets.publishing.service.gov.uk/government/uploads/system/uploads/attachment_ data/file/685903/The_Green_Book.pdf, accessed 19.12.2019; and see M Kleiman and S Teles, 2006, Market and non-market failures, in M Moran, M Rein and R Goodin (eds) *The Oxford Handbook of Public Policy*, Oxford: Oxford University Press.

Considerations of market failure tend to dominate the economic literature, but actually it is rather less important than some of the other reasons why markets fail to deliver. The principal weakness of markets is that, wherever market distribution is the exclusive means of distributing essential goods and services, some people cannot pay. The usual retort from advocates of the market is that if that is the problem, people can be given the money instead, so that they can make their own choices. That argument suffers from two critical weaknesses – that it does not get around any of the other problems associated with market provision, and that in practice governments which depend on liberal markets and residual financial support also seem determined to offer poor people the most restrictive and inadequate financial support they can get away with.

It is much more important that markets are not universal. Markets work by choice, and choice means, always, that there have to be compromises – that decisions have to be made about what to do and what not to do, that not everything is possible at the same time, that people do not get everything they might need. Producers exercise choices about what they do. If providing a service is expensive, logistically difficult, demanding, inconvenient or offers lower returns than alternatives, then – unlike governments – producers can opt not to do it. That implies that there may well be a shortfall in supply – implying either that some people are not served at all, or that government is forced to step into the breach.

The central problem of poverty in a market society is not that resources are scarce, but that shortages are visited on people who have the least. The allocation of resources is, after all, is what markets are supposed to do. In any market, some people have an advantage, and others have a disadvantage. Another way of expressing this is that markets are unequal – because that is what 'advantage' and 'disadvantage' signify. In any economic market, the price of goods depends on willingness to pay, and willingness is a function not so much of personal choice as of relative capacity. The price of housing, to take a clear example, tends to depend less on the intrinsic physical merits of the accommodation on offer than it does on location, status and exclusivity.

Social security versus decommodification

Where markets are not enough to provide for poor people, governments have two main options to remedy the situation. One option is decommodification – taking the item out of the market, and distributing it by some other means. Health care, public housing or education are typically distributed through non-market rationing. Health care can be distributed, for example, by professional referral systems (filtering) or strict eligibility criteria, though some forms of health care rationing are based on triage (identifying not the greatest need or the worst health, but the greatest ability to benefit). Public housing is typically rationed through a needs-based assessment, though there have been other methods including varieties of queuing. Entry to higher education is often rationed by competitive examination. The literature on non-market rationing is fascinating in its own right, but a detailed discussion would take us off in directions which have little to do directly with poverty. The most pertinent point from that literature is a depressing insight: that despite the best intentions of policy makers, and often despite the design of services to avoid it happening, the impact of poverty is often to create barriers to access even in circumstances where resources are not ostensibly taken into account. In the case of education, there is a general problem of middle-class capture of resources: children from more privileged backgrounds tend to do better in all kinds of tests, and the differences made by home background continue to have an effect throughout a person's educational career. In the case of health, there is an 'inverse care law':[12] people from disadvantaged backgrounds tend to have greater needs than others, but even in a publicly funded, non-market health service, people from socially advantaged backgrounds tend to receive more care and better service. Public housing seems to offer the best hope of favouring the poor, partly because the service has much less appeal to the better off. Even here, however, there is a reflection of the structures of the market: the best housing goes not to those in greatest need, but to those who are best able to hold on for something more, and those are liable to be people on higher incomes.

The other main option is social security – financial benefits which make it possible for people to pay for goods. There are many different approaches to social security provision – the most important are insurance, income-testing, needs assessment and 'universal' benefits for a whole category of people. Insurance, on the face of the matter, depends on people earning enough in the first place to make contributions. The purer the insurance scheme, one might think, the more likely it must be that poor people are liable to be excluded. There is some evidence to support this. The system in Germany was designed

---

[12] J Tudor Hart, 1971, The inverse care law, in G Smith, D Dorling, M Shaw (eds), 2001, *Poverty, inequality and health in Britain 1800–2000*, Bristol: Policy Press.

to leave out people on very high incomes (who were expected to make their own arrangements) and those on low incomes, whose coverage by discretionary and local schemes is patchy. In France, it was the realisation that many people were left out of the contributory scheme altogether that led to the movement for 'insertion' or social inclusion. And yet, despite the gaps, the performance of such schemes has been remarkably effective. Governments have been readier to accept more generous benefits when they are paid for by contributions – even if the schemes are not adequately financed. (The French scheme is notorious for running deficits – leaving 'le trou de la Sécu', or the hole in the social).

Means-tested schemes, by contrast, look on paper as if they are most likely to support the poor. If the object of the exercise is to take money from people with most and to move it to people with least, means-testing seems to be the way to go. Once again, appearances are deceptive. Part of the problem is political: there is huge resistance to the process of redistribution in these terms. It creates the impression that support for the poor is a public burden, and with that perception comes moral condemnation and parsimony. The other part is practical. It is all very well saying that benefits should be confined to those who are poor, but how are they to be identified? Incomes are not stable characteristics of the target population; they are subject to complex, fluctuating conditions, made worse by flexible labour markets, multiple sources of income and rapid changes in circumstance. The general experience of selectivity – separating eligible from non-eligible claimants – is that it is complex, administratively burdensome, error-prone, and inevitably subject to problems at the boundaries. The more frequently it is done, the worse the problems get. A tax schedule which tests people's income once and distributes benefits to all is more practical than a set of schemes which means-tests each benefit individually.

There are no national systems that work solely on a single principle; all have a mix of different approaches and mechanisms. Income is 'fungible' – when it is lumped together from different sources, it all mixes in and people find it difficult to identify which part came from where. That has led to a discussion of incomes in terms of 'income packages', and packages are much more important than the adequacy or inadequacy of individual benefits.[13] Figure 10.1 is based on some

---

[13] L Rainwater, M Rein and J Schwartz, 1986, *Income packaging in the welfare state*, Oxford: Oxford University Press.

Figure 10.1: The impact of transfers on the risk of low-income poverty (single-person households in selected EU countries)

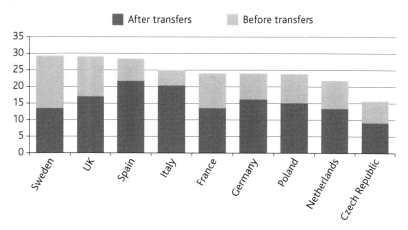

Source: Eurostat, 2016

indicative figures from Eurostat, showing the impact of transfers on single-person households on that household's 'risk of poverty'[14] – based on economic distance, itself a measure of inequality. The effect of transfers, from a wide range of sources, is generally to raise the income of people on low incomes (that does not have to be the case – transfers can be regressive). The test makes it possible to compare, in more or less equivalent terms, the aggregate difference made by different systems of welfare provision, rather than focusing on the impact of specific kinds of cash benefit.

The illustration should be helpful, but most of the reservations made earlier still apply – and besides, the underlying figures are concerned with income, not with living standards. If key elements of people's living standards are decommodified and publicly provided, such as education or health care, they disappear from the figures.

There is a view that poverty in rich countries can be attributed to the absence of adequate measures to prevent it.[15] There may be 'non-decisions':[16] a lack of action may result, not from deliberate decisions, but from the want of an appropriate agenda. What is true is that

---

[14] Eurostat, 2016, People at risk of poverty or exclusion, http://ec.europa.eu/eurostat/statistics-explained/index.php/People_at_risk_of_poverty_or_social_exclusion, accessed 2.5.2017.

[15] R Holman, 1978, *Poverty: explanations of deprivation*, London: Martin Robertson.

[16] P Bachrach and M Baratz, 1970, *Power and poverty*, Oxford: Oxford University Press.

governments in developed countries have come to see responses to poverty and the protection of people's circumstances as basic elements in the role of a democratic government, and if governments do not ensure that basic living standards are protected, they have failed.

11

Poor countries

What is a 'poor country'?

The difference between poor countries and others is a matter of degree rather than of absolutes. The gradients are not smooth, or easily predictable. Some middle-income countries have less poverty, some have more; some have rich and poor areas and regions. Several nations which have relatively strong economies have feet in different worlds – India, Brazil, South Africa and Mexico among them. There is a complex, slightly arcane economic literature about 'poverty dominance', comparing countries in terms of poverty head counts or indices.[1] It matters because a demonstration that one country is poorer than another can be crucial for applications for funding, but the standards applied are based on some fairly broad approximations, and the huge disparities in country size and regional variation can act to disguise the real differences.

Poverty is widespread, and most of the poor people in the world are not in countries where poverty is found in the greatest concentrations. The numbers of poor people in China and India are generally larger than the figures for sub-Saharan Africa (though Nigeria, one of few countries to have increasing numbers of very poor people, seems determined to outdo them both); and quite apart from the giants, most of the world's poorest people, Sumner argues, are now to be found in middle-income countries.[2] The countries with the greatest concentration of poverty might be identified in different ways. One simple indicator is the average income of people who live in those countries – the Gross National Income per capita. Another, used in the Sustainable Development Goals, is an income threshold of $1.90

---

[1] For example, M Ravallion, 1992, Poverty comparisons: a guide to concepts and methods, in Living standards measurement study, Working Paper 88, Washington DC: World Bank; N Siersbaek, L Østerdal and C Arndt, 2016, Multidimensional first-order dominance comparisons of population wellbeing, in C Ardnt and F Tarp, *Measuring poverty and wellbeing in developing countries*, Oxford: Oxford University Press, Chapter 3.
[2] A Sumner, 2016, Global poverty: deprivation, distribution and development since the Cold War, Oxford: Oxford University Press.

per day. This figure needs to be handled with tongs. Nearly thirty years ago, the World Bank lighted on the measure of $1 a day as a test of absolute or extreme poverty, with exchange rates adjusted for 'Purchasing Power Parity' or PPP. The World Bank's website offers an explanation of how the figure was arrived at. It is intended to give the impression that it is a subtle, informed calculation, based on existing national poverty lines:

> In 1990, a group of independent researchers and the World Bank proposed to measure the world's poor using the standards of the poorest countries in the World. They examined national poverty lines from some of the poorest countries in the world, and converted the lines to a common currency by using purchasing power parity (PPP) exchange rates. The PPP exchange rates are constructed to ensure that the same quantity of goods and services are priced equivalently across countries. Once converted into a common currency, they found that in six of these very poor countries the value of the national poverty line was about $1 per day per person, and this formed the basis for the first dollar-a-day international poverty line.
>
> After a new round and larger volume of internationally comparable prices were collected in 2005, the international poverty line was revised based on 15 national poverty lines from some of the poorest countries in the World. The average of these 15 lines was $1.25 per person per day (again in PPP terms), and this became the revised international poverty line.[3]

This is misleading. The original work did not settle directly on $1 a day; it offered two lines, of $275 and $370 a day.[4] The higher figure was based on lines used in six countries, including for example Indonesia and Morocco; $275 was the level being used in India. The other countries were described in the original report as representing a range of countries with relatively low incomes,[5] but in a later report

[3] World Bank, n.d., How is the global poverty line derived? How is it different from national poverty lines? https://datahelpdesk.worldbank.org/knowledgebase/articles/193310-how-is-the-global-poverty-line-derived-how-is-it, accessed 19.12.2019.

[4] World Bank, 1990, World development report 1990: poverty, pp 27, n29.

[5] World Bank, 1990, p 27.

(and in the quotation just cited) this has been altered to claim that it was based on the poorest countries,[6] which it was not. The figure of $1.25 a day for the later work was arrived at after obtaining data from 76 out of 88 countries,[7] and the median level for those countries was $2.00.[8] The authors deliberately selected a lower figure from a more limited set of countries. They made a choice, from a range of possible choices, about which lines they wished to incorporate, and they settled on each occasion on a neatly rounded figure. This was a political judgement, not a scientific one.

Hoy and Sumner refer to a range of poverty lines – $1.90, $2.50 as a median of poverty lines in developing countries, $5 as the median poverty line for all countries, and $10 as an indicator of the level of income needed to escape permanently from poverty.[9] All the counts are sensitive, some would say excessively so, to the indicators that are chosen.[10] Recently the World Bank has put in lines at $3.20 and $5.50 to reflect poverty standards in lower-middle and middle-income countries. The results are in Table 11.1:[11]

Table 11.1: World Bank figures on global poverty

	Millions		% of the world's population	
	1990	2015	1990	2015
Below $1.90 a day	1,895	734	35.9	10.0
Below $3.20 a day	2,914	1,938	55.1	26.3
Below $5.50 a day	3,541	3,386	67.0	46.0

Source: World Bank, n.d.

Many writers have been critical of the standard, both the level it is set at and the reliance on income. Estava and his colleagues write, for example:

---

[6] M Ravallion, S Chen and P Sangruala, 2008, *Dollar a day revisited*, Washington DC: World Bank, p 3.

[7] Ravallion, Chen and Sangruala, 2008, p 9.

[8] Ravallion, Chen and Sangruala, 2008, p 12.

[9] C Hoy, A Sumner, 2017, *Gasoline, guns and giveaways*, Washington DC: Center for Global Development, https://www.cgdev.org/sites/default/files/gasoline-guns-and-giveaways-end-three-quarters-global-poverty-0.pdf, p 2, accessed 19.12.2019.

[10] For example, A Cimadamore, G Koehler and T Pogge, 2016, *Poverty and the Millennium Development Goals*, London: CROP/Zed, p 6.

[11] World Bank, n.d., povcalnet, http://iresearch.worldbank.org/PovcalNet/povDuplicateWB.aspx, accessed 30.7.2019.

How can malnourishment be rising when the number of people in poverty is declining so rapidly? The answer is that poverty is measured in terms of money, usually money spent (consumption). … It's nearly impossible to exist in the market economy anywhere in the world on less than $1.25 a day. Thus 'poverty' by construction tends to measure the percentage of people who live outside the market economy rather than the percentage of people who live poorly.[12]

Despite the crudity of the process, the figures do actually convey something important. The income threshold is an indicator of poverty, but it is only an indicator, and it points to poverty of a particular kind. If people are not getting $1.90 a day, it generally means not that they have a low monetary income, but that they hardly have a monetary income at all. That implies that they are not part of a formal economy (though there has been a growth of very low paid urban jobs in some countries, making that less true than it was). Participation in a formal economy has lots of implications for the kinds of life that people will lead and their ability to have needs satisfied. However, there is no guarantee that, once people do move into a formal economy, they will cease to be poor. We need other indicators to get a sense of what is happening.

The United Nations Development Programme's Multidimensional Poverty Index has broken away from the conventional approach, taking into account education, health and living standards.[13]

- Education
  - School attendance
  - School attainment, by households
- Health
  - Child Mortality
  - Nutrition
- Living standards
  - Access to electricity
  - Access to drinking water
  - Sanitation

---

[12] G Estava, S Babones and P Babcicky, 2013, *The future of development*, Bristol: Policy Press, pp 82–3.

[13] S Alkire and S Jahan, 2018, The new global MPI 2018, United Nations Development Programme, http://hdr.undp.org/en/content/new-global-mpi-2018-aligning-sustainable-development-goals, accessed 30.8.2019.

○ The use of fuel for cooking
○ Having roof, walls or floor
○ Having assets to support:
  ▪ mobility (for example car, bicycle, motorcycle)
  ▪ information (TV, radio, phone, computer)
  ▪ livelihood (animal cart, refrigeration).

Education, health and living standards each count for one third of the total index. Some of the tests of living standards have changed since the first versions – the compilers had difficulty with 'livelihood', where they had to drop attempts to operationalise and quantify information about land or livestock.[14] That kind of compromise is commonplace in global statistics.

Table 11.2 shows all the countries with an MPI above 0.4.[15] Every country in this list is also a low-income country, with an average GNI pc below $3 a day, but the list is not the same as a list of countries based solely on income would be. The countries with the highest MPI figures are all African, and so are the countries with the highest MPIs after them. The size of the population can be expected to lead to some distortion in the figures (most of the figures in that column

Table 11.2: The poorest countries in the world (as ranked on the MPI)

	MPI score	% of people below $1.90 a day	Population (millions)
Niger	0.590	44.5	19.2
South Sudan	0.580	42.7	12.6
Chad	0.533	38.4	12.3
Burkina Faso	0.519	43.7	19.2
Somalia (2017 est)	0.518	n.a.	14.7
Ethiopia	0.489	27.3	102.4
Central African Republic	0.465	66.3	4.7
Mali	0.457	49.7	18.5
Madagascar	0.453	77.8	22.4
Mozambique	0.411	62.4	27.2
Burundi	0.403	71.8	9.9

Source: UNDP, 2019

---

[14] Alkire and Jahan, 2018, p 5.
[15] UNDP, 2019, *Global Multidimensional Poverty Index 2019: illuminating inequality*; UNDP, 2018, *Human development statistical update 2018*, New York: UNDP.

come from the World Bank, whose estimates are slightly lower than some other sources). Larger countries may well have high numbers of people in poverty, whose position is concealed by the rest – the 2019 report from the UNDP breaks down figures from India, Haiti, Cambodia and Ethiopia. There is an obvious illustration of the impact of subdividing nations in the inclusion of South Sudan in the table; when it was part of Sudan, the situation of South Sudan was lumped in with the rest, and its poverty has been recognised here primarily because it became independent. (A similar example might be the division of Pakistan between East and West; it was only with the independence of Bangladesh that it became clear how different the two parts of Pakistan were.)

Saying that a country is poor says more than that there are a lot of poor people there. If poverty is about individual experiences, only people can be poor, and poverty is not something that can be said to affect areas, communities or nations. We talk about 'poor areas' or 'poor communities' because there is something about the prevalence of poverty in an area which affects the people in it – and the effects of widespread poverty are often more generally felt than for poor people alone. If poverty is relational, there has to be something about the character of economic, social and political relationships in that country which affect the opportunities, entitlements, and welfare of the people who live there. A poor nation is not a nation where every single person is poor, but one where the range and experience of poverty denies the members of that nation the resources, services, amenities and quality of life that they might enjoy in other countries. For people in relations of poverty, the problems they experience in poor countries go beyond the problems of poverty in rich countries – not only a lack of entitlements, but the lack of a structure (such as a formal economy) in which such entitlements can be realised. For people who are not poor in such countries, the problems of poverty still affect their lifestyle – the facilities and amenities they can use, the public spaces they share with others, the risks they are exposed to. Public services and infrastructure, such as roads, schools, electricity supply and water, are likely to be inferior to the facilities in better-off nations. Government services are liable to be under-resourced and difficult to mobilise for positive action. The situation is made more difficult still by a range of other factors. Nearly all of these countries have experienced some kind of armed conflict in the course of the last 20 years. All of them had to go through the IMF's structural adjustment policies, which enforced debt repayments while removing protections from the economy.

Pathological explanations

'Pathological' explanations attribute the problems of poverty to processes that occur within the body that suffers them. That term is usually used in the context used in Chapter 10, considering the poverty of individuals – explanations which attribute poverty to the character or conduct of the poor. The same term can also be applied to pathological accounts of poor countries, attributing poverty to such factors as culture, elites, corruption or institutional failure. Part of the reasoning behind this, Rosling argues, is attributable to a 'destiny instinct', our tendency to interpret events as part of a coherent narrative.[16] Stories of the sort are used to excuse moral responsibility, to claim that helping poor countries is pointless, to claim that the country has to sort itself out before any help can be useful. Acemoglu and Robinson declare their intention to focus on 'extractive institutions' – governments which treat government as an opportunity to enrich themselves at other people's expense[17] – but their detailed examples – considering the role of institutions, external influences, history and happenstance – come uncomfortably close to saying that everything matters.

Pathological explanations are disputable enough in personal accounts of poverty; they are even harder to take when they are applied to territories and the institutions of government. It is hard to tell causes apart from effects: factors reinforce each other. The influences on development are complex, and all explanations are partial. When we start counting all the other influences – the things that have not happened, all the things that have happened within a country and everything that has had an impact from outside – anything that boils the explanation down to a single cause, no matter how plausible that cause may seem, should not be trusted. (I would make the same reservation about the claim by Frances Fox Piven, cited in the Introduction to this book, that a concept of relational poverty provides us with a causal explanation for poverty.[18] As a general rule, social scientists need to be very cautious about attributing causation to anything.)

If some countries are less developed than others, there is not necessarily anything about that which needs to be explained. Development can generate itself spontaneously, but there is nothing

---

[16] H Rosling, 2018, *Factfulness*, London: Hodder and Stoughton, Chapter 7.

[17] D Acemoglu and J Robinson, 2012, *Why nations fail*, London: Profile Books.

[18] F Piven, 2018, Introduction, in V Lawson and S Elwood (eds), 2018, *Relational poverty politics*, Athens, Georgia: University of Georgia Press, p ix.

about the process or the world economy that guarantees that this will just happen. Where communications and infrastructure are poor, the scope for trade is limited. Where people's education is limited, opportunities for developing certain types of industry are closed off. Where finance is not available, people cannot use the facilities to develop an industry. The lack of effective local government or community organisation often means that collective facilities are not available. Take-off – or at least, strong, sustained growth – relies on a combination of infrastructure development, communications, education, skills and appropriate economic conditions; where these things have not happened, it is difficult to bring them about. Gunnar Myrdal argued that there was 'cumulative causation' – a vicious circle – which reinforced the disadvantage of poor countries.[19] Easterly is sceptical about the view that poor countries are 'trapped' in poverty – some move into poverty, just as others move out.[20] Kraay suggests that even where countries appear persistently to be poor, this disguises constant changes in the patterns of economic production.[21] That means that poverty is not inevitable – but it does not mean that poor countries do not start at a disadvantage. Whether or not there is such a trap, the surest predictor of low income is starting out with low income. Development depends on development. Some of the most effective policies in development have been introduced to make a difference in a whole society – education, essential health care, the creation of infrastructure.

Then there are explanations concerning factors that stop things happening. The AIDS epidemic has had a devastating effect on regions of Africa. Ill health and malnutrition prevent people realising their potential; *Voices of the Poor* emphasises the importance of the body and physical health for poor people, because people who have nothing else are left with that and that alone. These are certainly serious problems in their own right, but serious problems are not a reason for development not to happen. Several countries have made the transition from relatively low to relatively high incomes; others are in the process of doing so. That does not show that low income is not an impediment to development, but it does show that 'traps' can be overcome.

---

[19] G Myrdal, 1957, *Economic theory and underdevelopment regions* (London: Gerald Duckworth).

[20] W Easterly, 2006, *The white man's burden*, Oxford: University Press, pp 34–6.

[21] A Kraay and D McKenzie, 2014, Do poverty traps exist?, *Journal of Economic Perspectives*, 28(3): 127–48.

Collier identifies four traps for the poorest countries: conflict, a natural resources trap, being landlocked with bad neighbours, and bad governance. The idea that conflict impedes development hardly needs explanation, and bad governance should be correctable, but more of that in a moment. Countries which are landlocked depend on the infrastructure – and the cooperation – of their neighbours.[22] The impact of natural resources is not a problem of poor resources, but the opposite: rich natural resources may lead to poor development. Collier argues that it leads to conflict, exploitation, poorer terms of trade in other forms of production and lack of accountability in government.[23] Mosley discusses the position of a range of poor countries affected by such a trap.[24]

It is tempting to see some other issues as obstacles to development. Drought and natural disaster are illustrative; they present immediate problems in their own right, and further reasons why a country is unable to develop. Amartya Sen's analysis suggests that some caution is needed before we say that. Natural disasters have happened in a range of developed countries, too – the Japanese tsunami, Italian earthquakes, Australian bushfires. The central issue is not that there are such problems, but that when they happen people are able to deal with them – the issues of vulnerability and resilience. Hans Rosling makes the telling point that deaths from natural disasters have progressively fallen, not because there are fewer disasters, but because the populations affected are not as poor as they were in the past.[25] People's capabilities are derived from their entitlements, and those depend on the economic, social and political context.

Bad governance is often seen as central. It is endemic in many poor countries (as well as in some transitional and emerging economies), and Easterly is fairly scathing about attempts to work with bad governments when they are so often at the root of the problem. 'Bad government has a lot do with the low growth of poor countries … bad government has a lot to do with their being poor in the first place.'[26] Some countries have been the victim of government incompetence. Some are 'kleptocracies', run by thieves and gangsters for their own benefit. Some problems in poor countries – and some not so poor ones, like parts of Nigeria – can reasonably be attributed to the

---

[22] Collier, 2007, Chapter 4

[23] Collier, 2007, Chapter 3.

[24] P Mosley, 2017, *Fiscal policy and the natural resources curse*, London: Routledge.

[25] Rosling, 2018, Chapter 5.

[26] Easterly, 2006, p 116.

breakdown of public order. Some have been torn apart by civil war. We have been here before. In the 1970s and 1980s, the World Bank was convinced that good economics would drive out bad government. Mosley writes:

> If only the Mobutus and the Marcoses and the Mois ('politics', in the mind of the econocrats) could be got rid of, ran the reasoning, that would expand the supply side of the economy as nothing else could, and the proper working of the price mechanism would pull the world out of recession. … this mechanism simply did not work in many parts of the world, Africa in particular …[27]

Problems of governance are often translated into concerns with corruption. Corruption is a wide-ranging, and fairly amorphous, concept; for practical purposes, it makes sense to concentrate on the most pervasive form, where officials exercise public authority in their own interests. Public officials siphon off funds intended to provide services. People have to approach politicians and people of influence to put a case forward or to have their interests considered. Police harass citizens and require them to hand over cash. Poor people have to pay bribes to officials to get basic things done – including, for example, whether they can get supposedly free medical care. The problem is made worse by poverty. Action Aid argues:

> Corruption is a consequence of poverty as well as a cause. … In Cambodia, for example, the typical civil servant only earns US$25 per month, only one fifth of the cost of living in Phnom Penh. Teachers in Uganda earn only US$50–$55 per month, far below the cost of keeping a family, even in the rural areas. … almost every dimension of governance is correlated with income, with higher incomes being both a consequence and a cause of better governance.[28]

There are different views about what kind of problem corruption is. Part is certainly a matter of governance. Public officials are not doing what they are supposed to do, or doing what they are not supposed

---

[27] P Mosley, B Chiripanhura, J Grugel and B Thirkell-White, 2012, *The politics of poverty reduction*, Oxford: Oxford University Press, p 36.
[28] R Greenhill and P Watt, 2005, *Real aid*, Johannesburg: Action Aid International, p 11.

to do. Correcting this depends on making their actions more clearly subject to rules – transparency, accountability and redress. Collier gives a striking example from Uganda: informing schools and the local press about the money that they ought to be receiving increased the actual receipt from 20% of the intended funds to 90%.[29] However, this is not only a matter of government. Robert Chambers discusses the exploitation of people from rural areas. There are problems of robbery – deception, blackmail and violence; a relative lack of bargaining power; and a likelihood that resources directed to the poor will be diverted. Local elites interpose themselves between the poor and attempts to offer aid or resources: 'Most government, parastatal and private sector campaigns and programmes are either designed intentionally for the elites, or so designed and implemented that they are likely to be intercepted by them.'[30]

The demand for bribes is not so easy to deal with through transparency, but it may be dealt with in other ways. Corruption, Klitgaard suggests, has a lot to do with bending rules. Some rules should not be bent; others should be. It follows that not all corruption is a problem, and the effect of trying to eradicate it completely might be undesirable. Good governance may be about holding corruption in, rather than getting rid of it altogether.[31] An example might be bribes that are used to obtain a service. Free medical care which people have to pay a bribe to get is not free; it may be better to introduce a charge than to pretend that charges do not happen, and at least that way people in need stand some chance of getting support. Markets, some economists argue, are inevitable; wherever something is in short supply, people who can will try to offer a higher price. If there is going to be a market, it might make more sense for that market to be brought out into the light.

Every poor country has a problem of governance; in many cases, that is attributable to the problems of capacity discussed earlier. There are not fewer problems to deal with in a poor country than in a rich one; there are more. The capacity of any government depends on its resources, on the information it has available, on the methods it can bring to bear, on the roles it can hope to take on. The poorer the population is, the more limited the government is going to be, and the more difficult the task it faces. On the other hand, Mosley suggests, the governments of poorer countries have fewer real choices about how

---

[29] Collier, 2007, p 150.

[30] R Chambers, 1983, *Rural development*, London: Longman, p 131.

[31] R Klitgaard, 1998, *Controlling corruption*, Berkeley: University of California Press.

money might be spent if not on the poorest: 'the more prosperous the recipient country, the greater is the likelihood that gains from increased income will be diluted by "substitution effects" into unproductive government expenditure.'[32]

Structural explanations

It is very disputable whether the problems of poor countries can ever be understood solely in terms of the country itself. These countries do not exist in isolation from others: while it is difficult to argue against the view that countries like Haiti, Congo or Somalia have been misgoverned, it is no less true that they have suffered at the hands of others, particularly the colonial powers. Julius Nyrere, the former leader of Tanzania, was asked at the World Bank in 1998: 'Why have you failed?' His response was a model:

> The British Empire left us a country with 85 per cent illiterates, two engineers and 12 doctors. When I left office, we had 9 per cent illiterates and thousands of engineers and doctors. I left office 13 years ago. Then our income per capita was twice was it is today; now we have one-third less children in our schools and public health and social services are in ruins. During these 13 years, Tanzania has done everything that the World Bank and the International Monetary Fund demanded ... Why have *you* failed?[33]

The relationships between poor and rich countries reflect a lengthy history. That history is not unequivocally of one type, but much of it is a story of colonialism, slavery and exploitation. The British Empire promoted economic and moral development and eradicated slavery by main force – but if one speaks to people in the countries on the sharp end of their operations, they are more likely to remember that Britain had probably invaded them, taken their resources and maintained its rule through violence or duplicity. In many respects, the conduct of Western nations has been rapacious: Belgium treated the Congo as a cash cow, Portugal's colonial wars were used to justify repression at home, and France extracted reparations from Haiti for daring to revolt against slavery. Many poor countries became independent from

---

[32] P Mosley, 1987, *Overseas aid*, Brighton: Harvester Wheatsheaf, p 87.
[33] Cited in K Kaunda, 2000, Africa has paid its dues many times, *New Statesman*, www.newstatesman.com/node/193470, accessed 19.12.2019.

the colonial powers in the period following World War II – Britain's former colonies included India, Pakistan, Bangladesh, Nigeria, Kenya, Uganda, Tanzania, Malaysia, Sierra Leone, Ghana and others in the West Indies and Oceania. While there are aspects of current provision which reflect the legacy of colonial rule, in most respects the experience is too diverse to sustain generalisation. [34]

In the periods after independence, some governments argued that national boundaries should be irrelevant – Nkrumah's and Kenyatta's Pan-Africanism – while others (sometimes the same ones!) assumed that they would have a central capacity and power that would enable them to do what they thought fit.[35] Several countries made the state dominant in industrial production, whether because they were influenced by the example of Stalin in believing that it was possible for the state to push a country to development, or because this offered opportunities for favouritism and personal control.

Some of the contemporary literature argues that the former colonies have continued to be locked into a subordinate, and often unfair, relationship with their former masters. The industries that they have, the trade links that they have established and the terms on which they trade are a survival of colonial relationships. The former colonies provide raw materials, cheap labour and convenient markets for goods. For André Gunder Frank, underdevelopment reflects an underlying relationship of exploitation by the richer countries.[36] This is sometimes referred to as structural dependency – a different use of the term from the concept referred to in Chapter 7. It is 'dependency' because the servant economies do not have the capacity to develop in their own terms, 'structural' because the bindings are based in the framework of economic relationships rather than the mechanics of power politics. Other relationships between poor and rich countries are considered further in the next chapter.

Mechanistic structural explanations need to be treated with as much caution as pathological ones, for the same reasons. There are never single causes for everything. The argument from complexity can be made against most of the alternative structural arguments – the idea

[34] J Midgley and D Piachaud (eds), 2011, *Colonialism and welfare*, Cheltenham: Edward Elgar.

[35] M Williams, 1984, Nkrumahism as an ideological embodiment of leftist thought within the African world, *Journal of Black Studies*, 15(1): 117–34.

[36] A Gunder Frank, 2014, The development of underdevelopment, in M Seligson and J Passé-Smith (eds), *Development and underdevelopment*, Boulder, CO: Rienner, Chapter 23.

that everything is down to capitalism, or to ideology, or to colonialism, or whatever. Wherever explanations are reduced to a single cause, we can be reasonably confident that they're wrong. That is not to say that the factors have no influence, but a single explanation is never good enough.

Responding to poverty in poor countries

Much of the work done with poor people around the world is done by focusing on the countries where they live. That is not the same thing as concentrating on the poorest people, because most poor people are not found within the poorest countries. If we look only at the countries in Table 11.1, the poorest countries account for a little above 100 million of the poorest 1000 million in the world. Only one country in that list has very large numbers of people, which is Ethiopia. If we want to find the largest number of people on very low incomes, we need to look at some of the biggest countries – India, which has over 300 million poor people, and China, next largest with about 84 million. If we pick out only three more countries, Nigeria (98.5 million), Bangladesh (60.5 million), and the Democratic Republic of the Congo (53.7 million), we have more than half the poorest billion. There is a simple reason why the two lists of countries are different: higher concentrations tend to be found in smaller areas. (It will also be true, at sub-national levels, that there will be some concentrations within the countries that are greater still – that has to happen if the dispersion of poverty is not absolutely even everywhere.) If we were dealing not with countries, but with populations of equivalent size, the distribution and concentration would look very different.

The Sustainable Development Goals, like the Millennium Development Goals before them, seem to imply that the global totals of poverty are the figures we should be focusing on. The argument for focusing on small, poor countries is not about reaching the largest possible numbers of poor people – a simpler way to do that would be to focus efforts on the big players. Where poverty is more concentrated, the problems change in character. The limited capacity of communities, regions and economies is a problem for everyone in a poor country. It would be possible of course to respond to those problems piecemeal, project by project, village by village; but ultimately, the problems are problems for governments, and for international organisations working through governments.

The burden carried by the governments of poor countries is considerable. We seem to expect them to manage with limited capacity, few resources and – rather than offering support – while carrying obligations to the international community. Some countries have managed to do this regardless, but it hardly seems reasonable for the world's poorest countries to pull themselves up by their bootstraps. Hanlon and his colleagues comment, echoing a point made by Martin Luther King: 'you cannot pull yourself up by your bootstraps if you have no boots.'[37]

Despite that, there are some grounds for optimism. Government has a complex set of roles and duties. In richer countries, this typically includes the promotion or provision of public services. Where there are roads, water supplies, medical care and pensions, they all help to reduce the prevalence and severity of poverty. This kind of provision tends to get overlooked in discussions of poorer countries, because the combination of mass poverty with limited government capacity seems to make the idea of mass provision unrealistic. Nevertheless, some developing countries have undertaken provision in these terms – the health service in Sri Lanka, the introduction of universal basic education in several African countries, the growth of Conditional Cash Transfers in South America and southern Asia, the programme of public housebuilding in Venezuela. Governments can, and do, make a huge difference to people's lives.

As more and more developing countries are taking on these roles, things are getting better. More countries are democracies. Fewer children are dying. Incomes are increasing. Communications are improving. Radelet argues that Africa has benefited from more democratic and accountable governments, better economic policies, major changes in relationships with the international community and a new generation of policy makers. The Gates Foundation has taken a determinedly optimistic view of prospects over the next fifteen years. Health will improve, Africa will be able to feed itself, and no countries will have the average level of income ($1045 p.a.) that currently defines them as being poor. 'The lives of people in poor countries will improve faster in the next 15 years than at any other time in history. And their lives will improve more than anyone else's.'[38]

---

[37] J Hanlon, A Barrientos and D Hulme, 2010, *Just give money to the poor*, Sterling VA: Kumarian Press, p 4.

[38] W Gates and M Gates, 2015, Gatesnotes: 2015 Gates Annual letter, www.gatesnotes.com/2015-annual-letter?WT.mc_id=01_21_2015_DO_GFO_domain_0_00&page=0&lang=en, accessed 19.12.2019.

12

Rich and poor countries

There is a fundamental, far-reaching imbalance in the position of rich and poor countries. Singer and Ansari point to the unequal distribution of:

- military power;
- financial and economic power;
- technological expertise;
- industrial production;
- commercial power;
- the influence of multinational corporations; and
- food security – the developed countries dominate here, too.[1]

The main exception they point to is oil. Natural resources in general have proved to be a curse for many countries; they offered the imperial powers an irresistible lure, and, Easterly argues,[2] left the countries a legacy of vested interests that resisted all attempts to redistribute the resources subsequently. Corrupt practice, too, is rife. Much of the finance that flows between developing countries and the developed world is illicit, reflecting criminal activity and illegal extraction of funds. In terms of volume, illicit flows have been said to account on average for about 20% of the trade of developing countries, and while some passes through less wealthy countries, about half of the money ultimately ends up in tax havens or developed countries.[3]

After military power, the disadvantage of poor countries is arguably most visible in the system of international trade. The arguments for international trade are powerful ones. The most basic theoretical justification is the idea of comparative advantage. In the process of commercial trade, it will usually emerge that one partner will be better doing one thing, the other will be better doing something else. If they

---

[1] H Singer and J Ansari, 1992, *Rich and poor countries*, London: Routledge, p 12.

[2] W Easterly, 2006, *The white man's burden*, p 109.

[3] Global Financial Integrity, 2019, Illicit financial flows to and from 148 developing countries: 2006–2015, https://secureservercdn.net/45.40.149.159/34n.8bd.myftp upload.com/wp-content/uploads/2019/01/GFI-2019-IFF-Update-Report-1.29.18. pdf?time=1561339974, accessed 24.6.2019.

both concentrate on what they're good at, and exchange goods and services on that principle, they can both be better off than they would be if they did it all by themselves.

There are several arguments for protection – that is, for preventing or deterring the importation of goods. An example is the claim that countries need 'food security'. The concept was introduced at the World Food Summit in 1996 to mean that 'all people at all times have access to sufficient, safe, nutritious food to maintain a healthy and active life'. At that level, it is fairly uncontentious. It becomes contentious when the idea gets translated into a demand for national self-sufficiency in food production and distribution. The whole point of international trade is that countries are interdependent, and that they benefit mutually through the trade of commodities. Self-sufficiency in any area assumes that countries meet their own needs – a situation that may imply lower levels of production and supply than would be available through specialisation and development. There are sometimes good reasons for pursuing self-sufficiency in essential commodities – for example, securing the supply of food in the event of war. (The control of agricultural production and distribution in the UK during the 1950s and 1960s directly reflected the experience of total war in the previous decade.)

Another is the argument for developing infant industries. Free trade doesn't take place from a position of equality. The developed countries have clear advantages in terms of productive capacity, skills and technology. Ha-Joon Chang thinks the argument that development depends on international trade is just plain wrong. 'Virtually all the successful developing countries since the Second World War initially succeeded with nationalistic policies, using protection, subsidies and other forms of government intervention.'[4] Free trade, he writes,

> is *not* the best path to economic development. Trade helps economic development only when the country employs a mixture of protection and open trade, constantly adjusting it according to its changing needs and capabilities.[5]

International trade does not necessarily work to the benefit of all parties. If everything works as it is supposed to, the capacity to produce will be closed down in some places so that others can develop. The

---

[4] H-J Chang, 2007, *Bad Samaritans*, London: Random House Business Books, pp 28–9.
[5] H-J Chang, 2007, p 68.

process of specialisation and concentration can be painful. It implies that some industries will fade while others succeed. That is one of the central arguments in the European Union for the 'social fund', which was designed to compensate poorer regions for the loss of industry and commercial activity which went with the development of a unified market. A related problem is found in regional economics: some areas can become progressively better off at the expense of others, which go into decline.

Beyond that, specialisation leads to inequalities, and inequalities lead to imbalances of power. For poor countries, Collier argues, this can mean that the country loses talented and trained labour, while the country becomes dependent on resources from other countries.[6] Russia's dominance in energy supply has had a major effect on many of the nations surrounding it. There are good political arguments for maintaining domestic productive capacity in many fields that might in theory be supplied more efficiently through a process of comparative advantage – energy, defence and agriculture among them. (That is one reason why the European Union has sought to link the development of an economic union together with the development of political unification in a federal structure.)

This all assumes that things work out as they are supposed to, but that may not be true. When trade agreements are made, free trade is not necessarily what happens. Developing countries have frequently complained that the terms on which they are obliged to trade are not reciprocated. The rules are rigged; their arrangements have to be open to developed countries, but the markets of developed countries are not open to them.[7]

The case against protection is partly theoretical, and partly practical. The theoretical arguments for more open trade are strong ones, and the pressure from international organisations has consistently been aimed at opening countries to international trade. Protection increases the price of commodities to the country that imposes barriers. Collier suggests that protection is often a veil for corruption: customs offices are used to milk funds.[8] Where there are regional trade organisations, further factors come into play. In a rich regional customs union like the EU or NAFTA, the effect of the trade barriers is to keep out labour-intensive goods from the developing world, and that favours the member states within the customs union which have the cheapest

---

[6] Collier, 2007, p 175.

[7] Make Trade Fair, 2002, *Rigged rules and double standards*, Oxford: Oxfam International.

[8] Collier, 2007, pp 161–2.

labour. In a customs union between poorer members, the effect of trade barriers is to exclude capital intensive goods requiring higher skills to produce, and that favours the position of the richest country. So rich customs unions tend to promote convergence between their members, and poorer ones tend to promote divergence.[9] There may still be a case for protection, but it has to be finely judged, and it may create as many problems as it resolves.

Debt

The imbalances in trading relationships reinforce a general problem for the governments of poorer countries relative to the position of richer ones. Governments and countries need to have access to the structures of capital – the ability to mitigate risk and to shift the burden of costs over time. To do this, they need to incur debts. There are three routes by which this is commonly done. One is that governments can, like any business or individual, seek to obtain capital from creditors on the understanding that they will repay the loan with interest. The second is that others in the country may incur debts, on a similar basis. The government of Greece has had major problems in the European Union not only because previous governments took high levels of debt, but because its banks did. The third mechanism is that effective debts can be concealed through other methods of raising finance. The issue of a banknote is, effectively, a promise to pay; if a government pays for its activities by issuing more currency, the value of that currency will ultimately be determined through a combination of its value as an investment and the level of economic production that the national economy achieves.

The combination of these different approaches has led to several poor countries being 'highly indebted'. The 'HIPCs' – Highly Indebted Poor Countries – have arrived at their status because they 'face an unsustainable debt burden that cannot be addressed through traditional debt relief mechanisms', and the IMF is offering debt relief – mitigation of the costs of servicing the debt, which is repaying the interest plus some capital. About a quarter of this debt is held towards commercial creditors, who have been particularly slow in complying with the IMF's requests.[10] It falls a long way short, however, of true

---

[9] Collier, 2007, pp 163–6.

[10] International Monetary Fund, 2019, Debt relief under the Heavily Indebted Poor Countries (HIPC) initiative, www.imf.org/external/np/exr/facts/hipc.htm, accessed 19.12.2019.

debt relief; the HIPC programme is about making debt repayment more realistic, and there have been criticisms that some indebted countries (Niger and Zambia) will actually have their debt repayments increased by participation in the programme.

Investors sometimes depict interest payments as a reward for risk; it is certainly not to be expected that lending to a government should carry no risk If these countries were businesses, and they were unable to pay their debts, one of two things would happen. Either the debt would be rescheduled – for example, that interest would be suspended, and they would undertake to pay only a limited proportion of the debt – or the business would go out of trade with limited liability, leaving it open for the firm to be taken over or re-established in a fresh start. There are some limited precedents for defaults. Some American cities have defaulted on debts: New York nearly did so in 1975, Cleveland actually did in 1978. The decision of the Argentinian government to default on debts occurred by its previous, illegitimate military government has been challenged in US Courts, and Greece is being told by European institutions that it is not permitted to default (though one wonders, if they did, what sanctions could be brought to bear). Probably the only example of bankruptcy is Newfoundland, which surrendered its independence on the verge of bankruptcy in 1932 and became part of the Canadian federation.

Unlike commercial relationships, too, the debts incurred by governments cannot be reduced to a simple fiduciary relationship. Part of the problem is that debts commonly reflect the actions of previous regimes – including dictators, autocrats and gangsters who have no legitimacy beyond their recognition by the international community. This is a bit like being made to pay the debts of a previous tenant of your house – and arguably being subject to their punishment as well. Part concerns relationships with creditors, where debts become an expression of an imbalance of power. After its revolution of 1804, Haiti was the subject of a disgraceful arrangement: from 1825 onwards, when they sent gunboats, successive French governments demanded the payments of reparations for the loss of their colony, and the last reparations were paid in 1947. It has many times been proposed that France should repay the money it extorted; there is little prospect that it will.

Money from abroad

In a perfect world, countries should be able to make a reasonable amount of income from their economic activity by trading with other countries. In theory – the same theory that justifies international trade – it should be possible for everyone to gain. This is often an aim of policy, but there are no perfect worlds. Many countries have to look to other ways of securing foreign income.

There are three key sources. The first is foreign direct investment, or FDI; persuading foreign investors (and possibly foreign governments) to spend money and develop facilities in the country's territory. On the face of the matter, foreign investment is a good thing – it promotes development, growth and extends inclusion in economic activity. Ha-Joon Chang argues that, despite the neoliberal presumption in favour of FDI, its benefits are ambiguous. Foreign investors divert resources back to their own country, and often operate differential pricing. FDI is neither as necessary, nor as stable, as theorists suppose – and in practice, many of the countries which have developed have done it by privileging home-grown industries.[11]

Next there are remittances. Poor countries may not have material assets, but they do have people. When those people work abroad, it is common practice to send money home, to support those left behind. Remittances are a major part of the national income of some countries – more than 20% of the incomes of Nepal, Armenia, Haiti, the Kyrgyz Republic, Moldova; more than 10% for 13 others.[12]

Third, there is international aid or development assistance. Development assistance is a curious rag-bag of different types of support – some is humanitarian, some self-interested, some (such as aid to Afghanistan) apparently more related to strategic defence issues than to poverty or development. Some kinds of aid, Deaton comments, are easy to divert, whether that is by the donors who bend them to other policy objectives, or by those in office who cream off funds intended for the benefit of their people. Other projects, such as work with public health, are less easily diverted.[13]

Riddell makes a basic distinction between different types of aid.[14] Official Development Assistance or 'ODA' is aid given through governments or inter-governmental organisations. The OECD countries have been asked by the UN to provide 0.7% of their GDP in aid; only a handful of countries (Norway, Sweden, Denmark and the UK) actually do so. About a third of ODA is channelled through

[11] H-J Chang, 2007, pp 88–92.
[12] World Bank, 2018, http://data.worldbank.org/indicator/BX.TRF.PWKR.DT.GD. ZS, accessed 19.12.2019.
[13] A Deaton, 2013, *The great escape*, Princeton, NJ: Princeton University Press, pp 279–80.
[14] R Riddell, 2007, *Does foreign aid really work?* Oxford: Oxford University Press.

'multilateral' donors and international organisations. Development assistance is usually conditional on compliance with conditions set by the international organisations, and those conditions tend to reflect the views of the rich donor countries. A second class of aid is provided by non-governmental organisations (NGOs) or civil society organisations. Then, in a class of its own, there is emergency assistance, typically provided in responses to catastrophic events, and provided by governments or the non-governmental sector.

Some aid takes the form of goods in kind rather than finance. Technical assistance, which can account for a quarter of official aid, supplies developing countries with experts. Collier argues strongly in favour of technical assistance, used at the right time – but much of it isn't provided at the right time, and it is 'supply-driven', provided according to the specifications of the providers rather than being responsive to the circumstances of the country receiving it.[15] 'Tied aid' is used to require the recipient country to order goods from the donor country – more like giving goods rather than money. The United Nations declared in 1970 that aid ought not to be tied, but donor nations tend to like the system, partly because it is equivalent to giving goods rather than finance, partly because it can help to support producers in the donor country. If tied aid does raise concerns, it is mainly that states have traditionally inflated its value and tried to pass it off as fulfilling their general international obligations – the US is committed by its own laws to the principle of tied aid, and 70% of US aid is spent on US domestic organisations.[16] That is not to say that tied aid is a bad thing or that it has no value, but it does not have the same value as a direct payment to a deprived country.

International aid has been forcefully criticised by neoliberals, who see it as market-distorting and liable to create a sense of dependency.[17] Moseley points to an apparent paradox: that while half the aid programmes seem to work on their own terms, overall they have no visible effect on overall growth.[18] That position has not apparently changed much in the intervening years.[19] The data are disputable,[20] but

---

[15] Collier, 2007, pp 114–15.

[16] R Greenhill, P Watt, 2005, *Real aid*, Johannesburg: Action Aid International, p 26.

[17] J Foreman, 2012, *Aiding and abetting*, London: Civitas.

[18] P Mosley, 1987, *Overseas aid*, Brighton: Harvester Wheatsheaf, Chapter 5.

[19] R Picciotto, 2006, Development effectiveness at the country level, German Development Institute, www.die-gdi.de/uploads/media/8-2006.pdf, accessed 19.12.2019.

[20] S Howes, S Otor and C Rogers, 2011, *Does the World Bank have a micro-macro paradox or do the data deceive?* Canberra: Australian National University.

in any case the paradox is only 'apparent'; there is little reason to assume that development assistance is actually directed to the promotion of economic growth, and less to suppose that the selection of programmes is based on strategic key intervention in national economies. The country receiving most aid currently is Afghanistan, and that reflects its political and strategic importance more than its poverty. (Military assistance is discounted from the ODA totals, but as the example suggests, the boundaries are fuzzy. Riddell notes particularly a blurring of the lines between emergency humanitarian assistance and military intervention.[21]) India, which in the view of many is a transitional or emerging economy rather than an underdeveloped one, receives the third largest amount.

There are criticisms, too, from supporters of aid. Action Aid argues that much of what passes for aid is 'phantom aid' – whether or not it is there in spirit, it never materialises. Phantom aid includes money that is not targeted for poverty reduction; debt relief, which does not add anything to the income of poor people; technical assistance, where the money largely goes on employing consultants from developed economies; tied aid; money spent on taking immigrants into the donor country; and money spent on domestic administration. For example,

> Just 11% of French aid is real aid. France spends nearly US$2 billion of its aid budget each year on Technical Assistance, and US$0.5 billion on refugee and immigration expenditures in France. Forty per cent of French aid is provided as debt relief, much of which is an accounting exercise rather than a real resource transfer.[22]

Action Aid's report on *Real Aid* was received with some disdain, and some annoyance, in official quarters,[23] but their central point was worth making: a substantial proportion of development aid is not spent in the countries intended to benefit from it.[24]

---

[21] R Riddell, 2007, Chapter 19.

[22] Greenhill, Watt, 2005, p 17.

[23] For example, R Carey, 2005, Real or phantom aid?, www.oecd.org/fr/cad/realor phantomaidbyrichardcareydeputydirectorofdacsecretariatdacnewsjune-august2005. htm, accessed 4.7.2019.

[24] *The Guardian*, 2016, How much aid money is spent in donor countries? www. theguardian.com/global-development/datablog/2014/feb/13/aid-money-spent-donor-countries-get-data, accessed 19.12.2019.

Ideas from abroad

Given the focus in discussions of poverty on material deprivation and economic relationships, it is not surprising that the relationships between rich and poor nations are generally discussed in the same terms; but the political dimension should not be neglected. There was a time when the dominant ideologies were imperialist: there was a natural and moral superiority in the colonial powers, who had a paternal duty to the lesser orders. Then there was marxism. Lenin argued that the relationships between the imperial powers and the colonies was exploitative, and a relationship of structural dependency; Stalinism, which seemed particularly attractive to some African leaders, offered the possibility of promoting socialist development through centralised planning. That led to a heavy reliance on public ownership and governmental direction by dictatorial governments.

In the 1980s, the combination of excessive centralisation and weak governance in many of these countries came together with the critique of state engagement that had surfaced with the growth of neoliberalism in several richer countries. It was described as the 'Washington Consensus'. The 'consensus' did not actually exist; the term was introduced by John Williamson to describe the new economic orthodoxy, and the label stuck. The orthodox view was based on:

- fiscal discipline;
- reordering public spending priorities;
- tax reform;
- liberalising interest rates;
- competitive exchange rates;
- liberalising trade;
- liberalising foreign direct investment;
- privatisation;
- deregulation;
- the establishment of property rights.[25]

This ideology was at the root of a process of 'structural adjustment' – by the end of the 1980s, structural adjustment programmes had

---

[25] C Gore, 2000, The rise and fall of the Washington Consensus as a paradigm for developing countries, *World Development*, 28(5): 789–804; J Williamson, 2004, A short history of the Washington Consensus, www.iie.com/publications/papers/williamson0904-2.pdf, accessed 19.12.2019.

been negotiated with more than 60 developing countries. Structural adjustment was intended partly to promote orthodox financial conduct – cutting inflation, limiting government spending and the use of credit – and partly to encourage the growth of markets, through privatisation, ending subsidies and using price incentives and commodification to govern. Institutional reforms in politics and economic management were supposed to reinforce the approach.

Despite the approval of many economists, the consequences were as likely to obstruct economic development as to promote it. Cutting government spending runs the risk of depressing an economy, by reducing demand for goods and services. Reducing support for employment leads to less economic integration, and less engagement in the formal economy. The IMF is divided about the outcomes of structural adjustment:

> The IMF is effectively two institutions. It has a research department that has broken with the Washington consensus and programme teams that operate in the field as if we were still in the 1990s.[26]

The evidence on structural adjustment is mixed, and that is a conclusion in itself. The economic benefits, even where reforms were instituted enthusiastically, were patchy at best, and the evaluations are full of excuses for their shortcomings.[27] The numbers of cases where improvements were reported were outnumbered by those where they had little effect, and by those where the effects were plainly negative.[28] Leaving important economic decisions to markets does not necessarily make them better; it makes them unpredictable. The consequences of structural adjustment too often were increased unemployment, hardship and poverty. Similar problems have been generated by the muddled insistence of the European Union's financial authorities on 'austerity'.

The international organisations have moved on, and the 'Monterrey Consensus' supplements market liberalisation with social issues

---

[26] L Elliott, 2016, The World Bank and the IMF won't admit that their policies are the problem, *The Guardian*, https://www.theguardian.com/business/2016/oct/09/the-world-bank-and-the-imf-wont-admit-their-policies-are-the-problem, accessed 19.12.2019.

[27] D Dollar and J Svensson, 2000, What explains the success or failure of Structural Adjustment Programmes? *Economic Journal*, 110(466): 894–917.

[28] World Bank, 1994, *Adjustment in Africa: reforms, results and the road ahead*, Washington, DC: World Bank.

including health and education.[29] Rodrik suggests that the Washington Consensus has not been abandoned, but rather 'augmented' by a range of further principles:

- Corporate governance
- Anti-corruption
- Flexible labour markets
- WTO agreements
- Financial codes and standards
- 'Prudent' capital-account opening
- Non-intermediate exchange rate regimes
- Independent central banks/inflation targeting
- Social safety nets
- Targeted poverty reduction.[30]

Some of these are difficult to disagree with: no-one, bar the most diehard libertarians, is going to argue that corporations should have no governance procedures, or that social safety nets are a bad thing. However, 'flexible' or insecure labour and the regulation of finance look like more of the market-based policies that have generated so many problems. Flexible labour markets can reinforce the problems of marginality and sub-employment. The WTO has rigged the markets in favour of the rich countries. The IMF has continued to favour targeting over universal measures, despite fairly consistent evidence that targeted poverty reduction (a term often taken to mean 'selective') is inefficient.[31] The 'augmented' consensus shares, then, a common vice with the Washington Consensus: the assumption that one size fits all. This book has emphasised a view of poverty as a complex, multidimensional set of issues, arguing that the problems are wicked, and constantly changing underfoot; that simple answers do not work; and that policies which seem to be beneficial in some ways can have negative effects in others. The central failures of this policy stemmed from ignoring those simple facts.

---

[29] United Nations, 2003, Monterrey Consensus on Financing for development, https://www.un.org/en/development/desa/population/migration/generalassembly/docs/globalcompact/A_CONF.198_11.pdf, accessed 11.11.2019.

[30] D Rodrik, 2006, Goodbye Washington consensus, hello Washington confusion? *Journal of Economic Literature*, 44: 973–87.

[31] J Griffiths and G Brunswijck, 2018, IMF conditionality: still undermining healthcare and social protection?, https://eurodad.org/IMF-conditionality-undermining-healthcare, accessed 19.12.2019.

The Millennium Development Goals and the Sustainable Development Goals

The relationship between rich and poor countries is not solely, or even primarily, determined in terms of bilateral arrangements. Trade, debt and finance are mediated through an increasingly complex structure of international organisations. For poor countries, the most immediate relationships tend to be with the two key financial institutions, the International Monetary Fund and the World Bank. Both offer finance for governments, with strings attached. Beyond that, however, there is a long series of organisations supporting development – the Asian and African Development Banks, ECLAC, the United Nations Development Programme; a range of international organisations, such as the European Union; and specialist organisations, such as the International Fund for Agricultural Development or the World Health Organisation.

Despite the variety and range of such organisations – and conflicting advice, even within the same agency – a remarkable degree of uniformity has emerged. There are common patterns of practice, of approach, or expectations. Most donors are not in the business of competing with each other (even if the accusation is sometimes levelled at them). They have common aims, they are increasingly likely to work in partnership, they share core information, and often they share methods.

The Millennium Development Goals have been the most visible aspect of this approach; they were meant to be. They took the form of a series of eight domains:

1. Eradicate extreme poverty and hunger
2. Achieve universal primary education
3. Promote gender equality and empower women;
4. Reduce child mortality
5. Improve maternal health
6. Combat HIV/Aids, malaria and other diseases
7. Ensure environmental sustainability
8. Global partnership for development.

Each domain was represented by a small number of selected objectives, and each objective was in turn represented by a small number of indicators.[32] The list was gradually expanded until there were 65 indicators altogether.

---

[32] United Nations, 2007, Millennium development goals, http://www.un.org/millenniumgoals/, accessed 19.12.2019.

The Sustainable Development Goals have increased the number of domains from eight to 17:

1. End poverty in all its forms everywhere
2. End hunger, achieve food security and improved nutrition, and promote sustainable agriculture
3. Ensure healthy lives and promote well-being for all at all ages
4. Ensure inclusive and equitable quality education and promote life-long learning opportunities for all
5. Achieve gender equality and empower all women and girls
6. Ensure availability and sustainable management of water and sanitation for all
7. Ensure access to affordable, reliable, sustainable, and modern energy for all
8. Promote sustained, inclusive and sustainable economic growth, full and productive employment and decent work for all
9. Build resilient infrastructure, promote inclusive and sustainable industrialization and foster innovation
10. Reduce inequality within and among countries
11. Make cities and human settlements inclusive, safe, resilient and sustainable
12. Ensure sustainable consumption and production patterns
13. Take urgent action to combat climate change and its impacts
14. Conserve and sustainably use the oceans, seas and marine resources for sustainable development
15. Protect, restore and promote sustainable use of terrestrial ecosystems, sustainably manage forests, combat desertification, and halt and reverse land degradation and halt biodiversity loss
16. Promote peaceful and inclusive societies for sustainable development, provide access to justice for all and build effective, accountable and inclusive institutions at all levels
17. Strengthen the means of implementation and revitalize the global partnership for sustainable development.

Depending on how you count them, there are now 169 objectives, supported by 100 global indicators and 149 further indicators which national governments have been invited to compile.[33]

---

[33] Sustainable Development Solutions Network, 2015, Indicators and a monitoring framework for sustainable development goals, https://sustainabledevelopment.un.org/index.php?page=view&type=400&nr=2013&menu=35, accessed 19.12.2019.

At the time of writing, it is too early to say much if anything about how effective the SDGs are going to be, but there are some important lessons to draw from the experience of the MDGs before them. The MDGs were met with understandable scepticism: they were too ambitious, they could not avoid the same kinds of failure that had dogged previous international aspirations. *The Economist* suggested that the aspiration to halve poverty was 'a promise the international community cannot possibly keep, and so was perhaps unwise to make'.[34] The unexpected success of the MDGs has become the justification for the SDGs, which are more ambitious: if we can shoot high and hit the target, the argument goes, then maybe we should shoot higher still.

In theory, goals of this sort work by focusing attention on the issues which are identified in the higher-level objectives. 'Indicators' are just what they say they are – numbers that indicate, or pointers, rather than complete answers to a problem. If the objective is being met, the pointers should line up with them. The danger of that view is that if too much focus is devoted to the indicators themselves, policy can be diverted to improving the figures rather than genuine overall improvements. Managers improve performance indicators by 'gaming' – changing procedures to make the figures look better. This criticism has been made, for example, about figures on primary education in Brazil:

> the real reason for the focus on the age criterion alone and the priority given to primary school students aged seven to fourteen, with the concomitant neglect of primary school students above the age of fourteen, seems not to be the correction of the particular vulnerability of this group ... The real reason seems to be to more quickly achieve MDG2's numerical targets. ... If the main purpose of Brazilian educational policies was to exhibit victorious figures to the international community, showing the success of a more universal primary education for Brazilian children on paper, then the criterion of age alone may be justified. But if the main purpose of the Brazilian educational policies

---

[34] *The Economist*, 2005, Aspirations and obligations, www.economist.com/node/4385253, accessed 19.12.2019.

is to provide a universal, quality primary education in reality, age cannot be the sole or the most adequate criterion …[35]

There are certainly countries where governments might wish to make things look a lot better than they are, and there are some countries where the rulers want to persuade their domestic population that everything is going swimmingly, but that impression is usually maintained by not producing the figures, rather than making them look better than they are. If anything, countries probably get more aid by presenting their deficiencies more prominently, rather than covering them up.

Producing indicators can make considerable demands on the information capacity of poorer countries, who are being asked to develop increasingly sophisticated and elaborate methods of collecting and analysing data. This may lead to problems; there are still parts of the world where population, residence or access to facilities is based on educated guesswork. Many poorer countries cannot answer questions about, for example, what proportion of their population have access to water, and the international organisations have moved from attributing nominal figures, instead extending the results from sample studies to neighbouring regions. In principle, using more indicators might seem to make the findings more robust and the direction of travel clearer – if there are more indicators, it is less likely that policy will be led astray by any defective piece of information. In practice, however, increasing the range of indicators can also water down priorities, because it gives governments the opportunity to deflect criticism from areas of weaker performance to others. Wildavsky complains that long lists of stated objectives can compromise aims, excusing bad performance in one area by better performance in another. They become 'mechanisms for avoiding rather than making choices'.[36] *The Economist* makes the same criticism of the SDGs:

> Moses brought ten commandments down from Mount Sinai. If only the UN's proposed list of Sustainable Development Goals (SDGs) were as concise. … the efforts of the SDG drafting committees are so sprawling and misconceived that the entire enterprise is being set up to fail. … The

---

[35] T Campos, C Duarte and I Soares, 2016, MDG2 in Brazil: misguided educational policies, in A Cimadamore, G Koehler and T Pogge (eds), 2016, *Poverty and the millennium development goals*, London: CROP/Zed, p 167.

[36] A Wildavsky, 1993, *Speaking truth to power*, 4th edn, New Brunswick, NJ: Transaction Books, p 29.

MDGs at least identified priorities and chivvied along countries that failed to live up to their promises; a set of 169 commandments means, in practice, no priorities at all.[37]

Despite the importance attached to them, it is not at all certain that the MDGs have actually had much effect in any of these directions. Goals and targets have been used effectively by governments which have the power to enforce edicts; these goals and targets, by contrast, come with nothing more than the power of persuasion. Dealing with the problems of poverty, and the problems of poor countries, calls for much more: if improving performance was as easy as stating a goal, then previous attempts to promote economic growth could have been met by stating a target figure. The thing that mattered about the MDGs was not the MDGs themselves; it was the adoption of a different approach to improvement. Where targets have worked, it is because people have been able to decide how to achieve them. 'Management by objectives' specifies intended outcomes while leaving it open to agencies what the precise methods will be used to achieve them. And that, more or less, is what happened under the cover of the MDGs. What made the difference was not the target, but the growing understanding that top-down direction by the international organisations does not work.

Poverty reduction strategies

There were certainly improvements while the MDGs were in force, but it does not follow that the MDGs produced them. At more or less the same time, an alternative strategy was being pursued: the Poverty Reduction Strategy Papers, a process which required many countries – more than 60 – to introduce participative strategies for economic development. The evaluative framework applied by the World Bank set five principles for the PRSPs. Strategies should be:

- '*Country-driven*, involving broad-based participation
- *Comprehensive* in recognizing the multidimensional nature of poverty and proposing a commensurate policy response
- Based on a *long-term perspective* for poverty reduction

[37] *The Economist*, 2015, The 169 commandments, www.economist.com/news/leaders/21647286-proposed-sustainable-development-goals-would-be-worse-useless-169-commandments, accessed 19.12.2019.

- *Results-oriented* and focused on outcomes that benefit the poor
- *Partnership-oriented*, involving coordinated participation of development partners.'[38]

This was very different from the kind of policy which preceded it. 'Structural adjustment' sought to impose particular structures and policies on debtor countries – structures of property ownership, industrial finance and the withdrawal of the state from direct economic production.[39] There are still legacies of this kind of approach within the PRSPs – and some commentators saw the PRSPs as a continuation of the same sort of ideological, top-down direction.[40] Gore suggests that the circumstances in which PRSPs are formed may tend to push countries to anticipate the funders' preferences. He suggests that 'The PRSP process is a compulsory process in which governments that need concessional assistance and debt relief from the World Bank and the IMF find out, through the endorsement process, the limits of what is acceptable policy.'[41] Hulme, putting it more cynically, cites an unnamed official: 'a compulsory process wherein the people with the money tell the people who want the money what they need to say to get the money'.[42]

There were two key differences between the PRSPs and what came before. The first was the emphasis on process, rather than specific content. The IMF's evaluation explained what they were looking for:

- 'realism in the setting of goals and targets as well as in managing expectations;
- the importance of openness and transparency;
- the importance of flexibility, to allow for different country circumstances;

---

[38] World Bank Operations Evaluation Department; IMF Independent Evaluation Office, 2005, *The poverty reduction strategy initiative*, Washington DC: World Bank.

[39] C Gore, 2000, The rise and fall of the Washington Consensus as a paradigm for developing countries, *World Development*, 28(5): 789–804; and see K Donkar, 2002, Structural adjustment and mass poverty in Ghana, in P Townsend and D Gordon (eds), *World Poverty*, Bristol: Policy Press.

[40] G Mutume, 2003, A new anti-poverty remedy for Africa? www.un.org/africarenewal/magazine/february-2003/new-anti-poverty-remedy-africa, accessed 10.10.2019.

[41] C Gore, 2004, MDGs and PRSPs: are poor countries enmeshed in a global-local double-bind? *Global Social Policy*, 4(3): 277-83, p 282.

[42] D Hulme, 2015, *Global poverty*, London: Routledge, p 162.

- the desirability of debate about alternative policy choices; and
- the importance of patience and perseverance with implementation.'[43]

The PRSPs were never mainly about poverty; they were about governance. Transparency was a key part of the process – in the evaluations, it was more important than success in meeting the objectives. For example, in the Joint Staff Advisory group report about the PRSP in Benin, the Staffs recognised the problems of persistent low income, the limited progress on previous PRSPs, the vulnerability to risks and external shocks weakness of government, the failure of government to address problems of corruption. Nevertheless they concluded that

> Staffs believe the PRSP III provides an adequate framework for poverty reduction in Benin. The strategy addresses the critical constraints and challenges facing Benin and builds on Benin's comparative advantages. The objectives under the strategy are well articulated and the vision is clear.[44]

In Nepal,

> PRS objectives are unlikely to be achieved … Staffs welcome the candid assessment of the slow down in implementation, which the APR [Annual Progress Report] relates notably to political uncertainty, resistance from some groups, security constraints and weak monitoring.[45]

The judgement was that the PRSP had failed either to meet aims or to manage governance effectively – but the assessment welcomed the paper's openness about it.

---

[43] IMF Independent Evaluation Office, 2003, *Evaluation of poverty reduction strategy papers and the poverty reduction and growth facility*, https://www.imf.org/external/np/ieo/2002/prsp/013103.PDF, accessed 19.12.2019.

[44] IMF, 2011, *Benin: joint staff advisory note on the poverty reduction strategy paper*, https://www.imf.org/en/Publications/CR/Issues/2016/12/31/Benin-Joint-Staff-Advisory-Note-on-the-Poverty-Reduction-Strategy-Paper-25304, accessed 19.12.2019.

[45] IMF, 2006, *Nepal: poverty reduction strategy paper annual progress report – joint staff advisory note*, https://www.imf.org/en/Publications/CR/Issues/2016/12/31/Nepal-Poverty-Reduction-Strategy-Paper-Annual-Progress-Report-Joint-Staff-Advisory-Note-20184, accessed 19.12.2019.

Another key difference was the emphasis on the local ownership of policies. The PRSPs were based in principles of partnership and dialogue – a 'deliberative' model rather than an ideological one. States were encouraged to see themselves, not as the sole representatives of public power, but as one of several actors engaged in a process, along with NGOs, independent enterprises and civil society. The process of negotiation with partners – and the corollary, of a more modest interpretation of the role of the state – was emphasised through participation, partnership and the multidimensional approach, which calls for acceptance of a range of definitions of problems.

As the role of the PRSP process has diminished, it has become more difficult to judge the extent to which governments are directly involved in development planning; several governments had made long-terms plans through to 2020 or 2030, which are still in force. Kenya, for example, has Kenya Vision 2030, introduced in 2008; Indonesia's long-term development plan to 2025 is supported by medium-term development plans, currently 2015–19. In Bangladesh, the last intervention of the PRSP process was for the Sixth Five Year Plan. The IMF/World Bank Joint Staffs note the extensive participation of civil society on consultations on the Sixth Five Year Plan, the explicit recognition of problems in a range of fields, the problems related to governance in energy, health care and government corruption. The targets for growth, infrastructure and urban development, energy, water supply and environmental protection are all judged to be 'ambitious', and sometimes too ambitious.[46] As it turned out, Bangladesh's growth rates were lower than the targets – 6.5% instead of 7.3% – but there have been substantial improvements in health care, sanitation and life expectancy. Bangladesh is now well into its Seventh Five Year Plan, under its own steam.

Poverty Reduction Strategies were not done well or effectively everywhere. The procedures associated with strategic planning could be technocratic; some documents were long, abstruse and often difficult to follow. Material which is most likely to appeal to the international evaluators or to donor organisations is not necessarily going to grip the popular reader. But the current trend is not to address those problems, or to broaden participation; it is for strategies and goals to be determined by the international agencies instead.

---

[46] IMF, 2013, *Bangladesh: joint staff advisory note on the poverty reduction strategy paper*, https://www.imf.org/en/Publications/CR/Issues/2016/12/31/Bangladesh-Joint-Staff-Advisory-Note-on-the-Poverty-Reduction-Strategy-Paper-40387, accessed 19.12.2019.

The Sustainable Development Goals have been central to this.[47] ECLAC, for example, aims to

> Integrate the SDGs firmly into national and territorial planning systems, including on taxation, budgets and public investment. At least 19 governments in the region have medium- or long-term development strategies and the task of aligning these strategies with the SDGs represents an important step towards building sustainable development in the region.[48]

The direction of movement is to be regretted. Taken one by one, the SDGs may be good aims, but they impose values, goals and targets from the top down. The Poverty Reduction Strategies were supposed to build them from the bottom up. The SDG process excludes many of the people or organisations who might have been expected to make a contribution.

---

[47] For example, UN Economic and Social Commission for Asia and the Pacific, 2017, *Achieving the sustainable development goals in South Asia*, New Delhi: UN, https://www.unescap.org/sites/default/files/publications/UNESCAP%20-%20SRO-SSWA%20SDG%20Report_Sep2018.pdf; UN Economic Commission for Africa, 2015, *Africa regional report on the sustainable development goals*, Addis Abbaba, Ethiopia: UNECA, https://www.uneca.org/sites/default/files/uploaded-documents/SDG/africa_regional_report_on_the_sustainable_development_goals_summary_english_rev.pdf; UN Economic Commission for Latin America and the Caribbean (ECLAC), 2016, *The 2030 agenda and the sustainable development goals*, Santiago: ECLAC, https://sustainabledevelopment.un.org/content/documents/24961barcena.pdf, accessed 19.12.2019.
[48] ECLAC, 2016, p 47.

13

Responses to poverty

Responsibility for poverty

Who should take responsibility for helping the poor? One of the most prominent perspectives in developed economies is based on an individualist view which blames poor people for their poverty, expects them to improve their situation through their own efforts, and imposes punishments when they fail to do so. There are three parts to that. The first of those statements is based on a moral condemnation of poor people. Commentators and politicians condemn the poor partly because poverty is deeply stigmatised, partly because blaming the poor excuses the rest of us from moral responsibility. The statement at the end is a consequence of moral condemnation. Punishments are sometimes couched in the language of 'incentives' – that people need to be 'incentivised' or offered inducements to move out of deprivation – or 'conditionality', too often taken to mean that if people remain poor they will be subject to penalties, further deprivation, searches and surveillance by those in authority or criminal prosecution. That seems to assume that poverty is a condition that people choose and that the basic problem with it is that it isn't bad enough.

The middle part is that poor people should be expected to improve their situation themselves. This is a very different kettle of fish from the other two parts, because it is something that lots of people would accept from different political perspectives. On one hand, those who believe in the power of markets and free commerce tend to think that the best prospect for the poor is to offer the freedom, choice and entitlements that come from engagement in the economy. On the other, there is a strong radical tradition which argues for empowerment of the poor, increasing their capacity both individually and collectively, the right to make their own decisions and the resources to make them possible.

A different way of answering the question is that poverty is everyone's responsibility. This can sound hollow – if everyone is responsible, no-one is. The moral position behind it is that people are interdependent, that we are all our brother's keeper, that we all have to do what we can. The moral condemnation of the poor is a travesty of what individualism ought to be doing – individualism ought to be about respect for persons, human dignity and individual rights.[1] But responding to poverty is not all down to individuals: communities, clubs, organisations, employers, businesses, unions, authorities, NGOs and so on all have parts to play. Part of the thinking behind the Poverty Reduction Strategy Papers is that the role of governments is to plan, coordinate and complement these efforts, through partnership, joint working and dialogue.

Then there is the role of government. Unavoidably, in a book which focuses to some extent on the position of the nation state, this has to be seen as a major part of the work of responding to poverty. Governments are not all-powerful, they do not have a monopoly of legitimacy or wisdom, and (particularly in poor countries) they may lack the capacity to deal with the problems they face. Most of the world's democracies have been founded in the expectation that governments will work to improve the lives of people who live in their territories. Democracy is about what can be achieved substantively for people's welfare, not just about process and procedure.

The literature on comparative social policy focuses, understandably enough, on the differences between governments – the kinds of policy and approach which seem to work best, the methods that are available, and what governments might practically do. It should not be surprising that governments do things differently. They have different problems, they have different resources to deal with them, and established practice is likely to reflect history, convention and usage. Often they have different cultures and ways of understanding the problems. If every country is developing policies in its own right, we ought to expect variations in the approach to public services, as there are in other fields. However, what we find instead is a remarkable degree of similarity: seen, for example, in the growth of insurance-based pensions, universal health provision, universal primary education and conditional social assistance. What is surprising is not that countries do things differently, but the opposite – that so often they do the same things as other countries, in much the same way.

Part of the explanation for that is down to the direction of international organisations, the hegemony of colonial powers and the practice of policy transfer. There are accepted practices, and common approaches, and a great deal of imitation, often within regions – governments tend to watch what their neighbours do, and if not their immediate neighbours, then at least what happens in countries which

---

[1] P Spicker, 2013, *Reclaiming individualism*, Bristol: Policy Press.

share common languages. Then there are pressures on governments that are part and parcel of the work they do. Ultimately, governments are responsible for poverty when no-one else can be. Once governments accept basic responsibilities for people who are deprived or disadvantaged, it is difficult for them to hold this to a minimum, and there has been a general movement over the last hundred years for governments to take on increasing responsibilities for poverty and social welfare.[2] One contributing factor has been the development of social arrangements for mutual assistance. We tend to see governments as the originators of social policies; in point of fact, most contemporary governments have built on structures developed through independent, voluntary, charitable and religious action, as well as occupational and commercial activity in the same fields. The task these governments faced has been to decide whether they should complement, supplement or replace existing networks with their own initiatives. Another set of factors come from the issues which governments face when they try to deal with provision incrementally or partially: inevitably, there are problems in maintaining the boundaries and denying services that fall beyond any initial restrictions that governments try to impose. Underlying both trends is a common thread, which is the growth of democracy – not just an accountable government, but accountable government that is characterised by communication and deliberation. Amartya Sen has argued that democracy, freedom and development are inextricably intertwined.[3] The basic argument is a powerful one: politics, economics and society are hard to separate, and wherever there is a democracy, the development of welfare provision runs close behind.

A fourth response to the question of who should take responsibility, one which is reinforced by the previous chapter, is that the international community – international organisations and foreign governments – also bears a heavy responsibility for the position of the poor in the world. That responsibility is met in many ways, including direct investment, development aid, support for international organisations and trade agreements – and also, more controversially, with schemes like tied aid, technical assistance and supported immigration to the donor country. There is often some ambivalence about this kind of support. On one hand, there is often a mistrust of the responsible governments and a fear that resources which are provided for aid may be siphoned off for other purposes. On the other, many governments

---

[2] P Spicker, 2000, *The welfare state: a general theory*, London: Sage.

[3] A Sen, 1999, *Development as freedom*, Oxford: Clarendon Press.

interpret the process of aid to imply that they have to work through governments, rather than independently. Action Aid argues that only the responsible government has the knowledge, expertise and scope to deliver such help, and they are critical of donors who try to do things differently.[4]

This does lead to difficulties in delivering support for poor people in poor countries. In developed countries, there are often confederations of employers or trades unions, mutual aid societies and third sector agencies ready to take on some part of the work. However, because government is the provider of last resort, and generally governments carry responsibility for whatever gets left out, governments have found it hard to step back and leave it to others. The resulting pattern has been described in terms of 'corporatism', incorporating independent activity into networks of support: government negotiates, bargains and steers, a range of apparently independent operators are asked to coordinate their activity with others and with the state, and government has to make arrangements to fill in the rest.[5] Something similar has been promoted through the planning process of the Poverty Reduction Strategies.

In the case of developing countries, however, the partners and agencies they are dealing with are not so clearly subject to government rule. The partners include international organisations, foreign governments (typically through bilateral aid agreements), international non-governmental organisations (NGOs) and trans-national companies (TNCs). Any of those partners can work through national governments – most of them do – but they may have the alternative of going directly to the beneficiaries. If a foreign NGO or TNC wants to improve education in an area, it can build a school. If a foreign government wants to do the same, things get more complicated. The protocol is that they will go through the domestic national authorities. The rationale for that restriction is fairly clear – it puts limits on the scope of foreign governments to interfere in the domestic affairs of a sovereign country – but the effects can be perverse. If a foreign government wanted to act differently, working for example through a private company, a bank or an NGO, it would be difficult to stop them. Governments can make payments to their own citizens living in the second country; they can make payments to people residing in their own territory for transmission to the second country, in the form of remittances or tax allowances; they can offer loans; they can

---

[4] R Greenhill and P Watt, 2005, *Real aid*, Johannesburg: Action Aid International.

[5] M Harrison, 1984, *Corporatism and the welfare state*, Aldershot: Gower.

pay compensation to aggrieved foreign citizens. There are further alternatives. For example, they can invite people to come to them, as happens with educational provision; they can send out their own technical experts, or volunteer staff, like the US Peace Corps. What they can't do, it seems, is to pay benefits or to provide services directly to citizens of a different country.

These policies mark an acceptance that it is the responsibility of government to make provision for the poor, to organise things so that the level of poverty is reduced and the experience of poverty is mitigated.

The experience of developed economies

As developing countries have moved to extend patterns of provision and service for their citizens, the issues and problems they face have come increasingly to resemble those previously faced in the developed world. It is difficult to draw any direct equivalence, and this should not be taken too literally, but when the UK introduced its National Health Service, its income per capita was not so very different from the position of Egypt or Ecuador now. Countries like Brazil, Turkey and Mexico have growing economies; they have been developing social safety nets, and seem relatively well placed and well disposed to develop services further; and while much poorer countries such as Angola, the Philippines or Mongolia still have some way to go, it is not beyond imagination that they will move that way too. The dilemmas of managing scarce resources, targeting, providing safety nets, balancing markets and public provision, though they have been translated by political ideologues into a tale of never-ending 'crisis' and retrenchment,[6] are all very familiar.

The experience of the developed world shows very clearly that markets are never enough. Free marketeers have put forward two 'fundamental theorems' of welfare economics, which claim to show both that markets can deliver, and that only markets can deliver.[7] They are wrong on both counts. In relation to the first, the problem is not down to what economists call 'market failure'. It is that there is nothing in markets, either in principle or in practice, which means that there will be enough goods, resources and services to go round.[8]

---

[6] C Pierson, 2006, *Beyond the welfare state?* Brighton: Polity.

[7] M Blaug, 2007, The fundamental theorems of welfare economics, historically contemplated, *History of Political Economy*, 39(2): 185–207.

[8] P Spicker, 2013, *Reclaiming individualism, Bristol*: Policy Press, Part 3.

More fundamentally, markets are all about choices – not just the choice to have things, but the choice not to have them. That must mean that the system is incomplete: in conditions of scarcity, there will be things that people do not have – land, housing, education, health care, and so on. And that is intolerable. The gaps might be filled universally, as happens in education, or on a residual basis, as happens with provision for homeless people, but in a democracy, the gaps have to be filled.

The persistence of poverty demonstrates the complexity and diversity of the issues that have to be considered. The range of conditions can seem overwhelming – as can the realisation that, despite the best efforts of some governments (and the worst efforts of others), poverty continues to be a problem. One of the earliest insights from Chadwick's work on the 'new Poor Law' of the 19th century was the realisation that the relief of poverty could not be distinguished from the response to illness.[9] If people were sick, they might have to claim as poor; if they were poor, they might have to claim as sick. People have to go where they need to go to get support. If the system for sickness does not allow for disability, then people with disabilities have to present themselves as sick; if there is no provision for either, but there is provision for unemployment, then sick and disabled people will present themselves as unemployed (and vice versa). There are similar arguments concerning the need to distinguish disability and incapacity.[10] That insight is why Beveridge made his famous 'assumptions' – for a system of social security to work, there had to be a health service, and full employment.[11] Everything is connected, and the boundaries can't be held.

In terms of system design, targeting is not the way to help people most effectively. Korpi and Palme describe a 'paradox of redistribution': 'The more we target benefits at the poor only and the more concerned we are with creating equality via equal public transfers to all, the less likely we are to reduce poverty and inequality.'[12] Gugushvili and Laenen are sceptical about the generalisation; the evidence is inconclusive.[13]

---

[9] E Chadwick, 1842, *Report on the sanitary condition of the labouring population*, Edinburgh: Edinburgh University Press, 1965.

[10] P Spicker, 2003, Distinguishing disability and incapacity, *International Social Security Review* 56(2): 31–43.

[11] Beveridge Report, 1942, *Social Insurance and Allied Services*, Cmd 6404, London: HMSO.

[12] W Korpi and J Palme, 1998, The paradox of redistribution and strategies of equality, *American Sociological Review*, 63 (5): 661–87, p 682.

[13] D Gugushvili and T Laenen, 2019, *Twenty years after Korpi and Palme's paradox of redistribution*, Leuven: KU Leuven.

As so often happens in comparative studies, drilling down into the details shows a range of exceptions, differences in different fields and distinctive sets of policies in countries that are shaped by their distinct experiences. We can probably say, nevertheless, that some welfare states generally outperform others, and that systems which rely heavily on residual selectivity do not perform well. The system in the US does particularly badly; it combines parsimoniousness and punitive approaches with expensive and cumbersome administration.[14] Systems in northern Europe generally do best,[15] and Goodin and his colleagues make a case for the Netherlands:[16] they combine elements of social protection and a strong emphasis on earned entitlements with high minimum standards and a degree of egalitarianism. Just because poverty hasn't been completely eradicated doesn't mean that it can't be reined in.

Mixed systems generally perform better than pure ones. Neophytes who look for the first time at the arcane systems of service delivery immediately realise that everything could be simpler, more efficient and more straightforward. And so they could be, if everything worked like it should, if only everyone cooperated with the administration, if the professionals liaised more effectively, if people's lives were a little less complicated, and so on ... Stop right there. Benefits, services and mechanisms for delivery are complicated for good reasons – because they are dealing with complex human dilemmas, because they need to be robust and fair, because what they are trying to do is difficult. There is a trap in simplification: it cannot avoid the boundary problems already referred to, but it does make people on the boundaries particularly vulnerable to the loss of service. In any situation where people are vulnerable, where systems are imperfect, where information is incomplete, there has to be redundancy – some fallback, some protection, some slack. Neat, pat formulas inevitably fail.

There are also some basic practical constraints. Systems that rely on comprehensive, detailed knowledge of the population just don't work. All-singing, all-dancing computer programmes can't deal, as Richard Titmuss realised, with the moral and human complexities of personalised distribution. It was an attempt, he complained, to pass over to computers questions that we had not worked out the

---

[14] R Goodin, B Headey, R Muffels and H-J Dirven, 2000, *The real worlds of welfare capitalism*, Cambridge: Cambridge University Press.

[15] F Vandenbroucke, R Diris and G Verbist, 2013, *Excessive social imbalances and the performance of welfare states in the EU*, Leuven: KU Leuven.

[16] Goodin et al, 2000.

answers to – how to deal with complex human problems.[17] Relying on precise information, adjustments to personal circumstances and rapid delivery is beyond the capacity of any government, because the people most closely affected cannot describe their situation or answer official questions in these terms. That is a major problem with selectivity – the pattern of targeting that relies on separating the people who are entitled from those who are not entitled. Selectivity is problematic everywhere. It invariably leads to misclassifications – errors of inclusion, where people do receive services they're not supposed to receive, and errors of exclusion, where services fail to get to the people they're intended for because of the rules, conditions and processes that have to be overcome to get them.

The experience of the developing world

From the Poverty Reduction Strategies, we can say something about the way that the governments of developing countries understand and approach their situation. Despite the label, the strategies were never really about poverty as such; they were partly about governance, as I have explained, but they were also about development. For example, strategies that were nominally concerned with the position of the poor would commonly contain provision to manage principal industries, banking and finance, including the establishment of a stock exchange. Where they focused on problems that are more specific to the poor, they typically proceeded not by identifying what needs to be done and how much of it there should be, but by creating structures, institutions and initiatives that can be seen as responding to the issues – water, health care, education – in broad terms. In other words, the main responses to poverty are indirect. Some of them might be justified as being 'key' or strategic interventions, based on a selection of priorities which might be considered to have broader and wider effects in transforming the economy. No-one seems to have been arguing in these documents, however, that the objective of policies to help poor people might be to direct resources to the poor.

That does not mean that redistributive policies are not being followed, but to find policies of that sort, it is necessary to look in a different direction. As disillusionment set in with the process of structural adjustment, international organisations began to recognise that other elements were necessary to the agenda of development –

---

[17] R Titmuss, 1968, Universal and selective social services, in *Commitment to welfare*, London: Allen and Unwin.

particularly health and education.[18] In the case of health, the World Bank and the World Health Organization have been encouraging the use of Essential Health Packages.[19] In the case of education, several countries have attempted a 'big bang' in enrolment, making basic education available to millions of children. (In Uganda, one of the pioneers, enrolment increased from 3.4 million to 6.9 million in five years. The approach presents considerable problems – where do the schools and teachers go? Where do four and a half million extra children sit, eat, or drink?[20]) Another particularly interesting trend has been the growth of cash transfers in a range of emerging economies. Most countries in South America and others, including Mexico, India, Indonesia and South Africa, have started to introduce systems of social assistance, often combining basic cash support with conditions that promote health and education. Barrientos and Hulme call it a 'quiet revolution'.[21]

There is much that the developed countries can learn from the developing world. Because studies of poverty in developed countries and developing countries have gone in different directions, it happens at times that they have gone about things in different ways. For much of the 20th century, influenced by the work of Rowntree or by the US poverty line, most of the leading papers on poverty were based on an understanding of poverty in terms of low income, and there are still many people in the field who will assert that poverty can only be understood in these terms. Over the course of the last twenty-five years or so, the certainty that fuelled these studies has rapidly eroded, and few commentators would try to argue that poverty was not multidimensional. Beyond that, there is a view which has become well established, and has suffused this book: the recognition of poverty, not just as a matter of economic resources, but of capacity, rights and social relationships.

The second key lesson follows from the first. The emphasis on participation in identifying priorities is partly about developing the mechanisms which are needed to negotiate poverty as a complex,

---

[18] United Nations, 2003, *Monterrey consensus on financing for development*, www.un.org/esa/ffd/monterrey/MonterreyConsensus.pdf, accessed 19.12.2019.

[19] World Bank, 1993, *World development report 1993: investing in health*, Washington DC: World Bank.

[20] World Bank, 2002, *Achieving universal primary education in Uganda: the 'big bang' approach*, http://documents.worldbank.org/curated/en/878251468316474104/pdf/241070BRI0REPL1BLIC10EduNotesUganda.pdf, accessed 10.10.2019.

[21] A Barrientos and D Hulme, 2009, Social protection for the poor and poorest in developing countries, *Oxford Development Studies*, 37(4): 439–56.

wicked, many-headed set of problems. It is no less about the political status of the poor. During the 1980s and 1990s, while academics in social policy in developed countries were fixated on issues of definition and measurement, studies in development were exploring new ways to empower the poorest. As Sen argues, if poverty is a matter of rights and entitlement, the responses lie not just in mechanisms and social action, but in capacity, effective social protection and listening to the voices of the poor.[22]

There is considerable scepticism in the political discourse about that capacity, and that leads to a third lesson. In the richer countries, there has come to be a general expectation that people are already able to escape poverty, and if they do not, it is treated as a reflection on the poor – their willingness to take action, competence and bad choices. There are good reasons to reject this view of the world – far more is attributable to the economic, social and political context than this allows for. But the myth is pervasive, and the same arguments are often extended to developing countries: poor people are where they are because of laziness, lack of will power, immorality, corruption or dependence. The picture is hard to recognise in most poor countries, where poverty demands constant energy, and entrepreneurial activity is often essential to survival. Nevertheless, this kind of moral condemnation permeates debates about poverty, development and aid. In part, moral condemnation also serves the useful function of excusing people from moral responsibility for action. In part, too, it reflects a desire to extend the same arguments (often, free market arguments for non-intervention) to poverty in all its forms.

There is a relevant difference here between rich and poor countries. Relatively more people are poor in poor countries than in rich ones. In rich countries, poor people are in the minority; in the poorest countries, they may be in the majority. That means that in rich countries, poverty can be seen as a residual problem – that is, a problem of dealing with people who have been left out of the advantages of development. In poorer countries, that position is harder to sustain; the problem has to be seen as a structural one, unless the whole country is seen as a leftover. And yet the relative position of poor people is similar in both cases: poor people are lacking resources, lacking status, excluded and left out. So what emerges is not a difference in nature, but a difference in degree – a continuum, from the poorest to the richest.

---

[22] A Sen, 2001, *Development as freedom*, Oxford: Oxford University Press.

The basis of structural and pathological explanations for poverty was discussed in Chapters 10 and 11. The continuum of poor to rich countries depends on much more than the residual pathology of poor countries. All the arguments in Part 1 – the development of formal economies, infrastructure and take-off, the recognition of rights or patterns of social exclusion – imply that development ought to be seen in structural terms. Equally, the idea that richer countries do not need further structural change – a position implicit in Murray's[23] or Mead's[24] contention that people are poor despite their social opportunities in rich societies – seems hard to sustain. The lesson to draw from the comparison of rich and poor countries is that poverty has, inescapably, structural elements, and so that solutions which focus exclusively on pathology cannot hope to address the circumstances.

The fourth lesson, which emerges most clearly from recent initiatives in social protection, is the priority of basic social provision. Managing with minimal resources is not about cutting back, or moving to the market; what is happening in health and education is the establishment of a basic minima as the foundation of fundamental rights. That should also tell us something about the true meaning of austerity – not just spending less than before, not rolling back the frontiers of the public sector, but spending minimal amounts to achieve the maximum possible effect. As Basic Health Care packages show, that is done most effectively in a universalist framework.

Lastly, the position of poor countries tells us something about the limitations of conventional social science in offering recommendations for policy. One of the recurring themes of this book is that many effective strategies to deal with poverty – economic development, markets, trade, targeted support and so on – work to some extent, but they can trail further aspects of poverty in their wake. They are part of the solution, but they can just as easily be seen as part of the problem. It is often the case in studies of poverty that while some people are passionate advocates of particular types of response – aid, microcredit, trade, and so on – others are equally passionate in rejecting them. The arguments are stronger, on both sides, because they are based on a wealth of experience in different countries: people like Sachs or Easterly[25] know what they are talking about, but they take strongly opposed positions. The difficulty for any critical reader

---

[23] C Murray, 1984, *Losing ground*, New York: Basic Books.

[24] L Mead, 1986, *Beyond entitlement*, New York: Free Press.

[25] W Easterly, 2016, *The economics of international development*, London: Institute for Economic Affairs.

is that, on the whole, they are all probably right – depending on context, situation and circumstance. Unfortunately, what they have to say cannot necessarily be taken from one place and applied in another. It is a point which might equally be made about richer countries. Policies are particular, not general. Different countries might pursue similar objectives, Castles argues, but they do it through distinctive combinations of policy and practice.[26] Both the understanding of the problems and the responses that might be made to them need to be understood in their specific context, rather than relying on the generalised principles of economics or sociology.[27]

---

[26] F Castles, 1998, *Comparative public policy*, Cheltenham: Elgar.

[27] S Schram, 2004, Beyond paradigm, *Politics and Society*, 32(3): 417–33; P Spicker, 2011, Generalisation and phronesis, *Journal of Social Policy*, 40(1): 1–19.

Conclusion:
Poverty and social science

Over the course of the 20th century, the concept of poverty adhered to by social scientists became progressively more distant from the experience of poor people. When Charles Booth compiled his reports on poverty in the 1880s, the political discussions of the time homed in on his 'poverty line'[1] (not, in point of fact, a 'line' at all[2]). Rowntree's subsequent work on poverty refined that concept, centring our attention on subsistence and household incomes.[3] Most of the work done between the 1960s and 1990s focused on income. The main models that were used by social scientists – subsistence needs, baskets of goods and income thresholds – were developed to analyse a limited set of problems, examining the position of poor people within specific countries and polities. The use of a common income threshold across countries was an attempt to extend this kind of discussion to comparative studies; the development of various indices, such as the Human Poverty Index or the indices used by the International Fund or Agricultural Development, were others.[4]

While this was going on, however, alternative approaches and understandings of poverty were being developed – among them, the emphasis on entitlements and basic security emphasised in international organisations,[5] the concept of exclusion developed in France and subsequently adopted by the EU and the UN,[6] and forceful accounts of the experience of poverty in developing countries which emphasised the structure of power. Another key influence was the development of a methodology for examining poverty, most strongly advocated by

---

[1] C Booth, 1902, *Life and labour of the people in London: first series, poverty*, vol 1, London: Macmillan.

[2] P Spicker, 1990; C Booth: The examination of poverty, *Social Policy and Administration*, 24(1): 21–38.

[3] B S Rowntree, 1901, *Poverty: a study of town life*, London: Macmillan.

[4] See P Spicker, S Alvarez Leguizamon, D Gordon (eds), 2007, *Poverty: an international glossary*, London: Zed.

[5] For example, J Wresinski, 1987, Grande pauvreté et précarité économique et sociale, *Journal officiel de la République française*, 6 fev. 1987.

[6] For example, A Bhalla and F Lapeyre, 1999, *Poverty and exclusion in a global world*, Basingstoke: Macmillan.

Robert Chambers[7] and subsequently adopted for the World Bank's seminal studies on *Voices of the Poor*.[8] Those studies pointed to a range of issues such as precariousness, social isolation, gender and disempowering institutions, which conventional studies of poverty, still focused on resources and income, had hardly touched on. Over the course of the last 25 years or so, there have been new measures, new approaches and a range of policy initiatives – the Poverty Reduction Strategies, the Sustainable Development Goals or the integration of anti-poverty work with human rights.

The flaws in mainstream approaches to poverty were less obvious during the 1960s and 1970s, when poverty studies were concerned primarily with a single country. As the focus of social policy has shifted to a comparative or international base, the conceptual problems have become more salient, and more difficult to resolve. In order to make direct comparisons, there has to be some phenomenon that is capable of being compared, and the idea of poverty has to be operationalised to some extent in cross-national terms. The absolute approach has justified doing this on the basis that poverty reflects common human needs, sometimes framed in terms of subsistence,[9] sometimes 'basic needs',[10] possibly basic security.[11] Different countries have different levels of poverty; they may have different manifestations of the problems, but the essential core nature of poverty remains the same. Treating poverty as a matter of consistent, directly comparable outcomes makes it possible directly to compare issues in rich and poor countries. The Sustainable Development Goals use a common standard for everyone, and there are writers in the field, such as Martin Ravallion,[12] who will make a staunch defence of using a common approach. Unfortunately, judging everyone by the same standards has also been widely rejected in the theoretical literature. There are powerful arguments for relativism – the importance of norms, the social definition of poverty and the role of inequality – which militate against the use of such standards.

---

[7] For example, in R Chambers, 1997, *Whose reality counts?* London: Intermediate Technology Publications.

[8] D Narayan, R Chambers, M Shah and P Petesch, 2000, *Voices of the poor*, World Bank: Oxford University Press.

[9] Rowntree, 1901.

[10] ILO, 1976, *Employment growth and basic needs*, Geneva: International Labour Office.

[11] Wresinski, 1987.

[12] M Ravallion, 2015, *Toward better global poverty measures*, Washington DC: Center for Global Development.

In a relative approach, poverty is defined socially, and it can refer only to the norms and standards that are applied in the society where it occurs. Townsend argued that the resources which are customary or necessary are different in different societies.[13] If that is right, poverty cannot be compared directly: if the resources, amenities and facilities needed to escape poverty in different societies are different, and poverty is defined in terms of those resources, then poverty itself is different in different countries. A strongly relative position based on resources means – it must mean – that the standards which apply to rich countries cannot be treated as if they applied to poor ones, or vice versa, because that would be inconsistent with the social definition of the subject. There are indices which try to codify relative differences – the European test of 'economic distance' does this by identifying the risk of poverty as a proportion of the median income in each country[14] – but what they are codifying is a different level of resource in different places. 'Consensual' approaches have been used to identify the distinctive pattern of goods and services that are accounted 'necessary' in different places. If poverty means something different in different countries, like is not being compared with like. That also has the discomforting implication that inferior standards will be applied to poorer countries. In the UK, people were asked if they were able to save or have family celebrations;[15] in Bangladesh, they were asked whether every person had a pillow or a quilt;[16] in Benin, people were asked if they had a change of clothes or any furniture.[17]

Amartya Sen has tried to resolve this dilemma by allowing for the differential expression of common circumstances. He argues that poverty has to be judged in terms of people's different 'capabilities'.[18] The ways in which those capabilities are expressed depends on the circumstances where people live: so, for example, the capability for 'mobility' might be met through a bicycle, a bus, a car or a boat, and the question of which is appropriate depends on where and how things are done. Sen's capability approach was developed explicitly

---

[13] P Townsend, 1979, *Poverty in the United Kingdom*, Harmondsworth: Penguin, p 31.

[14] M O'Higgins, S Jenkins, 1990, Poverty in the EC: 1975, 1980, 1985, in R Teekens, B van Praag (eds) *Analysing poverty in the European Community*, (Eurostat News Special Edition 1–1990), Luxembourg: European Communities.

[15] For example, J Mack and S Lansley, 2015, *Breadline Britain*, London: Oneworld.

[16] A Ahmed, 2007, Consensual poverty in Britain, Sweden and Bangladesh, *Bangladesh e-Journal of Sociology*, 4(2): 56–77.

[17] S Nandy, M Pamati, 2015, Applying the consensual method of estimating poverty in a low income African setting, *Social Indicators Research*, 124(3): 693–726.

[18] A Sen, 1999, *Commodities and capabilities*, Oxford: Oxford University Press.

as an attempt to reconcile the tension between absolute and relative positions; it seems to make it possible to claim that commonalities are being identified, even if they are expressed in different ways.[19] The difficulty with Sen's proposed solution is that the elements being considered are still not commensurable – at the moment that capabilities such as 'communication' or 'transport' are operationalised, they mean different things. Translating capabilities into commodities suffers from the same problem as consensual approaches; the specific resources that are considered essential in different places are different.

A change in focus

The study of poverty has been hobbled by three inter-related assumptions, all of which are, I think, fallacious. The first is that poverty is a condition or state of being, which can be considered primarily from the perspective of individuals. This is often combined with the assumption that there is a threshold below which people can be said to be poor, and above which they are not poor – that there must be some kind of identifiable discontinuity between the position of the poor and the rest,[20] which can be checked and consequently aggregated to provide authoritative estimates of head counts, poverty gaps (how far people fall below the thresholds) and 'poverty dominance'.[21] Much of the argument of this book will only make sense if one accepts a key premise: poverty is a collective experience, not just an individual one. The capabilities and commodities available to individuals and households cannot be identified in terms that make it possible to explain what distinguishes poor countries from richer ones. The literature on development attests that it is the network of social and economic relationships that defines people's lifestyles, not the position of individuals. Societies and nations matter.

The second assumption is that poverty can be understood, or at least summed up, in terms of resources. The problem here is not that resources do not matter, but that resource-based accounts are necessarily incomplete. They are reductionist. They leave out lots of the things we might want to know about poverty – not to mention a goodly part of the content of this book. Much of the experience of poverty is not centrally about resources or commodities at all: it is

---

[19] A Sen, 1983, Poor, relatively speaking, *Oxford Economic Papers*, 35(2): 153–69.

[20] See D Piachaud, 1993, The definition and measurement of poverty and inequality, in N Barr and D Whynes (eds) *Current issues in the economics of welfare*, London: Macmillan.

[21] J Foster and A Shorrocks, 1988, Poverty orderings, *Econometrica*, 56(1): 173–7.

about issues such as rights, exclusion, gender, communities, structures of authority and inequality. Empirical evidence about resources can still be useful, but in itself it does not give us enough information to allow for an adequate comparison. That is why so many institutions and organisations have moved to compiling information about 'poverty and social exclusion' instead.

The third assumption is that issues of social organisation, such as status, relationships of exclusion or the lack of rights, are secondary. They are treated as the causes or consequences of poverty, rather than the defining elements of it – a matter of 'accidents' rather than 'essentials'. The structure of social and economic relationships is central to the meaning of poverty; resources have to be understood in terms of such relationships.

This book has made a case for a change in focus from conventional approaches to poverty, and that invites a few critical questions. What would an analysis of poverty look like if we focused on relational issues rather than resources? If poverty has to be understood in relational terms, how do we find the relevant data to analyse the problems? And if the nature of poverty is not what we thought, what does this mean for policies that are supposed to deal with poverty?

To a very large extent, the focus in this book on a relational perspective simply reflects what social scientists and institutions dealing with poverty are doing anyway. There has been a growing awareness of the complex, multidimensional and relational elements of poverty. Most of the agencies which are working with poverty internationally have given up on artificially narrow conceptions of poverty; they have to deal with the world as it is. It should be clear by now that poverty is not primarily an income or resource-driven concept, and that material deprivation cannot sensibly be distinguished from social deprivation. The discourse of social exclusion has come into use as a way of referring to the aspects of poverty that traditional social science has failed to engage with, and many institutions have shifted to talking about social exclusion instead, because that is a way of legitimating the consideration of relational issues. The substantive issues that are being covered would not need to change – only the language that we use to discuss them. The practice has already changed; the theory needs to catch up with it.

Much the same argument applies to the use of data. There may be grounds to be critical about some of the interpretations that people put on resource-based empirical data, but there is no need to adopt a wholly new approach to acquiring data about poverty; what we have is adaptable to the purpose. The data we hold are not based on a precise, faithful measurement of agreed phenomena – any study which does that misses the point. What they do, instead, is to give us indicators. Resources, income, assets, infant mortality or years of schooling do not define poverty, but they are valuable indicators of it. As the complexity and subtlety of concepts of poverty have shifted, the pattern of indicators held by international organisations and national governments has progressively changed to recognise the importance of social and economic relationships. Poverty is being described by a wide-ranging and increasingly varied range of indicators, signposts rather than 'metrics' and precise descriptors, along with a rich vein of qualitative recording and empowering social research. A relational perspective cannot overcome all the problems that plague comparative research, and it may still be vulnerable to the objection that different societies express similar phenomena in different ways; it might have to deal with issues that are not commensurable. In some circumstances, there will be evidence of common relational issues – a lack of legal rights, non-participation in political processes, exclusion from landholding, the disadvantages of women in education – but issues such as the abuse of authority, weak community organisations or stigma are hard to count whatever we do. The most we can ask for is that at least we are looking for indicators in the right place.

There has been no less of a shift in the development of policy responses. Many of the measures that are being taken – measures based on participation, voice, empowerment, and so forth – reflect the widespread and familiar knowledge that relationships matter. The experience of exclusion, lack of rights, lack of power or inequality; the issues of gender, disability, and the status of disadvantaged minorities; the problems of isolation, communities without power and physical insecurity – any of these is likely to be reflected in the position of poor people in different countries.

Understanding poverty as a relational concept does not make it easier to handle; if anything, it emphasises the inherent complexity of the topic. Work on the dynamics of poverty invite us to think of it as a complex set of processes, in a constant state of flux.[22] Many of the relational issues discussed in the course of this book – issues such as lack of power, exclusion, access to entitlements or problems with authority – manifest themselves in many ways, and are always subject to change.

---

[22] S Yaqub, 2000, *Poverty dynamics in developing countries*, Brighton: University of Sussex Institute of Development Studies; M Vaalavuo, 2015, *Poverty dynamics in Europe: from what to why*, Luxembourg: European Commission.

A relational perspective is not a sovereign remedy for every problem. The best it offers is a way of resolving some of the conceptual dilemmas. I have not tried to construct a fresh, authoritative 'definition' of poverty, because that process can be self-defeating. One of the central reasons why poverty has proved so elusive as a concept is that it is not a fixed state, that can be understood in isolation from its social context; it is defined and experienced in terms of the relationships that poor people have with other people. There may be cultural differences in the perception of poverty, but the root of the social construction of poverty is about something else; poverty is a matter of a pattern of relationships, like class or gender, that may be developed in any society. Poverty needs to be understood as a status – a set of roles and experiences – defined by the constellation of social, economic and political relationships where it is experienced.

The more emphasis that we put on such relationships as elements of poverty, the more difficult it becomes to suppose either that poverty is primarily a matter of resources, or that poverty in rich countries means something fundamentally different from poverty in poor countries. Social relationships are just as much part of the experience of poverty in poor countries as they are in rich ones. It is no less true that social norms and relationships in rich countries lead to people being locked out of access to resources just as surely as if they were in poor ones. The position of poor people cannot be understood without a consideration of relationships of disadvantage, insecurity, exclusion, and lack of entitlement. They are part and parcel of what it means to be poor.

Index of subjects

A

absolute poverty, 23–4, 26
abuse of authority, 20, 22, 45, 46, 47, 59, 83, 105, 200
access to land, 2, 24, 70, 141

B

Basic Health Care Packages, 99, 134, 191, 193
basic needs, 23, 196
basic security, 16, 31, 33, 74, 75, 76, 103, 195, 196

C

capabilities, 16, 25, 27, 28, 57, 58, 62, 93, 155, 164, 197, 198
capitalism, 35–41, 44, 45–7, 56, 113, 160
caste, 46, 68, 78, 86
child labour, 4, 5, 22, 128
citizenship, 69, 84, 88, 91–3, 94, 123, 127
class, 16, 18, 27, 31, 35, 39, 46, 47, 67, 69, 80, 124, 143, 201
colonialism, 46, 51, 113, 118, 158–60, 171, 184
commodification, 9, 39, 62, 142, 172
commodities, 25, 32, 61, 62, 140, 141, 164, 165, 198
communications, 25, 35, 36, 53, 56, 57, 58, 62, 64, 86, 116, 126, 154, 198
community development, 68, 200
community organisation, 20, 46, 85, 105, 154, see social capital
comparative social policy, 118–21, 184, 194, 196, 197, 200
conditional cash transfers, 98, 100–1, 161, 191
consensual approaches to measuring poverty, 21, 22, 197, 198
corruption, 29, 81, 83, 117, 128, 153, 156, 157, 165, 173, 180, 181, 192
crime, 29, 78, 157

D

debt, 29, 44, 45, 50, 55, 152, 166, 167, 170, 174, 179
decommodification, 54, 142, 145

democracy, 9, 85, 125–31, 146, 161, 184, 185, 188
dependency, 4, 16, 18, 31, 47, 59, 103–4, 139, 169
deprivation, 4, 15, 18, 19, 24, 27, 31, 32, 33, 70, 90, 98, 104, 105, 107, 183, 199
developed economies, 24, 39, 42, 43, 51, 56, 120, 140, 170, 183, see richer countries
developing countries, 43, 54, 58, 60, 68, 72, 76, 80, 91, 98, 113, 115–6, 135, 139, 149, 161, 163–7, 169, 172, 186–7, 190–3, 195
development, 6, 10, 35, 36, 37, 38, 41, 44, 45, 46, 49, 53–65, 73, 75, 86, 87, 89, 92, 106, 118, 126, 129, 131, 135, 138, 139, 150, 153, 154, 155, 158, 159, 164, 165, 168, 174–5, 177, 179, 181, 182, 190, 192, 193, 200, see economic development; human development
development assistance, 168–70, 185, see international aid
development studies, 11, 114, 198
disability, 28, 68, 70, 75, 79, 80, 82, 87, 92, 96, 98, 105, 139, 188, 200
disadvantage, 1, 2, 5, 7, 10, 16, 25, 34, 42, 46, 47, 49, 50, 58, 67–70, 72, 105, see inequality
dynamics of poverty, 84, 107, 200

E

economic development, 6, 45–6, 51, 53–62, 126, 135, 164, 172, 178, 193
economic distance, 16, 26, 31, 32, 33, 71, 145, 197
economic participation, 42, 62, 78, 82, 100, 106, 183
economy, structure of, 6, 35–45, 45–51, 53–59, 60–1, 65, 74, 81, 86, 89, 91, 116–7, 118, 133, 134, 139, 152, 154, 156, 166, 190

Index of names